P9-EJH-340

TWAYNE'S WORLD AUTHORS SERIES

A Survey of the World's Literature

Sylvia E. Bowman, Indiana University

GENERAL EDITOR

CANADA

Joseph Jones, University of Texas

EDITOR

Malcolm Lowry

(TWAS 217)

TWAYNE'S WORLD AUTHORS SERIES (TWAS)

The purpose of TWAS is to survey the major writers —novelists, dramatists, historians, poets, philosophers, and critics—of the nations of the world. Among the national literatures covered are those of Australia, Canada, China, Eastern Europe, France, Germany, Greece, India, Italy, Japan, Latin America, the Netherlands, New Zealand, Poland, Russia, Scandinavia, Spain, and the African nations, as well as Hebrew, Yiddish, and Latin Classical literatures. This survey is complemented by Twayne's United States Authors Series and English Authors Series

The intent of each volume in these series is to present a critical-analytical study of the works of the writer; to include biographical and historical material that may be necessary for understanding, appreciation, and critical appraisal of the writer; and to present all material in clear, concise English—but not to vitiate the scholarly content of the work by doing so.

MALCOLM LOWRY

By RICHARD HAUER COSTA

Texas A&M University

Twayne Publishers, Inc. :: New York

FOR J. F. HOPKINS

whose friendship for 32 years
has proved Faulkner right:
Enduring is the most
beautiful of words.

In any event, to talk about masterpieces now is to think of oneself as possessing not merely wholly original powers but a kind of inviolability from the age. Except for Nabokov's *Pale Fire* which is a unique invention in the early 20th-Century "modern" manner—the last thoroughly successful instance was Malcolm Lowry's *Under the Volcano* (1947).

ALFRED KAZIN, 1969

Acknowledgments

For permission to quote from materials in the Malcolm Lowry Special Collection, University of British Columbia at Vancouver, I am indebted to his widow and the executor of his estate, Margerie Bonner Lowry. I should also like to express my gratitude to Mrs. Lowry for her spendid commitment to her husband during his lifetime and to the furtherance of Lowry studies since his death, and her prompt responses to my requests for information, much of which was of a delicate nature.

For permission to quote from the published works, I thank these publishers, listed by volume: *Under the Volcano, Hear Us O Lord from Heaven Thy Dwelling Place, Ultramarine,* and *Selected Letters of Malcolm Lowry,* Lippincott; *Dark As the Grave Wherein My Friend Is Laid,* New American Library; *October Ferry to Gabriola,* World; *Lunar Caustic,* Jonathan Cape and Grossman. For permission to quote from *Ushant: An Essay* by Conrad Aiken, I thank Little, Brown & Co.

I should also like to thank a number of journals and magazines for permission to adapt for this book essays which originally appeared there: *The University of Toronto Quarterly, The Nation, The University of Windsor Review, Focus No. 2,* a publication of J. Howard Woolmer, New York City, and *Journal of Modern Literature,* Temple University.

Finally, I should like to express my gratitude to these individuals and institutions who helped me substantively to apply a 25-year interest in Malcolm Lowry to the writing of this book:

To my friend, the poet Earle Birney of Vancouver, whose suggestions made in correspondence and during chats in West Lafayette, Ind., Utica, N.Y., and New York City were of substantive help.

To Conrad Aiken, who graciously received me at his home in Savannah, Ga., for two long chats during Easter week, 1967. He brought to my tentative ideas about the Lowry-Aiken symbiosis the wisdom, often chastening, possible in the man who was the major literary influence on Lowry.

To Lowry's friend—now mine—the novelist David Markson whose friendly counsel has given me untold encouragement.

To my friend, Professor Dale Edmonds, Tulane University, whose exhaustive Ph.D. dissertation on Lowry (University of Texas at Austin, 1965), began academic scholarship on Lowry at that level. His articles and chats did much to help me crystallize my own ideas.

To Philippe Thoby-Marcelin, the Haitian poet and novelist, who by an accident of geography came to be a neighbor in Upstate New York, for his reminiscences of the Malcolm Lowry he came to know well during the latter's stay in Port-au-Prince, Haiti, in 1947.

To Professor Maurice Beebe, now of Temple University, who in his Joyce seminar at Purdue University spurred me to my first substantive work on Lowry, a paper on the Joyce-Aiken-Lowry literary kinship which I expanded into the opening chapter of this book.

To Dean W. David Maxwell, College of Liberal Arts, and Professor Harrison E. Hierth, Head of the Department of English, Texas A&M University, for their enthusiastic support in a successful bid for an in-lieu-of-teaching summer grant in 1971. To Utica College of Syracuse University and to Purdue University for summer grants that enabled me to travel to the University of British Columbia and examine the materials of the Lowry Collection; to Mrs. Anne Yandle of the U.B.C. library staff for directing a massive amount of xeroxing of Lowry materials; to Miss Judith Combs, U.B.C. library staff, for additional help at the last minute; to my friend and colleague Karl Elmquist for painstaking proofing of final galleys.

I should like to acknowledge my indebtedness to Sylvia E. Bowman, general editor, Twayne World Authors Series, and Professor Joseph Jones, Austin, Texas, editor of the Canadian Section, TWAS, and to Mr. Erik J. Friis of the Twayne editorial staff, for intelligent and conscientious editorial supervision.

And finally, to my wife Jo for uncountable evidences of forbearance, not the least of which was in becoming a Lowryan too.

RICHARD HAUER COSTA
College Station, Texas

Contents

Chronology

1909   Clarence Malcolm Lowry born July 28 at "Warren Crest," North Drive, Wallasey, England, to Arthur Osborne Lowry and Evelyn Boden Lowry.

1927   May: went to sea as cabin boy and traveled to Singapore and back through Siam, Malaya, the Philippines, Ceylon, the Indian Ocean, and the Suez Canal. Kept a sea journal which he was to rely heavily upon in the writing of his first novel, *Ultramarine*.

1928   Wrote first letter to Conrad Aiken after reading latter's novel *Blue Voyage*.

1929   Summer: took sea voyage, as a passenger, to West Indies, returning by roundabout route to Boston, where he met Aiken; the two spent what Aiken called "that wonderful summer of '29" at Aiken's home in Cambridge, Mass.
        Fall: entered Cambridge University.

1930   Summer: made trip to Norway as fireman on Norwegian freighter; met Nordahl Grieg, author of novel *The Ship Sails On;* received Grieg's permission to write a play based on the novel.

1932   Graduated from Cambridge with third-class honors in the English tripos; received B.A.

1933   *Ultramarine* published by Jonathan Cape, London.
        December: married American girl, Jan Gabrial.

1933–   First work published in America: stories in the Whit Bur-
1934   nett-Martha Foley magazine, *Story*.

1935   Went to New York alone; brief commitment to Bellevue Hospital.

1936   Went to Los Angeles alone.
        November: went to Mexico with Jan Gabrial; began work on *Under the Volcano*.

1937   May–July: reunion with Aiken in Cuernavaca, Mexico,

with each making notes for autobiographical episodes in later work—Lowry's *Under the Volcano,* Aiken's *Ushant;* wife Jan left him.

1938 Returned to Los Angeles.

1939 July: went to Vancouver, British Columbia, Canada.

1940 Was divorced.

December 2: married American novelist Margerie Bonner. Settled in Dollarton, near Vancouver, in squatter's shack off Burrard Inlet.

1941 *Under the Volcano* refused by twelve publishers and withdrawn from agent; fourth version begun.

1944 June 7: house at Dollarton burned down; went east to stay with friend from Cambridge days, Gerald Noxon, near Toronto.

Christmas Eve: completed version of *Under the Volcano* that would be accepted for publication.

1945 February: returned to Dollarton and started to rebuild house.

June: sent manuscript of *Under the Volcano* to agent.

Fall: went to Mexico with wife.

1946 January 2: wrote long letter to publisher Jonathan Cape protesting deletions and revisions in *Under the Volcano* manuscript called for by Cape's reader.

Spring: *Under the Volcano* accepted by Reynal & Hitchcock in New York and Jonathan Cape in London the same day.

May: returned with wife to Dollarton.

December: sailed from New Orleans with wife on a freighter for Haiti.

1947 February: went to New York; *Under the Volcano* published by Reynal & Hitchcock; returned to Dollarton.

November: sailed from Vancouver, through the Panama Canal, to France, on French freighter.

1949 Returned to Dollarton and began stories in *Hear Us O Lord from Heaven Thy Dwelling Place* and film script of Fitzgerald's *Tender Is the Night.*

1950– In Dollarton working on four novels, *Dark As the Grave*
1954 *Wherein My Friend Is Laid, October Ferry to Gabriola, Mordida,* and *The Ordeal of Sigbjørn Wilderness;* the short stories and poems.

Chronology

1954 August: left Dollarton for New York and, after a brief and last reunion with Conrad Aiken, sailed with wife for Genoa on Italian freighter.

1954– Winter: in Taormina, Sicily.
1955

1955 Went to England and moved to Ripe, Sussex.
1957 June 27: died unexpectedly.
1961 Posthumous publication of *Hear Us O Lord from Heaven Thy Dwelling Place.*
1962 First American publication of *Ultramarine* in slightly revised form. Publication of *Selected Poems of Malcolm Lowry.*
1965 December: simultaneous publication of Lowry's *Selected Letters* and first hardcover reissue of *Under the Volcano.*
1968 Summer: publication of *Dark As the Grave Wherein My Friend Is Laid.*
Fall: publication of *Lunar Caustic* in England.
Winter: screen rights to *Under the Volcano* sold to the Hakim Brothers.
1970 Fall: publication of *October Ferry to Gabriola.*

Introduction:
One Great Confession

> It makes no difference whether the poet
> knows that his work is begotten, grows, and
> matures with him, or whether he supposes
> that by taking thought he produces it out of
> the void. His opinion of the matter does not
> change the fact that his own work outgrows
> him as a child its mother.
>
> Carl G. Jung
> *Psychology and Literature*

ONE often reads of how, with the completion of a book, its author sheds it, snaps forever the umbilical cord which made it for a time an appendage of his soul. Conceived this way, each book is self-contained, after publication no longer a part of the man. Only the new work breathes life from him. Goethe, however, referred to his works as "fragments of a great confession." If I may take the phrase out of its context, it will apply with special force to the curiously interlinked works of the late British-Canadian writer Malcolm Lowry. He worked over novels, stories, poems, all at the same time, and his methods of revision would be a nightmare to a controlled writer. Except for an apprentice novel, *Ultramarine,* written under Conrad Aiken's tutelage while Lowry was still an undergraduate at Cambridge, his single "completed" book was *Under the Volcano,* published in 1947 only after a decade of revisions. *Under the Volcano,* according to a kind of literary game plan reported by Lowry in letter upon letter during the lean years after his one major success, was to be the *Inferno* part of a trilogy to be called *The Voyage that Never Ends. Lunar Caustic,* which survives as a novella about a derelict seaman committed to Bellevue Hospital, was to be expanded into the *Purgatorio.* The *Paradiso* was called *In Ballast to the White Sea,* a manuscript which, as Conrad Aiken, one of the few ever to see it, told me, was much longer than *Volcano*. That manuscript, like others in Lowry's star-crossed life, was destroyed in a fire that leveled the couple's cabin on the beach at Dollarton, British Columbia, on June 7, 1944. At his death, Lowry had legitimately relevant material on the *Paradiso*. A novella, "The Forest Path to the Spring," explicitly redemptive as nothing else in the Lowry *corpus*, was published posthumously in Lowry's only story collection, *Hear Us O Lord from Heaven Thy Dwelling Place* (1961). "Forest Path" is a rarity for Lowry, a tour de force that is worthy of comparison in kind, if not degree, with *Walden*, a prose ode to rebirth.

Scattered manuscripts of two long novels, two novellas, and many sketches and fragments, including scores of poems, were assembled after Lowry's death. Two of these, *Dark As the Grave Wherein My Friend Is Laid* and *October Ferry to Gabriola*, were stitched together for publication in 1968 and 1970, respectively. All of the posthumous Lowry material is alike in one sense: it is fragmentary, unready, except in brief passages, for publication. In manuscript form in the Special Collections Library, University of British Columbia, these vagrant works testify to Lowry's method of composition: five, ten, or even twenty versions of a sentence, paragraph or chapter going at once, and nothing ever being finished.

Lowry was a strange combination of the conventional and unconventional as a writer. He was conventional in the almost old-fashioned sense of a man who never wished to be anything but a writer. He was unconventional in the sense of a man in whom overriding ambition and overriding addiction were combined. To such a one, life in ordinary society led only to disaster. The Canadian poet Earle Birney, who knew him intimately during the years in the squatter's shack at Dollarton, told me in conversation that Lowry was incredibly accident prone and that his wife Margerie dared not allow him even to cross a street unaccompanied. Lowry's lifelong sense of being haunted, of being a sounding board for visions, produced at his best a species of ecstatic, lyrical prose that has all but gone out of existence. I write this with the painful awareness that no amount of myth building ought to be allowed to take the place of a writer's achievement that is measured by a solid row of books.

We are, in a sense, the beneficiaries of the fruits of Lowry's defects as a working novelist. It is hard to imagine another contemporary writer in English who so thoroughly analyzed and anatomized the materials of his art. In reading the *Selected Letters,* especially those written after the publication of *Volcano,* one wonders how Lowry found time to work on the half dozen books invariably in progress, so full of their explication is his correspondence. If Hemingway was right when he declared that what a writer talks about he does not write, Lowry's preoccupation could only have been damaging. Nevertheless, the long letter he wrote to the English publisher Jonathan Cape on January 2, 1946, protesting a Cape reader's recommendations for cutting and altering, is so thorough and complete that Granville Hicks was probably justified in praising it as "the most careful exposition of the workings of the creative imagination" he had ever encountered. The poet Stephen Spender has gone on record as advising that Lowry's letter, which occupies forty-two pages in the *Selected Letters,* be made the standard preface for every new edition of the novel.

The manner in which the novel finally meshed is the main concern of the first half of this book. More than 1,100 pages of working notes—two large boxes in the University of British Columbia collection—testify to the fact that Lowry reworked everything. If one includes the short-story version, published in a special Lowry issue of *Prairie Schooner* (Winter 1963–64), there are five drafts of *Under the Volcano* in the U.B.C. collection. The "first draft" is the typescript of the short story. The "second draft" contains 364 pages of typescript, divided into twelve chapters. The "third draft" is a clear copy of the second, embracing some minor changes bringing the page total to 404, but not yet effecting the key change in the interrelationships of the three principals. This is the version—I refer to it as the Mexican Version— rejected by twelve of New York's most prestigious publishers in 1940–41. The "fourth draft" is of significance for the interlinear changes penciled in. These changes point to the final, the published version, which recently was purchased from Lowry's Cambridge friend, Gerald Noxon, by the University of Texas at Austin. The "fifth draft," of course, is the critical success and minor best seller of 1947. I refer to this draft in those chapters where distinctions between drafts are vital as the Published Version. Unless otherwise noted, all quotations from *Volcano* are from the published book.

It is impossible to fix exactly the dates of the revisions of *Under the Volcano*. We do know that from Lowry's initial conception of the material, arrived at in late 1936 (probably during the month of Malcolm's and Jan Gabrial Lowry's arrival in Mexico), until the final proofreading of the galleys in late 1946, *Under the Volcano* was an obsession. On the evidence of the story "Through the Panama" and the unfinished novel *Dark As the Grave*, the obsession continued for several years after acceptance and publication.

In the interests of clarity, I shall cite text from only two of the unpublished drafts. In Chapter 4 I refer to the short-story version as *short story* and the clear copy of the unsuccessful Mexican manuscript of 1940–41 as the *Mexican Version*.

The second half of the book is an examination of Lowry's fifteen years in Canada and the prose writings—nearly all unpublished during his lifetime—of that period. My aim in Chapters 5, 6, and 7 is to show how intertwined were his works and his life and how inability to create the larger-than-life configurations of *Under the Volcano* defeated him in much of the subsequent fiction.

Chapter 8 attempts to deal with the mystical-messianic aspects of Lowry, his belief in himself as something very like a "Jungian conductor." This chapter is necessarily tentative in thrust and content. I have had no training in Jungian psychology; I make a link between Lowry the man and Jung's notion of the Archetype as a means of correlating aspects of the side of him that was inveterate collector of what one critic calls "daymares."

My discussion of Lowry's poetry is limited to a long note at the beginning of "Notes and References," immediately after the text proper,[1] 177–80. Lowry published almost none of the poems during his lifetime and there is nowhere to my knowledge any indication of the importance he attached to them. Since my book does not approach his work from a genre standpoint, a discussion of them within the text would have thrown off badly the shape of the book. Earle Birney's forthcoming edition of the Lowry poems is likely to be definitive.

CHAPTER *1*

The Literary Kinship

> Give not over to future generations the
> glad duty of acknowledging him for what he
> is. Take that joy to yourself, in your own
> generation; and so shall he feel those grate-
> ful impulses in him that may possibly
> prompt him to the full flower of some still
> greater achievement in your eyes. And by
> confessing him, you thereby confess others;
> you brace the whole brotherhood. For ge-
> nius, all over the world, stands hand in hand,
> and one shock of recognition runs the whole
> circle round.
>
> Melville, writing of Hawthorne

I *Addiction as Transcendence*

F. SCOTT FITZGERALD once observed (in *The Crackup*) that
the test of a first-rate intelligence is the ability to hold two
opposed ideas in the mind at the same time, and still retain the
ability to function. His own mental crackup occurred, he believed,
at the point where he was no longer able to balance the conviction that all was hopeless with the determination—even the illusion—that one ought to make things otherwise. The supreme
exemplar in modern fiction of self-knowledge that is cut off from
the ability to act is the creation not of Fitzgerald but of an ex-
patriate British novelist, Malcolm Lowry. His most notable creation, Geoffrey Firmin, the Consul, the hubris-ridden yet earth-
bound protagonist of Lowry's single masterpiece, *Under the
Volcano,* may have been the first character in fiction to reflect
fully the noblesse oblige of the addict, the kind of pride that must
be asserted to seek in drink a means of transcending the agony
of consciousness.

The plot can be simply told. On the eve of his departure from Mexico, Jacques Laruelle reflects on the tragic deaths of a man—Geoffrey Firmin, the Consul—who had been his friend, and the Consul's former wife Yvonne, who we learn had been his mistress. Laruelle's musings occupy a haunting elegy of an opening chapter, an honoring of the memory of the Consul. As the novel proper opens, Yvonne has returned to Mexico to attempt reconciliation. The time is November, 1938, and the entire action of the story takes place on the last day of their lives. The whole efficacy of the novel depends on Lowry's ability to cast Firmin as a Promethean figure. He is not merely a theatrical drunkard flinging himself at destruction; he rises from the page as a tragic, real, rounded man of mind and emotion, sharply etched from the inside. The Consul's drinking creates a chain of ungrasped opportunities, of negotiable obstacles that are never cleared for the communication of his deep love for Yvonne, a fearful partition which she on her side is unable to break through. Drunkenness causes Firmin's loss of Yvonne, of Hugh, his half-brother, of his grasp upon reality, and finally of his own life, when he is thrown over a cliff into a barranca, literally under the volcano, by a gang of Mexican Fascists.

In life, Lowry underwent the kind of Molochian ordeal in 1936–38 that enabled him to *become* the Consul. Lowry's was a ritual burning in Mexico, the country that the rootless and self-destructive side saw, as one of his poems has it, "pyre of Bierce and springboard of Hart Crane," [1] the age-old arena of racial and political conflicts of every nature. He subsisted on the monthly cheques sent him by his father, Arthur O. Lowry, a well-off Liverpool cotton broker: only about $90 but enough to supply him his principal needs in those days, mescal and tequila. He also languished in some of the dingiest jails of Mexico, watched his first marriage crack, but, above all, lived by total immersion the early plot of *Under the Volcano*, whose essential drafts he was still able, by some incredible mind-over-matter crucible, to complete. If it was to be his fate to die, like the Consul, in a ravine, his body tossed there with a dead dog, so much the better. Like Proust's Marcel who found that "I myself seemed actually to have become the subject of my book," Lowry was elevated—or, in terms of his career's crackup, *reduced*—to being his own character. He once wrote to Conrad Aiken, the man who became not only his major literary influence but his mentor and *in-loco-parentis* father: "I do not feel so much as if I am writing this book as that *I am myself being written.*" [2]

At another time, somewhat later, Lowry wrote his "Epitaph" with engaging candor:

> Malcolm Lowry
> Late of the Bowery
> His prose was flowery
> And often glowery
> He lived, nightly, and drank, daily,
> And died playing the ukulele.

Unfortunately, life was not so kind. Lowry did not die "playing the ukulele" but expired during the night of June 27, 1957, lying on the floor of a rural cottage in the village of Ripe, Sussex, England. He died of what the coroner, with perfect accuracy, termed "misadventure" but which was more specifically an alcoholic's death: strangling on his own vomit, a victim like many another before him and since of that now recognized lethal combination of food, alcohol, and barbiturates.

The death of Malcolm Lowry was like his life: an underground thing, a carefully guarded secret, a fighting of private demons in obscure places: down and out in London and Paris in the early 1930s; alternately dying by the tequila and drying out in dingy jails in the Mexican interior, 1936–38; finding temporary haven in a fisherman's shack on Burrard Inlet, at Dollarton, British Columbia, where, with his devoted second wife, he lived and worked for fourteen years, the best years, ten miles through wilderness to the nearest saloon.

The end of temporal life was not the end of Lowry's communications to the outside world. Like his hero Melville and another artist-addict, Fitzgerald, Lowry spoke from the grave. A stream of posthumous long and short fiction, poems, and correspondence has surfaced during the decade 1961–70.[3] It is too early to determine whether the issuance of two novels, a collection of interrelated stories, the small edition of poems so far published will spur the legitimate new interest in Lowry that the posthumous publications of *Billy Budd* and *The Last Tycoon* did for their authors. The life of Lowry's books is as strange—

and uneven—as the life of the man, and it is not too much to expect that when the entire corpus is finally available in undistorted form we may have one of the more complete laboratories of the possessed artist yet left behind.

II Pre-Volcano Lowry (1909–36)

There are gaps in the record of Lowry's life, especially in the pre-*Volcano* years, which may never be filled. His first wife, deceased, could have contributed to the fleshing out of the periods of uncontrolled drinking and apprentice writing in England, France, Spain, New York, and Mexico. Conrad Aiken, whose spiritual paternity Lowry acknowledged to the end and whom he honored as the model for the controlled side of the Consul, created in his autobiography *Ushant* an unforgettable memoir of the youthful Lowry, "visibly and happily alight with genius," but he has declined any fuller statement of their unparalleled symbiosis, artistic and human.

I am indebted to Margerie Bonner Lowry for the biographical chronology prefixed to this study and for the events in my brief statement of the pre-Mexico years.[4] The acknowledged masterpiece, while much more than the usual autobiographical first novel, is in a special sense a recapitulation of the destructive parabola traced by the first thirty years of Lowry's life as well as an exact forecast of what was to come.

Clarence Malcolm Lowry was born on July 28, 1909, at "Warren Crest," North Drive, Wallasey, England. His father was Arthur O. Lowry, a wealthy cotton broker, who also owned cotton and oil fields in Egypt, Peru, and Texas. His mother was Evelyn Boden, the daughter of a well-known Norwegian sea captain, the skipper of a famous sailing ship, *The Scottish Isles.* Captain Boden went down with his ship in the Indian Ocean. Many extraordinary stories were told about this man which the young Malcolm heard and which made a lasting impression. There are many analogues in *Under the Volcano* and in some of his early poems to the sources for his love of the sea—his maternal grandfather and his artistic progenitors, Melville, Conrad, and O'Neill.

His mother and father spent much of their time traveling and Malcolm was sent away to school as a boarder when about seven years old. He did not live at home from that time onward. He suffered a painful eye ailment which from age nine to thirteen caused him long periods of blindness. After long neglect, the ailment was diagnosed at school, and surgery corrected the corneal ulceration. After his eyesight was restored he became a strong athlete. He was the boy champion golfer of England when he was about fifteen. He played rugby and tennis, and was an especially strong swimmer. He enjoyed taking solitary walks, and the remembrance by Jacques Laruelle of walks with the young Geoffrey Firmin (*Volcano*, Chap. I) undoubtedly ties in with Lowry's boyhood hikes of as much as twenty or thirty miles a day. He attended a public school, The Leys, where he became editor of the school paper and contributor to it. Many of his early sketches were published at school under the pen name "Camel," based on "C.M.L." From as far back as he could remember he had always intended to be a writer. His three brothers entered the family firm after taking their University degrees, but the youngest— Malcolm—wanted nothing to do with the cotton business. After being graduated from The Leys he went to sea. His father wished him to go to Cambridge and he had been entered for Christ College there. But he was determined to go to sea and finally won his father over after a major domestic crisis. He promised that if he was allowed to go for a year he would then attend Cambridge and get an honors degree. Meanwhile, his father got him a job on a tramp steamer, out of Liverpool. I shall have more to say of the bad start the young man, driven to the dock in a Rolls-Royce, had with the other seamen. The sea voyage, which lasted a year, took him to Singapore, Vladivostok, and other Asian ports, and back via Siam, Malaya, the Philippines, Ceylon, the Indian Ocean, and the Suez Canal. During this voyage he kept a journal and from it he later, while at Cambridge, wrote *Ultramarine* as his thesis for his B.A. He received third honors in the English tripos from St. Catherine's College.

Before going up to Cambridge he read the translation of a Norwegian novel, *The Ship Sails On*, by Nordahl Grieg, a distant relative of the composer Edward Grieg. This book too was about a young man's first voyage to sea, and it made a deep impression on him; he considered it much better than his own book, and he decided he should meet Grieg. Also he wanted to go to Norway, his grandfather's birthplace. So, during the first long vacation at

Cambridge, he signed on as a fireman on a Norwegian tramp bound in ballast to Archangel on the White Sea. The ship never reached Archangel: they stopped at a small town in northern Norway, Aalesund, hoping to take on cargo; the captain failed in this and the crew was disbanded and paid off. While in this town Lowry learned that Nordahl Grieg was living under an assumed name in Oslo. At their meeting, Grieg told Lowry in reference to *The Ship Sails On* (as Aiken would a year later in reference to *Blue Voyage*) that Malcolm understood the novel better than he. With Grieg's permission, he worked for several years, on and off, on a play version of the book but never achieved what he considered was due the book. During this trip to Norway he kept a journal which later became the basis for a long novel, *In Ballast to the White Sea*. The 2,000-page first-draft manuscript and notes went up in flames with the Lowrys' first beach shack in June, 1944. He was never able to rewrite this novel. He tells the salient aspects of the Nordahl Grieg kinship in a long letter to David Markson (*Selected Letters,* 261–65).

It was during his first year at Cambridge that Lowry read *Blue Voyage* by Conrad Aiken. The effects of that book's deep impression on him—the crucial implications of the Aiken-Lowry symbiosis—are discussed fully in the remainder of this chapter and the next. Aiken's memoir in his autobiography *Ushant* is, apart from a surviving letter or two, the only direct report we have of Lowry's terrifying crucible in Mexico during 1936–38. Of such intensity was that twenty-month interlude that its felt life literally *burned* into being the outline and most of the crucial motifs of *Under the Volcano*.

III *The Way to Joyce*

Recent reissues in hard and soft covers of *Under the Volcano* [5] invariably stimulated many readers, including some eminent critics, to go to the book after having missed it earlier. Certainly the novel's rebirth will stimulate what the late R. P. Blackmur, speaking of *Ulysses,* called "the whole clutter of exegesis, adulation, and diatribe." [6] A *Times Literary Supplement* critic calls *Volcano* "a masterpiece as rich and humorous as *Ulysses* and far more poetic." [7] It is not idle to pair *Volcano* with *Ulysses* in any sense. A University of Toronto thesis by Anthony Kilgallin [8] finds echoes in Lowry's novel of Christ, Adam, Don Quixote, Dante, Faust, Oedipus, Lord Jim, Svidrigailov, Chichikov, *Moby Dick,* and of authors too numerous to mention here. In an ingenious attempt to demonstrate that *Under the Volcano* is a truly Joycean work, one of Lowry's friends, the novelist David Markson, finds a complete Homeric parallel incorporated into Chapter X.[9] Markson's epigram, to the effect that Lowry carried the Odyssean correspondences through "as an indication that one man's myth needn't become another man's poison," is justified only by its cleverness. All his writing life that aspect of the Lowry persona which emerges from the limited published works seemed to be trying to exorcize even the idea of James Joyce from its soul.

In a pre-*Volcano* letter to a friend, the Irish short-story writer James Stern, Lowry urges him to attempt the well-made novel, one written "without being full of inventories (like Joyce) . . . or quotations from quotations from other novels (like me, 7 years ago)." [10] When at last, after more than a decade of struggle with revisions of *Volcano,* Lowry was able to see his novel published, it was both acclaimed and discounted. Jacques Barzun could not digest what he called a "regurgitation" of *Ulysses,* and *The New Yorker* dismissed it in a paragraph as being "a rather good imitation of an important novel." [11]

Perhaps the charge that he was a reasonable facsimile of a better writer gave Lowry the impulse to put in the journal of one of his alter-egos the words, "And indeed I do sometimes hate Joyce." [12] As if to shut off altogether the flood of Joyce talk, Lowry declared he did not read *Ulysses* through until 1952, five years *after* the publication of *Volcano.*[13] Elsewhere, however, he has recorded that most writers, himself included, have come under the influence of Joyce. Most commentators on *Under the Volcano* find the novel either directly influenced by *Ulysses* or full of the resonances of that novel. John Wain writes that "the writer with whom Lowry has most in common is James Joyce," and adds, in one of those aphorisms that titillate rather than instruct, "To me, *Ulysses* is a great book that almost didn't come off. *Under the Volcano* is a great book that almost did." [14] Scholars have been content to let it go at that, perhaps thinking with Perle Epstein that his stylistic derivations from Joyce constitute "a critical commonplace." At any rate, although they readily acknowledge what Lowry did not—that *Volcano* is a descendant of *Ulysses*—almost no one has traced the lineage.

The purpose of this chapter is dual: to demonstrate that, despite his unwillingess to acknowledge it, Lowry *did* move, *especially* in technique, ever closer to *Ulysses*, but did so through an intermediary, a writer whom he has been as anxious to credit as he has been reluctant to genuflect toward Joyce; and lastly, to show that for a parallel to, a precedent for, the "tragic joy" of Lowry's novel—its insistent humor amidst hellish demons—one can indeed only turn to *Ulysses*.[15]

IV *Joyce—Aiken—Lowry*

In the summer of 1951, Lowry wrote a long letter to David Markson, then a Columbia University graduate student, who had asked about certain references to the occult in *Volcano*.[16] Lowry observed that Joyce had had a superstition about the name Lowry which occurs in the Hades burial scene of *Ulysses*, and, more significantly, that Joyce had been searching for a long poem, *Coming Forth by Day of Osiris Jones,* when he died. Biographical material confirms these claims,[17] but more important is the fact that, in the same paragraph of a deeply introspective letter, Malcolm Lowry should link his own name to Joyce's masterpiece and then link himself to a poem by Conrad Aiken.

On the published evidence, Aiken is the seminal influence. The Lowry letters document a debt to Aiken first proclaimed in the novella *Through the Panama*. Sigbjørn Wilderness notes in his journal that he is "capable of conceiving of a writer today, even intrinsically a first-rate writer, who *simply cannot understand . . .* what his fellow writers are driving at. . . ." While he heroically reads each night a few pages of William Empson's *Seven Types of Ambiguity,* Wilderness says that the only literary work he has ever enjoyed with esthetic detachment was a poem by Aiken. Lowry's first letter to Aiken begins, "I have lived only nineteen years and all of them more or less badly. . . ."[18] He quotes from Aiken's *House of Dust,* and within a few months a transatlantic correspondence is under full steam. The just-turned-twenty Lowry begs, even tries to bribe, the established poet-novelist to take the beginner into his household in the "other" Cambridge. In the summer of 1929, before going up to Cambridge, Lowry set sail for

Boston by way of the West Indies. He arrived at Aiken's doorstep with a battered suitcase containing an exercise book in which were notes for *Ultramarine,* the projected novel of his sea experiences. That summer a kinship was formed which was deeper than one of mere literary dimensions. "The fact is," Aiken recalled, "that we were uncannily alike in almost everything, found instantly that we spoke the same language, were astonishingly *en rapport;* and it was therefore the most natural thing in the world that a year later, when difficulties arose between him and his father, I was able to act as mediator . . . and . . . for the next three years, *in loco parentis,* I became his father." [19]

Malcolm Lowry is the brilliant, alcoholic Hambo in Aiken's surrealistic autobiography, *Ushant,*[20] and in the autobiographical novel *A Heart for the Gods of Mexico.* The next chapter will examine in detail the influence of Aiken, the man and friend, in the alchemizing of that almost comic Hambo figure into the creator of the Consul. Aiken's tutorship of the young artist seeking a viable technique was crucial. While Lowry saw in the quest for identity of such other voyager-writers as Melville, Conrad, O'Neill, and, especially, the Norwegian Nordahl Grieg, a compelling correspondence, he could find in none of them a congenial fabric and texture. For these Lowry went to his mentor, and in Aiken's first novel, *Blue Voyage,*[21] Lowry began his own literary voyage to Joyce. In *Voyage* and subsequent novels, the American writer translated the Joycean flow of consciousness and interior monologues into a subjective emphasis that becomes megalomaniacal. It was Aiken's careful study of *Ulysses* that illumined for him the most viable way of evoking consciousness from the flux of life. Frederick J. Hoffman believes it probable that the first publication of *Ulysses* in 1922 was Aiken's incentive for beginning *Blue Voyage.*[22] At any rate, he started the book in the winter of 1922–23, and it was published in 1927, about the time Lowry began writing to him.

Before turning to the works themselves for evidence of the movement of Lowry to Joyce through Aiken, one might mention an unusual application of the epigraph from Melville which opens this chapter. If I read his tribute to Hawthorne correctly, Melville urges a "confession" of a kind of chain of indebtedness from artist to artist. Both Lowry and Joyce appear aware of a chain of indebtedness. Lowry's correspondence is replete with tributes to his friend. Aiken's reputation is primarily as a poet and as a writer of a number of imperishable short stories, his novels being largely forgotten today (Walter Allen calls *Blue Voyage* a "stillborn" *Ulysses*,[23] and Anthony Burgess sees Aiken as a producer of "Prufrock figures"[24]). Lowry's preference to credit Aiken over Joyce as an influence on style is paralleled by Joyce's deference to the little-known Edouard Dujardin as the source of the interior-monologue technique that he brought to perfection in *Ulysses*. Richard Ellmann records that Mary Colum drew Joyce's pique when she chided him, shortly after the publication of *Ulysses*, for his insistence on resurrecting Dujardin. "Haven't you had enough fun with this?" she asked. "Haven't you pulled enough people's legs? And anyway, why deny your indebtedness to Freud and Jung? Isn't it better to be indebted to great originators like that than to——?"[25] Although Joyce later described his exchange of credits with Dujardin as giving "cake for bread"[26]— the Frenchman's methods being of importance only because Joyce sensed their potential—he shares with Lowry a seemingly compulsive predilection for favoring others than the "great originators." While Gide was arguing persuasively at the time *Ulysses* was published that it was neither Dujardin nor Joyce but Poe, Browning, and Dostoevsky jointly who were responsible for the interior monologue, Joyce continued to honor Dujardin and, in a sense, himself. Lowry in Chapter II of the *Volcano*—the actual beginning of the novel, the point where Yvonne returns unexpectedly to the Consul, thus presenting a possibility for his redemption—records their conversation in a technique which closely resembles that perfected by Flaubert in the agricultural fair episode of *Madame Bovary* (Part II, Chap. 8): the practice of juxtaposing multiple conversations. There, as is well known, the dialogue between Emma and Rodolphe is regularly interrupted by councillor Lieuvain's speech about political storms and agriculture. In *Volcano*, the strained conversation during the first moments of reunion between Yvonne and Geoffrey Firmin is consistently broken into by loud comments from another person, a gunrunner for the Mexican Fascists, the man who has helped make it possible for the third leg of the novel's triangle, Geoffrey's half-brother Hugh, to arrive in Mexico at the same time. As with Flaubert, the intersecting dialogue is about agriculture (". . . just a bunch of Alladamnbama farmers!"). Lowry over and

over affirmed the voice of Aiken in *Voyage* as responsible for
such multi-level effects. But Joyce, not to mention Flaubert, goes
unacknowledged. Joyce in the first quarter of the century was displaying to Aiken, who did not absorb them fully (Burgess says—
unjustly, I believe—that he lacked the "architectonic skill"), and
to Faulkner, who could, lessons in flux techniques which, while
they were tiny tempests in the teapot novels of Dujardin, had
certain earlier applications in *Bovary* and *Karamazov*. Here is
Flaubert's contrapuntal effect as Joyce has reworked it for a
description of a priest's journey through Dublin to aid the family
of a deceased parishioner:

. . . Father Conmee smiled and nodded and smiled and walked along
Mountjoy square east.

Mr. Denis J. Maginni, professor of dancing, & co., in silk hat, slate
frock coat with silk facings, white kerchief tie, tight lavender trousers,
canary gloves and pointed patent boots walking with grave deportment
most respectfully took the curbstone as he passed Lady Maxwell at the
corner of Dignam's court.

Was that not Mrs. M'Guinness?

Mrs. M'Guinness, stately, silverhaired, bowed to Father Conmee
from the farther footpath along which she sailed. And Father Conmee
smiled and saluted. How did she do?

(*Ulysses*, 217)

The priest's is the main action, but Joyce, like Flaubert, wants
to give the reader a kind of third dimension. He therefore in-
terposes between Father Conmee's walking and meeting with
Mrs. M'Guinness an encounter in another part of Dublin between
Maginni and Lady Maxwell. Early in *Blue Voyage*, Aiken
achieves a sense of simultaneity in the Joycean manner. While
Demarest and a British major are playing chess and discussing
"Ruy Lopez" and other matters of the game, several conversations intersect theirs, one between a man and a woman and
another among poker players as they hum the tune being played
on the ship's gramophone (*Blue Voyage*, 47–49).

Joyce is especially skilled in tracing the onset of erotic fantasies.
In the passage below, Leopold Bloom, seeking a return to Molly's
favor and favors, experiences crosscurrents of "outside" matters
and "inside" thoughts, the two playing on each other like intersecting monologues. He conjures up images of concupiscence

merely by scanning *Sweets of Sin,* a novel he considers buying for Molly.

. . . *Sweets of Sin.* More in her line. Let us see. He read where his finger opened.

—*All the dollarbills her husband gave her were spent in the stores on wondrous gowns and costliest frillies. For him! For Raoul!*

Yes. This. Here. Try.

—*Her mouth glued on his in a luscious voluptuous kiss while his hands felt for the opulent curves inside her deshabille.*

Yes. Take this. The end.

—*You are late, he spoke hoarsely, eyeing her with a suspicious glare.*

The beautiful woman threw off her sabletrimmed wrap, displaying her queenly shoulders, and heaving embonpoint. An imperceptible smile played round her perfect lips as she turned to him calmly.

Mr. Bloom read again: *The beautiful woman.*

Warmth showered gently over him, cowing his flesh. Flesh yielded amid rumpled clothes. Whites of eyes swooning up. His nostrils arched themselves for prey. Melting breast ointments *(for him! For Raoul!).* Armpits' oniony sweat. Fishgluey slime (her heaving embonpoint!) Feel! Press! Crushed Sulphur dung of lions!

Young! Young!

(*Ulysses,* 232–33)

One notes Joyce's impatience with the usual means of narrative expression. The suggestive words from *Sweets of Sin* have isolated Bloom's state of domestic unfulfillment. Joyce wants to show how half-formed thoughts enter and leave consciousness with almost impossible rapidity. The fleeting impression must be seized at its birth, even if inadequately. The mind keeps racing on.

In an equivalent scene from *Blue Voyage,* Demarest, in a kind of portrait of the pseudo-artist as a middle-aged man, reveals his erotic deprivation in a vision of the attractive widow Faubion. In quick order, Faubion breaks into Demarest's consciousness merely as a name in men's conversation, then as a participant in an erotic fantasy, and finally as the "vigorous synthesis" of all his past loves.

". . . I don't know, she strikes me as straight—that's all. Straight but fidgety."

"Straight but fidgety! No siree, Bob. I'm an old fool, and never knew a woman, if that girl isn't—! He lifted a twinkle, sidelong, toward

Demarest. Demarest sat down on the red plush divan. A sour smell came up from it; and the clicking of the water bottle in its wooden socket, and then the loosely delayed return click, hollow and slack, made him slightly giddy. He lifted his nose toward the pure stream of air from the port. Porpoises. Flying fish. Icebergs. Cobalt and snow . . . A slice of porpoise, Mr. Smith? Thank you no, Mr. Demarest . . . Wing of Faubion, Mr. Smith? A little off the breast, please, Mr. Demarest . . . Faubion gazed at him, morose and sombre, reserved but yielding, implacable but affectionate. Poising the bread knife, with waved edge damescent, he prepared to make Faubion an Amazon. One-breasted. Tell me when it hurts, Faubion. Does it hurt? . . . A-a-ah-mmmm—you're hurting—now! . . . Still hurting? . . . Phhh-not so—much . . . She turned her head far to one side, closing her eyes . . . This was the moment—this was always the moment; that delicious moment of utter anguished surrender: the flushed face turned extravagantly aside, eyelids shut, mouth relaxed with pleasure but curved with apprehension and rigid with pain . . . The dew on the forehead . . . Singular, that we should so desire this of all possible moments, a moment the essentially fleetingest of moments, that one must dedicate one's life to its pursuit. . . .

"She's damned attractive," Demarest said.

(*Blue Voyage*, 44)

Aiken is less staccato, more consciously literary, than Joyce. He follows Demarest through a crescendo of thoughts called up by the mere mention of a woman's name.

Joyce, accused by Lowry of writing inventories, uses every word to advantage in evoking the feel of a hearse going quickly by with a baby's coffin inside. The impact on Bloom, who lost his only son Rudy in infancy, is superimposed on that of another onlooker, and the effect is telegraphic.

White horses with white frontlet plumes came round the Rotunda corner, galloping. A tiny coffin flashed by. In a hurry to bury. A mourning coach. Unmarried. Black for the married. Piebald for bachelors. Dun for a nun.
—Sad, Martin Cunningham said. A child.

A dwarf's face mauve and wrinkled like little Rudy's was. Dwarf's body, weak as putty, in a white-lined deal box. Burial friendly society pays. Penny a week for a sod of turf. Our. Little. Beggar. Baby. Meant nothing. Mistake of nature.

(*Ulysses*, 94)

[33]

Bloom's mourning for his son has been renewed by a single word from Cunningham. Here is Demarest, visioning his own death and burial while listening to a song.

. . . "My Little Gray Home in the West." Flute, violin, piano and double-bass. The flute player, a young man with a pale, fine girlish face and a blond cascade of hair, hooked his lip earnestly over the flute: uncous lip. How white his hands were, too, on the black flute. *My lit-tle gray ho-ome in the West.* A brick vault in the cemetery, overgrown, oversnarled, with gaudy trumpet vine . . . Bones in the tropic dust. My little red house in the south. Bees and bones and trumpet flowers: nostalgia, Gauguin, heart of darkness. . . .

(*Blue Voyage,* 28)

Joyce, as usual, is short; Aiken is only a little longer. Both dash off the key phrases or words. Each wants to show the essential relatedness—the constant irrelevant relevancies—in things. The distinction between Joyce and Aiken is that between a virtuoso and a concert musician. Each, in Anthony Burgess's useful phrase, allows the technique to live a life of its own,[27] but only Joyce provides characters and situations which are sufficient to justify the display of experimental skills. One cares deeply about the interrelationship of Bloom, Stephen, and Molly. The interior monologues of Demarest illumine his plight, but it is of insufficient interest to raise the devices out of the test-tube stage; they remain interesting experiments.

This is not the place to examine the metamorphosis of Lowry's Consul into an archetypal figure compelling enough to justify the kind, if not the degree, of language virtuosity found in *Ulysses.* Lowry's stage, like Joyce's (and Aiken's) is domestic. The life of the Consul, like Bloom's, has less amplitude in itself, say, than that of one of Thomas Mann's heroes, Hans Castorp or Adrian Leverkühn. In the concrete elements of it there is not the constant pressure toward epical-allegorical aggrandizement. Yet both Lowry and Joyce have a range of tone that household drama never had. When the Consul describes the *delirium tremens,* he does so in language that suggests Joyce.

But d.t.'s are only the beginning, the music round the portal of the Qlipoth, the overture, conducted by the God of flies. . . . Why do people see rats? These are the sort of questions that ought to concern the

World. . . . Consider the word remorse. Remord. Mordeo, mordere. La Mordida! Agenbite. . . .

(Volcano, 218)

The last, of course, when combined with "inwit," means in Middle English "remorse of conscience." It is not by accident that Lowry applies it to the Consul *in extremis*. Midway through *Ulysses*, Stephen Dedalus encounters his sister Dilly at a bookstall. She has just spent her food money on a book.

> He took the coverless book from her hand. Chardenal's French primer.
> —What did you buy that for? he asked. To learn French?
> She nodded, reddening, and closing tight her lips.
> Show no surprise. Quite natural.
> —Here, Stephen said. It's all right. Mind Maggy doesn't pawn it on you. I suppose all my books are gone.
> —Some, Dilly said. We had to.
> She is drowning. Agenbite. Save her. Agenbite. All against us. She will drown me with her eyes and hair. Lank coils of seaweed hair around me, my heart, my soul. Salt green death.
> We.
> Agenbite of inwit. Inwit's agenbite.
> Misery! Misery!

(Ulysses, 239–40)

The cries of Leopold Bloom, wailed inwardly as he reads from the book selected for the wife who has forsaken him, and those of Stephen, as he contemplates his drowning sister, correspond to the series of multilingual equivalents for the remorse that has overcome the Consul. Language-as-discovery is supreme in both *Ulysses* and *Under the Volcano*. But the stages in Lowry's voyage to Joyce are still to be charted.

V *The "Fatherless" Dedalus; the Rootless Hilliot*

If all the stories of *Dubliners* can be considered a single assault aimed by Joyce at probing the nets of state, language, and religion in Ireland, Malcolm Lowry's early writing had a similar obsession. His first voyage at eighteen (year-long) to the Orient that provided the material for *Ultramarine*, a second as a fireman on a Norwegian tramp to visit his grandfather's birthplace in

Norway and to see the writer Nordahl Grieg, and a third, after his first year at Cambridge, to Boston and Conrad Aiken by way of the West Indies—all these had made Lowry a seasoned sailor and charged him with a flagging current that convinced him he would be "outward bound, always outward . . . to be fighting always for the dreamt-of-harbor." As he wrote of himself much later, consider the

plight of an Englishman who is a Scotchman who is Norwegian who is a Canadian who is a Negro at heart from Dahomey who is married to an American who is on a French ship in distress which has been built by Americans and who finds at last that he is a Mexican dreaming of the White Cliffs of Dover.

("Panama," 96)

Lowry, like Joyce, had always known what he wanted to say, but, unlike Joyce, never how to say it. A very early story, "Hotel Room in Chartres," [28] is suffused by the quest theme but takes tentative steps away from straight narrative toward Aiken—and hence, toward Joyce—in a scene where the lovers, after a quarrel, are reunited on a train from Paris to Chartres. The hero, just back from a sea voyage, listens to a group of French sailors as they sing and read aloud from a magazine whose main feature is a column of enticements to sexual liaison:

"Butterfly with wings of blue wishes to exchange thoughts and dreams, 30 years; pretty cultivated."
. . . as the train thundered through Maintenon on its way to the sea, he was joining all his ships once more . . . Exchange to Prester to join the Suley, to Birkenhead to join the Mentor, to Oslo to join the King Haakon. . . . A ship silent at dawn as they approached the port: at the deskboy's knock crawling fuddled with sleep from his bunk. . . . You don't want to bother with a washdown today . . . just square up the after deck . . . and get them derricks up.
"Modern Eve. 23. Sportive. Seeks good comrade for automobiling and true friendship."

("Chartres," 56–57)

The ex-sailor senses that his arrival in the compartment with a woman has inhibited the seamen. This causes him to lash out at the girl. She leaves him with his kinsmen and their bottle.

When they arrive in Chartres, he visions the station as a ship being dismantled. But the spire of the cathedral reminds him that they were first lovers there. The ending is land-locked but one suspects not for long. Rootlessness is at the heart of all Lowry's works.

But how to evoke it? A close friend of Lowry's, Gerald Noxon, recalls his classmate's attempts to complete *Ultramarine* while still at Cambridge. Their conversations were always about the technical problems of the writer.

The question always was, how should a serious novelist write in that year 1930? Naturally we discussed the kind of solutions put forward by such writers as Joyce, Faulkner and Hemingway. . . .

Basically Malcolm was unwilling to repudiate the legacy which he found awaiting him in the works of nineteenth-century novelists. While discarding the aridity of a purely realistic style, he was unwilling to adopt the kind of personal stenography which made the works of writers like Joyce and Faulkner superficially difficult for the reader but still insisting that his writing must be capable of carrying meaning at many different levels of intellectual and emotional communication which he discerned in Melville, for instance.[29]

Lowry was to borrow from Melville. He, like Melville, named his ships after archetypal themes (the *Rights of Man* became the *Oedipus Tyrannus* of *Ultramarine,* and even characters are named after Melville protagonists (the psychiatrist in *Lunar Caustic,*[30] a novella about a down-and-outer in Bellevue, is named "Dr. Claggert"). But the few moving passages of *Ultramarine* [31] are the ones that are Aikenian and Joycean. Dana Hilliot, a rich English youth about to go up to Cambridge, has shipped aboard the freighter *Oedipus Tyrannus* for Singapore. Anxious to win the approval of his shipmates, a rough, derisive lot, and to match their example in the bars and bordellos of the Chinese ports, Dana struggles to remain somehow faithful to all he left in England—most obviously, his girlfriend, and more subtly, his parents and upper-class heritage. His tensions are dramatized by the use of interior monologue as Dana—drunk, disorderly but never free of the obsessions of estrangement—steals a rickshaw.

Richard Barthelmess in *The Amateur Gentleman.* . . .
The wind came slowly at first, like my own intermittent breath, as

I ran down the Yamagata-dori in the shafts of the jinrickshaw. Like
the beginning of Debussy's *Hommage à Rameau*. Then it came in
quicker puffs: finally it bellowed as if ejected from the maw of some
dragon; it blew in the teeth of rickshaw-wallahs and in my teeth, and
I braced myself against it in the shafts like a shying horse. It snatched
at the bottom of lampposts whirling old copies of the *Singapore Free
Press* across the road . . . posters shouted: *Free Press, Free Press,*
murder of brother-in-law's concubine. Shrill light flickered behind
glimmering panes, where kimonos and soft fabrics slept. . . . The night,
pocked with bright stars, twitched its face and drew black blankets
over it. Ah, mother, mother, what is this man thy darling kissed and
cuffed thou lustingly engenderest to make his brag and rot crowned
with all honour and all shamefulness? The Amateur Gentleman? The
Yumato Hotel, nine million two hundred and fourteen bathrooms . . . ?
Me nice girl very nice very clean very sweet very sanitary? I don't
want my son coarsened by a lot of hooligans? My son whom thou
lustingly engenderest? Ah, sorrow, who dost borrow the lustrous passion
from the falcon's eye, but you cannot borrow your son because he is
being coarsened by a lot of hooligans. Ah, Zeus, hear me now. Zeus.
Zeus. Dis. Dios. Dii. Deorum, Deis or Dis. Dais. I. S. R. Miles, the
mathematics master, sitting at the head of the hall, presiding over
preparation, his eyes lecherous and rolling, the eyes of a ferret. One
had always suspected his homosexuality. Herod, he looked like. Herod
watching Salome. . . . Male Salome. Satsuma wares. Salome wears—
what? And they pierced his hands his side his feet, and dey heard dat
noise in Jerusalem street. . . . Harry Weldon in 1925 singing that at the
Derby Castle, Douglas. . . .

(Ultramarine, 124–25)

The interior monologue, its parts linked by newspaper headlines, sound-alike words, double-entendre on a film title, a ship's
siren, continues for three more pages. I have quoted at length
because this passage from a forgotten first novel is quite likely the
first extended stream-of-consciousness by Lowry on the Joyce-
Aiken model. In exuberance, it is suggestive of Stephen Dedalus's
mock-sermon which closes the Oxen of the Sun chapter of *Ulysses*.
Lowry's youthful protagonist moves in drunken fantasies from
his mother to a Singapore brothel to a series of Latinate cognates
for God to a remembered headmaster to the words of a song
about the Crucifixion. At the end of the Hospital chapter, according to Stanley Sultan,[32] Stephen makes a concise recapitulation
of his defiance of God, his complaints against church and state.

Where Hilliot lacks a father or God figure, Dedalus has Bloom who, in Sultan's analysis, is a messiah, the agent of God's grace, the Elijah who can bring the sinner to God.

Christicle, who's this excrement yellow gospeller on the Merion Hall? Elijah is coming. Washed in the blood of the lamb. . . . Come on, you triple extract of infamy! . . . The Deity ain't no nickel bum-show. I put it to you that he's on the square and a corking fine business proposition. He's the grandest thing yet and don't you forget it. . . . You'll need to rise precious early, you sinner there, if you want to diddle the Almighty God. . . . He's got a cough-mixture with a punch in it for you, my friend, in his backpocket. Just you try it on.

(*Ulysses*, 420)

The two young heroes—the "fatherless" artist Dedalus and the "fatherless" Hilliot—both express their profoundest dilemma, in each case, rootlessness, through innovations of novelistic technique forged by Joyce and utilized by Lowry after a kind of transfusion given him by Conrad Aiken.

VI *Learning the Lessons of the Master*

Malcolm Lowry's first novel, published when he was twenty-three, reveals little of the command and control of material and language displayed by James Joyce in *Dubliners,* written when he was the same age. *Ultramarine,* except for a powerful explosion of style here and there, reads like badly digested Melville-Conrad-Dana. To pursue an earlier metaphor, Aiken's transfusion to Lowry of the flux materials of *Ulysses* had failed in *Ultramarine;* Lowry understood the experimentalism of *Blue Voyage,* but could not make it work. Joyce usually writes in the third person, Aiken always. Dana Hilliot's first-person reflections were usually self-conscious.

I put down my glass noisily then picked it up again, and gazed mournfully at my reflection. Narcissus. Bollocky Bill the Sailor. Bollocky Bill, aspiring writer, drawn magically from the groves of the Muses by Poseidon . . . I looked more deeply in the glass. Christ, was this me? . . . Sadness! Misery! Self-disgust! Terror! No getting away from . . . the unfortunate Hilliot, this strong creature with a head of filthy, infected hair, and a maggoty brain and a rotting consciousness, who dreams of archetypal images. . . . Eugene Dana Hilliot! . . . Hear me, stinking cod, fulfilled of donge and of corruption! Tinfoil Jesus, crucified homunculus (who is also the cross), spitted on the hook of an imaginary Galilee!

(*Ultramarine*, 98–99)

Lowry mentions his early novel only with embarrassment in his letters. The lapses into long soliloquies, invariably punctuated with exclamation points, show little either of the ingenuity of Aiken or the variety of Joyce. Lowry's widow, Margerie Bonner Lowry, reveals that he always intended to make a thorough revision of *Ultramarine* which would have involved the Joyce-Aiken practice of keeping the viewpoint consistently in the third person.[33] All that can be served by pairing *Dubliners* and *Ultramarine* is to show that Joyce and Lowry, from the beginning, worked their art from opposite directions. In his stories Joyce circumspectly detaches himself from his characters while, at a safe distance, maintaining sympathy for them. Lowry is incapable of a gallery of characters; his tools are wholly subjective. If Joyce's mission as artist was to forge "the uncreated conscience of his race," it was Lowry's goal to illumine the consciousness of one shattered fragment of Western civilization, the hero manqué: the man of supreme sensibility who is fallen but does not choose to rise.

Stephen Spender tries to link *Ulysses* and *Under the Volcano* but ends in a series of contrasts.[34] He concludes that Joyce uses myth and symbols—the complex weave of his language—to absorb the characters into the cosmos. Joyce's outside-life preoccupation is distinct from Lowry's creation of the inner world of one doomed man. Both novels encompass a single day. Bloom and Stephen live through that single day in which the incredible "thinginess" of life swirls around and, in the final chapters, through them. Geoffrey and Hugh Firmin—the two equal one, Malcolm Lowry—*are* the stuff of life, and their apparent defeat on the Day of the Dead is also their redemption.

Spender concludes that the hero of *Ulysses* is the language in which the book is written, and that language is also the history of race. He adds that the hero of *Volcano* is the autobiographic consciousness of the Consul. The Consul is a nation invaded: devastated by a period of history—the story takes place in November, 1938, and the Battle of the Ebro in Spain is a recurring motif for man's inhumanity—and devastated by the paradox of knowing there is no life without love and yet being unable to accept love.

To acknowledge that the real hero of *Volcano* is any less the book's language than is the case with *Ulysses* runs against the grain of this study. It now remains to show that through his study of Conrad Aiken's experimental rendering of Joyce in *Blue Voyage*, Malcolm Lowry finally found his own voice. Professor Sultan demonstrates more clearly than any recent commentator how to puzzle out the fantasy-laden latter chapters of *Ulysses*. He shows that the longest chapter, the 170-page Nighttown episode, when read as a series of "daymares" which are artistic representations rather than case reports, can be readily grasped. His key, as will be seen, works equally well for those sections of *Blue Voyage* which are most Joycean and for those portions of *Under the Volcano* where the mind of the Consul, his sensibility heightened by vast quantities of mescal, wanders in a grotesquerie that is no less comic than tragic.

Sultan writes that "the fantasies of Bloom and Stephen are not simply communicated naturalistically but represented in terms dictated by the author." [35] Thus a long dream—a matter of seconds, according to psychologists—may extend over many pages between a comment and a response. In the Nighttown chapter, which takes place in Bella Cohen's brothel, one of the prostitutes asks Bloom for a cigarette. Bloom says, "The mouth can be better engaged than a cylinder of rank weed." The prostitute pokes fun at him: "Go on. Make a stump speech out of it." And, for nineteen pages of fantasy, Bloom does just that. The prostitute's next comment, after Bloom is "carbonized" in a fiery immolation, is perfectly apposite: "Talk away till you're black in the face."

There is nothing so elaborate as Bloom's in the fantasies of Demarest. Nevertheless, Frederick Hoffman is right when he finds certain of Aiken's inside narratives—Sultan would call them daymares—suggestive of the Nighttown episode.[36] Early in the novel the bachelor Demarest befriends Smith, an aging divorced man, and the two fall into conversation about "available" women aboard ship. Smith speaks of Faubion: "Attractive! . . . She's a ring-tailed screecher. She's got me going—yes, sir, she's got me going. She can put her slippers—" (*Blue Voyage*, 44). Smith's words are drowned by various ship noises and absorbed by his partner's reverie. Demarest visions a bearded, wizard-like Smith inside his coffin wailing for Faubion who approaches, flame-bodied, *bearing a slipper in each hand.* One page later, the day-mare is interrupted, and the men's conversation continued. Smith tells Demarest his marital history. His wife "flew the coop. With a little shrimp of a one-lunged candy salesman—married man, too" (*Blue Voyage*, 45). She is described to Demarest as young —twenty-one—and musical—she plays piano. This combination of descriptives leads to a three-page fantasy in which Smith's runaway bride's story is reenacted, but in Demarest's mind and terms. Smith is pictured as leaving his young Venus at home, bored and alone, by the piano. Her lover taps on the window as she plays "Waltz me around again Will-ee." Willy brings a box of candy. The wife and her lover depart. The scene shifts to Smith's return with the waltz "still hanging in the air." All that remain are a farewell note and an opened box of chocolates (*Blue Voyage*, 46).

Demarest's inner monologues often expand into imagined conversations with the objects of his heart's desires, most notably with Cynthia. At first, his words are aimed at shocking the young girl. Then he launches into a monologue on the relationship of suffering to art. This material alternates with actual discussions on art with Silberstein, a chewing-gum merchant. Hoffman speculates that Aiken had probably been influenced by Joyce's *Portrait of the Artist as a Young Man* where Stephen discusses art with Lynch and Cranly.[37] Eventually, the reader sees Demarest's suffering for what it is: a disguise for the desolation he shares with Leopold Bloom—erotic deprivation. As with Bloom in Nighttown, Demarest undergoes a fantasy trial for "erotomania." Bloom's trial is much the richer, of course. Where, in *Voyage*, the trial is merely amusing, it is, in the Nighttown chapter, a brilliant example of technique-as-discovery. As Sultan notes, "It presents Bloom's fundamental problem and the sin related to it. . . . It probes Carnal Concupiscence more deeply, especially the furtive and shameful pseudo-sexual activities to which he has descended."[38]

In Bloom's daymare, a series of women is summoned to testify to his erotic character. The scene explodes into burlesque. The distraught Bloom is additionally accused of sins against society, of being a black-robed anarchist. The judge orders the "well-known dynamitard, forger, bigamist, bawd and cuckold" to be hanged. Bloom is saved when Dignam, to whose funeral and survivors the kindly Bloom has contributed generously, rises from the grave to reveal that Bloom is in black, not because he is an anarchist, but because of the funeral.

The *grand-guignol* quality of the fantasies in the Nighttown episode is made possible, in part, by the drunkenness of Bloom and Dedalus. *Under the Volcano* is a novel whose hero is compulsively—irremediably—drunk three-fourths of the time. The fantasies in Nighttown are a palimpsest of the two men's mental preoccupations and the actual goings-on in the physical world around them. Aiken, in perhaps the first novel to show the full impact of *Ulysses*, also manages a superimposition of Demarest's fantasies on the cabin-deck world of the ship. In contrast, the result in *Blue Voyage* is a series of neat tricks. Malcolm Lowry, whose literary life began with his aping of *Voyage* in *Ultramarine,* can, in *Volcano,* go beyond anything his teacher accomplished in prose. He achieves in his portrayal of the Consul's mescal-inflamed consciousness a deftly patterned—wild but never improbable—medley of memories, free fancies, conversational snatches, absurdities, improvisations. Where Joyce combines the nuptial self-reproach of Bloom and the filial guilt of Stephen, Lowry achieves a composite in his view of the fall of a man of sensibility who is also subject to the earthy disasters of the addict. He maintains a maelstrom harmony between the physical world of the Consul—his delusive and daemonic universe—and the fantasy harbor where deliverance lies.

The best analogue to Nighttown is the "garden" scene (Chapter V) of *Volcano.* Here Lowry moves the Consul about his run-down Eden in search of a bottle of tequila he had hidden there. Trying to look nonchalant—for even as a boy Geoffrey made it a point of honor to appear more sober the drunker he became—the Consul finds the tequila, carries on a bitter exchange with his conscience, and gives in to the needed fortifier. He sees a keep-off-the-grass sign which, freely translated (actually mistranslated) from the Spanish, becomes the novel's major talisman of doom. He attempts to swap pleasantries with a dour American, significantly named Quincey, who mocks him. His dignity failing because of hiccoughs and an inability to button his fly (the latter, a likely parallel to the button-bipping sound in Nighttown), the Consul decides to talk instead to Quincey's cat. His words echo Joyce more strongly than at any point in the novel: "—Hello-pussy-my-little-Oedipuss-pusspuss. . . . My little Xicotancatl" (*Volcano*, 134).

And later, or, perhaps, earlier, for time shifts imperceptibly in this section:

Mr. Quincey's words knocked on his consciousness—or someone actually was knocking on a door. . . . Old De Quincey; the knocking on the gate in Macbeth. Knock knock: who's there? Cat. Cat who? Catastrophe. Catastrophe who? Catastrophysicist. What is it you, my little popo-cat? . . . Katabasis to cat abysses. . . .

(*Volcano*, 136)

No book since *Ulysses* can match Lowry's inspired punning. The garden scene is funny beyond compare. Yet, as Douglas Day observes, "The garden is the ruined Paradise, and Geoffrey a forlorn and corrupted Adam, forced by a malevolent God to remain forever there, at the place of his sin." [39]

One could go on indefinitely linking the "feel" of the two novels. It is enough to say that the essential lessons of flux—those pioneered and perfected by Joyce—are also commanded by Lowry. *Ulysses* and *Under the Volcano*, unlike in many ways, join in this: they are susceptible to reading on many levels—jam session to tragedy, entertainment to prophecy, cryptogram to allegory. Malcolm Lowry once spoke to a friend, the poet Earle Birney, in glowing terms of the comic excellence of Birney's novel *Turvey*. He quoted Joyce's complaints about critics of *Ulysses*: "They might at least have said it was damned funny." [40]

CHAPTER 2

The Son in Search of a Father

> I have known a city of dreadful night,
> Dreadfuller far than Kipling knew, or
>   Thomson. . . .
> This is the night when hope's last seed is
>   flown
> From the evanescent mind of the winter's
>   grandson.
>
> In the dungeon shivers the alcoholic child,
> Comforted by the murderer, since compas-
>   sion is here too;
> The noises of the night are cries for help
> From the town and from the garden which
>   evicts those who destroy!
>
>   . . . .
>
> And I crucified between two continents. . . .
>   Malcolm Lowry
>   "In the Oaxaca Jail" [1]

IT is a multiple irony of modern literary history that *Under the Volcano,* a novel Conrad Aiken both "posed for" and helped "coach" into being, is often spoken of in the same breath as *Ulysses,* a landmark behind whose shadow Aiken's own long fiction has been relegated.

Chapter 1 sought to show that Lowry, even without having read *Ulysses,* mastered Joycean technique through absorption in the writings of Aiken. This chapter will seek to demonstrate that Lowry began the complex evolvement that ripened in his characterization of the Consul through his relationship with Aiken the man and the father-in-place-of-a-father. I sought in Chapter 1 to trace by biographical circumstances and textual comparison the literary blood transfusion of Joyce to Lowry through Aiken. By a further combining of personal history and text I shall try to assert the crucial private role of Aiken in the alchemizing of the almost comic "Hambo" figure into the archetypal "Consul" figure.

I   Early Manhood: "Out-Mobying Melville"

The Malcolm Lowry who left the "English death" behind for the Mexican variety in 1936 and, *in extremis,* became his own character, the Consul, was a young man about whom little can be documented but much can be inferred. He was already, three years after his graduation, a legend at Cambridge, although from the accounts of T. R. Henn, then a Junior Fellow and once a tutor of Lowry's, he was a better story teller and ribald song-smith than student.[2] Once gone up to Cambridge, he saw little of his parents, Mr. and Mrs. Arthur Osborne Lowry. His father was a devout Wesleyan Methodist who kept urging Malcolm to read the story of the Prodigal Son.[3] His mother appears to have been a sweet woman, understandably dominated by her husband, a woman who lived just long enough—until 1947—to see the enthu-siastic U.S. reviews that seemed assurance that her favorite, the youngest of four sons, would be a major literary success. Lowry's defiance of family—and concomitant guilt—appears to have reached the breaking point when the elder Lowry, in a response to his son's pleas, arranged for him to ship aboard a freighter as a coal trimmer when he was seventeen. The presence of a "rich kid" on a schoolboy lark was not welcomed by the professional seamen. To complete the disaster, Arthur Lowry had his son chauffered to the dock in the family limousine. Lowry recalled these circumstances in *Ultramarine.*

As noted in Chapter 1, the meeting with Aiken "that beautiful summer" of 1929 in Cambridge, Massachusetts, not only gave Lowry a literary father but an actual one. He had crossed the Atlantic driven by mystic and literary reasons to meet the author of *Blue Voyage.* Aiken's dedication—to "C.M.L."—Lowry took to be to himself although, of course, his first transatlantic letter to Aiken came *after* he had read *Blue Voyage.* Sometime between his attendance at The Leys (where "Mr. Chips" was a master) and Cambridge Lowry had dropped his given name, Clarence.

"C.M.L." could have stood for "Clarence Malcolm Lowry," but they were also the initials of Conrad Aiken's first wife, Clarissa Lorenz, who recently devoted a poignant memoir to the Lowry of those years.[4] "Nothing in his cherubic countenance suggested the crucified genius" of *Under the Volcano,* she wrote. The stroke of fortune that brought Aiken to the "other Cambridge" later in 1929 for a lengthy residence made the literary and spiritual kinship permanent.

From his university days, Lowry seems to have dropped his family below his horizon except for the monthly cheques—twenty guineas—from "the old man," cheques which the elder Lowry sent to Aiken to prevent his son from spending them on drink. In the early thirties the Aikens went to live in Rye, Sussex, where, not far from the house where Henry James had lived, they took over Jeake's House, a seventeenth-century edifice named after a family of astrologers and necromancers.

Malcolm was fascinated by the place, and he spent all his vacations from Cambridge with the Aikens. For all her motherly feelings toward the just-come-of-age Malcolm, Mrs. Aiken

associated him with catastrophe. On his own admission, just to meet him was a disaster. Conrad for a long time suffered fracture headaches—souvenirs of a bibulous wrestling match with his protégé over the lid of the WC tank.

("Call It Misadventure," 106)

During these years, Malcolm provided a foreshadowing of the man who fifteen years later, his novel a major critical success, would stand, arms folded and seaman's legs spread and firmly planted, talking to no one at a publisher's cocktail party in his honor. He was given to clairvoyance and long silences, Clarissa Lorenz recalled,

and was never so isolated seemingly as when part of a group. Social occasions paralyzed him. Playing bridge or parlor games like mock murder trials, he would sit in a trance, lost in his private world of daemons and demons.

("Call It Misadventure," 106)

But, if one may judge by a snapshot taken by Clarissa Aiken at the earlier Cambridge, the period was a happy one. Lowry, despite horrendous misadventures with its several manuscripts,[5] completed and published *Ultramarine* in 1933. Aiken told me [6] that *Ultramarine*'s debt to *Blue Voyage* (1927) could best be proved by feeding both into an IBM computer. Aiken's creativity during the Lowry years (1928–36) was prodigious. He wrote the long poems *John Deth, The Coming Forth by Day of Osiris Jones, Preludes for Memnon;* the novel *Great Circle,* a work admired by Freud and kept on his bookshelf in his reception room in Vienna; and a story collection, *Among the Lost People.*

The immediate post-Cambridge Lowry has been best described by Clarissa Lorenz and by a close friend, the Irish short-story writer James Stern. In April, 1933, Malcolm joined the Aikens and the painter Edward Burra for a holiday in Spain. Clarissa Lorenz's description reads like a bibulous parody of *The Sun Also Rises* with Lowry, an uncastrated but booze-vulnerable Jake Barnes; Aiken, an older Bill Gorton; and the painter Burra, a kind of acid brush-wielding Mike Campbell. In fact, she notes an interesting reference to the Hemingway hero:

> He [Malcolm] and Conrad had been talking of little else but the first bullfight of the season. . . . My husband treasured a snapshot of a beaming, mustachioed aficionado crouching beside a live bull, the autograph reading, 'Don Ernesto Hemingvia, *toreando a un cabestro castrado en Pamplona.*'
>
> ("Call It Misadventure," 109)

Most important by-product of the holiday for Lowry, however, was to be the Lady Brett figure. She was "an exotic American girl" named Jan who joined the Aikens and Lowry at their Granada pension in the company of a French escort. She and Malcolm promptly entered into an indiscreet liaison. She had been a companion of Aiken's and would assume both a real and symbolic role in Lowry's life and fiction and in the symbiotic love-hatred between Lowry and Aiken which will be discussed later in this chapter.

Between his trip to Spain with the Aikens and the Mexican phase (1936–38), Lowry bummed about London and Paris for nearly two years, his drinking seeming the sole determinant of his fate. James Stern writes [7] of having read by chance in 1933 a book just published whose author's name meant nothing but whose subject matter meant everything:

The Son in Search of a Father

It was about an Englishman, an educated young man, who had signed on to a ship in Liverpool as a deckhand, or trimmer. Instead the writer had evidently, as the romantic phrase goes, "run away to sea." I thought that was wonderful . . . someone . . . who had done what I had always wanted to do.

("M.L.: A First Impression," 58)

Stern goes on to describe the unusual circumstances of his meeting with Lowry in winter of that same year, 1933. He was in Paris and ducked into a bistro to get in out of the rain. Always impressed by the immunity of Parisians to human eccentricity, he finds evidence of that characteristic in the obliviousness of the customers to a man lying supine on a sawdust-covered floor. The man is

flat on his back, evidently asleep, a robust-looking fellow with a week of stiff red stubble on his face, and across his stomach a guitar. Round his neck the recumbent figure wore a scarlet blue tweed, and on his legs a pair of dirty grey flannel trousers.

("A First Impression," 58)

The figure rises, gripping the guitar, and, with impeccably clipped speech, asks Stern if he, too, is English. They fall into animated conversation, the "very English English" is dropped, and the man announces that "the name's Lowry, Malcolm Lowry." It turned out that each had read the other's first book, Stern's being a volume of autobiographical stories about a young Englishman living in a remote region of Africa. Stern graphically describes how his new acquaintance lapsed into sea jargon. "Each of us," Stern observes, "convinced the other he was a budding genius. Of himself I believe Malcolm laughingly boasted that he would soon be 'out-Mobying Melville.'"

"Out-Mobying Melville" became Malcolm Lowry's most persistent persona throughout his late teens and early twenties. Specifically, Lowry sought to project a legend like that of Melville's youthful wanderer, Redburn. Twelve years after meeting Stern, Lowry in 1945 as Sigbjørn Wilderness, rootless in the airport of Los Angeles, returns in his thoughts to Melville-Redburn: "So Sigbjørn reflected must Herman Melville, masquerading as Redburn, have felt at Euston Station, in London, over a hundred years ago. . . ." [8]

II *Manhood: Two Women in His Life*

If Lowry's seaman's demeanor was a masquerade, as his friend, the poet Earle Birney, told me [9] that he always suspected, it was a convincing masquerade—at least to two women. One was the English novelist Charlotte Haldane; the other, the aforementioned Jan Gabrial.

Miss Haldane, in a novel *I Bring Not Peace* (London, 1932), created a heroic protagonist, James Dowd, who she says "was partly synthesized from my friendship with a remarkable young man, Malcolm Lowry, the most romantic undergraduate of that period in Cambridge. . . ." [10] The book, dedicated to Lowry, presents in Dowd a young man of discarded affluence who has fled for spiritual fulfillment to sea. Midway through the novel, he explains his rebellion by lashing out at his genteel friend Dennis Carling who has advocated leaving the "dirty work to dirty people":

"Dirty work? Hell, it is *not* all dirty. That only shows you've never done an honest day's work. Take the sea, now. Dirty? I should say it was. If you'd seen some of the messes I've cleaned up in my time, you'd be sick right here and now. Your stomach couldn't stick even the thought of it, let alone the smell. But as work, it's clean for all that. The life is clean. The chaps are swell. It's only you people who sit about in cafes and talk who're dirty. . . . There's no life in your life, no health, no good anywhere. It's all just rotting stinking putrefaction. . . ."

(*Not Peace*, 135–36)

As Miss Haldane's portrait of Dowd deepens, we learn that the apparently self-possessed sailor, openly contemptuous at anyone's dread of death, actually feared life. Existence, he had found

was like the sea, silent deep as the soul itself, fertile of beauty and horror. James was afraid of the sea, as he had been afraid of life, had run away from sea, as in the beginning, being no wiser, he had run away to sea. But there was no peace for him on earth, on dry land or water, and never would be peace until he learned surrender and acceptance.

(*Not Peace*, 310)

The Malcolm Lowry who roamed the pubs and bistros of London and Paris, in guilty rebellion against his aristocratic family and Cambridge background, was at this time a man of a false bravado born of a desperate inner seismograph. The sea which had failed James Dowd as a protective subterfuge also failed Lowry. He ran away from it—and from life—to the insular extremes of the North American continent—first to Mexico, then to British Columbia.

Jan Gabrial was an American girl from New York City who directly shaped the destiny of Malcolm Lowry for five years and, indirectly, for perhaps much longer. As noted in Clarissa Lorenz's memoir, they were introduced by Aiken in Granada in the pivotal year of 1933, were married in Paris that year, had a stormy time of it for two years before going off to Mexico together in the fall of 1936. The picture we get of her, if the descriptions of Hambo's wife Nita in the last pages of Aiken's *Ushant* are accurate, is largely negative. One could, between the lines of Aiken's autobiography, make a case for Nita. *Ushant*, with its oedipal suggestion in the pairing of Hambo, the self- and father-destroying son, and D., the "father" seeking to enjoy the wife of his "son" by a kind of vicarious sexuality, largely omits any suggestion that Nita could have been choked between two competing geniuses.

Aiken in conversation told me that Jan was Jewish, of a strong social consciousness, and "quite a pretty little piece at the time." [11] He acknowledged that her infidelities went on from the start of the marriage. The critic John Davenport, close friend and Cambridge classmate of Lowry's, told Aiken that a series of writer friends of Malcolm's replaced him in Jan's affections as Jacques Laruelle did with the Consul and Yvonne in *Under the Volcano*. Aiken added significantly: "Malc simply couldn't cope with a woman like Jan. His deep sense of sexual inadequacy—a characteristic of the Consul too [12]—probably stems from the situation with Jan."

A recent reviewer of the 1966 reissue of *Volcano* expresses the view that Yvonne "is clearly an amalgam of Lowry's two wives, both aspiring writers and not actresses, especially his first wife, Jan, who did live in Mexico with him at the time, who did leave him: with a dash of the idealized 'Jan' (for Janet) of *Ultramarine* (he married his first wife because of the coincidence)." [13] The Yvonne we meet in the published version is an amalgam of good and bad, though mostly good: the good she draws from Lowry's adoration of his second wife; the bad, from bitter memories of his first.

The Yvonne of the much rejected early versions is the closest we will ever get to an insight into the Jan-Nita figure whom Malcolm-Hambo, in Aiken's version, once begged with a pathetic gift of silver earrings not to leave him (". . . how could she possibly pay the slightest heed to the little gift . . . ? They were for her birthday—he murmured—handing them awkwardly and shyly through the camión window. . . . She accepted them with . . . repressed annoyance . . . and then the bus shot way. . . ." [14]); the closest we will get to the woman for whom he bore such love as to be able to have written the unsent letter of doomed love that, with all the power of an extended Elizabethan sonnet, established from the first chapter the principal motif of the book.

The Yvonne of the early drafts is the Consul's daughter rather than his burdened wife. The first Yvonne was not without her burdens. She speaks of her numerous abortions. She has come to Mexico out of a concern over her father's downward plunge into dipsomania. The scene when we meet her (Chapter II) is Acapulco, where in actuality Malcolm and Jan Gabrial Lowry came ashore in Mexico for the first time on the Day of the Dead, November of 1936. Yvonne's credentials as a Lowryan wanderer-figure are quickly established:

> . . . she slowly drew off her sheer stockings and let them drop in a heap beside her small blue dancing sandals, *with high, spiked, arrogant heels* [my italics]. She would have given anything for some creature's company now, for anybody's company, even the wireless operator's. . . . She was pretty, she was twenty-four; the questions she put to herself were none the less cogent for being unoriginal: what was she moving toward, but more important still, what was she running away from?

(*Volcano*, Mexican Version, Chap. II, 47–48)

The reference to Yvonne's "high, spiked, arrogant heels" parallels a reference to Nita in Aiken's *Ushant*—Nita, the man-baiting wife of Hambo (". . . she was no sooner seen, clipping over the marble tiles with those absurd high heels of hers" [15]). Her meeting with Hugh Fernhead, the early Hugh Firmin and, at this point, no relation to the Consul, is a Hollywood-style encounter of two lonely voyagers "in a dilapidated Mexican church . . . at dawn, during an earthquake." Its impact on Yvonne resembles that of James Dowd on Ann, the heroine of Charlotte Haldane's novel. Although Yvonne has known Hugh in Paris, Cambridge, Algeciras, and Granada without numbering him among her conquests, she now finds, half a world away from her memories, that she, like Desdemona, is subdued "to his honors and his valiant parts." As Desdemona's Venetian sophistication is turned to simple love by a warrior's tales of wars in exotic climes, so the disenchanted Yvonne becomes enraptured at Hugh's stories of sea quests to the Orient:

> . . . with his hair blowing in the breeze Hugh was talking about the sea itself, pointing to a ship out near the horizon, of the beauty of dawns in the Indian Ocean abaft the beam and, Yvonne, listening entranced, felt again that she had never really travelled at all, and she found herself longing to identify these finer scenes of Hugh's with her own experiences, and so utterly to enter into them that it would be as though they already shared them.
>
> (*Volcano*, Mexican Version, Chap. II, 60)

The point to be stressed is that while Lowry was undergoing Moloch in Mexico—a spiritual burning that included the loss of his wife, frequent confinements in some of the dingiest jails in Mexico, and untold physical torments, he was also *living* the early plot of *Under the Volcano*. But only occasionally could he rise from the mire of his private hell to see his agonies transformed into art, the first materials for a modern tragedy. One such occasion presented itself during their first month in Mexico when he and Jan took a bus ride to a fiesta in Chapultepec. That bus ride, as will be seen in a later chapter, provided him with the thematic touchstone for the emerging novel: the dying Indian, robbed and unaided, as despoiled mankind.

More frequently Lowry's lot was that of the down-and-outer, finding in the Cuernavaca of the 1930s a drunkard's paradise and hell,[16] where between and during alcoholic fugues Lowry portrayed the dark side of his soul in William Ames, the first Consul, and the idealized side in Hugh Fernhead, the first Hugh, with Yvonne occupying an ambiguous never-never land between the two as daughter and sweetheart.

III *The Lowry-Aiken Symbiosis*

Except for a gnarled letter or two salvaged from those demonic days, the most faithful account we have of the Lowry of 1936–38 is provided by Aiken in *Ushant*. It was nearly a decade after the publication of that book that Aiken revealed publicly, what was long known privately, that Hambo, the drunken wanderer, the youthful writer "so visibly . . . happily alight with genius" was a faithful portrait of Malcolm Lowry.[17]

Aiken told me that he regards this autobiographical narrative as the culmination of a statement on art and the artist which he began with *Blue Voyage* twenty-five years before. The episodes dealing with D. and Hambo—that is, with Aiken and Lowry— deliver a further dividend: a candid insight into the maelstrom union of coeval geniuses.

Aiken arrived in Cuernavaca in mid-May, 1937, with his third wife, the painter Mary Hoover ("Lorelei Three" in *Ushant*), and they stayed until July 7. Their railroad journey from Boston to Mexico is described in his novel *A God for the Heart of Mexico* (1939). In that book Hambo makes his debut: an absurdly stocky figure, flailing thick but undersized arms like a landlocked seal and carrying a forked stick like St. Christopher. Hambo is given little to do in the novel, although his predilection for tequila and queer hours is revealed. He is a witness at the climactic death of the doomed Noni, whose life had been ebbing away even as the voyagers approached their Mexican Eridanus.

In *Ushant*, however, published twelve years after the Mexican novel but begun long before it, Aiken reintroduces Hambo, this time as one leg of a sinister triangle represented by Nita, D., the father who had taken the father's place, and Hambo, the son who had taken the son's. The relationship had evolved into a necessary parasitism in which each took turns being starfish to the other's oyster. "Every angle of it had been studied in mirrors," Aiken wrote, "each of them with an eye . . . to making use of it first." Hambo's drunken words promise the fulfillment of a kind of reciprocal murderer's pact. Hambo cries out, "Now it was my turn to kill you," and points to his unfaithful wife Nita as the instrument of death, both wound and weapon:

"For of course we both knew that both of us were powerfully drawn to that open wound—you first, but with your own obligations to [your wife] . . . and therefore guiltily offering her up to me, but in effect proposing to share her . . . as foul a sort of voyeur's incest as any second-rate God could imagine."

(Ushant, 352)

D. acknowledges his "visceral and feculent scheme" but defends it as humane, for the marriage might "stop your drinking. Pull you together. Take you out of the endless chain of aguardientes, the daily round of cantinas, and the ultimate slobber of drunkenness in which you daily threatened to kill me." They discuss Nita's infidelity, presumably an effect—or was it the cause?—of Hambo's drinking, and Hambo half threatens to kill D. with his own hands. "My dear Hambo, you *are* killing me," D. answers. Hambo asserts his dominance: "You no longer know your boundaries. You are a nation invaded. And as I'm younger, and as I'm stronger, in appetite, in will, in recklessness, in sense of direction, it will be no use your trying to compete with me . . . you will no longer have a personality of your own." As the scene ends, they drink to betrayal and death (*Ushant*, 356).

The father and son not only discuss Nita's infidelity and their own but also the intense political climate of the late 1930s. "Hambo had drifted pretty far, politically, towards something like communism," Aiken writes. "He had been through something like a social conversion, and clearly felt a need for some sort of fraternal joining and belonging; and D.'s and Lorelei's more abstract political views were not calculated to make him happy" (*Ushant*, 351).

Lowry, in keeping with the starfish turn so characteristic of him, also exploited the mescal-inflamed talks in Cuernavaca that summer of 1937. In the earlier versions, these conversations between the Consul and his daughter's "young man" read flatly, for they are incompletely integrated into the flow of the narrative. The talks all sound like unintentional evidence of a "generational gap," with Yvonne addressing the Consul as "Dad" and Hugh, in phony-sounding obeisance, as "Sir." They read like dialogue in a late tract novel by H. G. Wells, where the characters stand for viewpoints, where positions are "rigged," and where spokesmen formally air lifeless viewpoints in gusty rhetoric.

In the published version, however, with the relationship between Geoffrey and Hugh wisely changed to that of half-brothers

—doppelgänger, really, for Malcolm Lowry—the invective-laden conversation between them at the end of Chapter X, just before the Consul flees his wife for the cantina refuge that will lead to his death, can be taken as the exact equivalent of the midnight acrimony between D. and Hambo in *Ushant*. Ostensibly, the argument is about communism, with the Consul lashing out at Hugh's "indoor Marxmanship" and at the futility of involvement in all those "people's revolutions" that were so much a part of the political picture in the thirties.

". . . Or the fallacy of supposing a point proved or disproved by argument which proves or disproves something not at issue. Like these wars. For it seems to me that almost everywhere in the world these days there has long since ceased to be anything fundamental to man at issue at all . . . Ah, you people with ideas! . . . All this, for instance, about going to China! Can't you see there's a sort of determinism about the fate of nations? They all seem to get what they deserve in the long run."

(Volcano, 309)

But at a deeper level, the debate is also between Geoffrey Firmin and embattled aspects of his psyche as represented by the fragments of his identity—by the artist manqué, by Hugh, the man the Consul was before disillusion and dissolution set in, by Yvonne, the responding lover for his last chance at love.

Aiken wrote recently that the bitter exchange at the end of Chapter VIII was a verbatim report of an argument between Lowry and himself in Cuernavaca, with the positions reversed: what the Consul says, Aiken said. It is not too much to suggest that the role of Conrad Aiken in Lowry's masterpiece goes beyond the pupil's free adaptation of the teacher's material—the William Blackstone alienation theme, for example, which Lowry took wholecloth after Aiken developed it during their first summer together, or the scores of Joycean puns ("hello—pussy—my —little—Priapusspuss, my—little—Oedipusspusspuss . . . my little Xicotancatl") which Aiken insists were given first utterance by himself. The civilized, sensitive, still idealistic figure of Geoffrey Firmin—the archetypal Great Man invaded by addiction and a doleful period of history—is largely built on the artistic and spiritual conflict between Aiken and Lowry. Aiken's true subject in his novels is his own effort to live with the gargoyle disharmony between man's egotism and unimportance; this effort takes the form of a search for consciousness in the void. Lowry seeks artistic and actual salvation in the unconscious ("Throw away your mind," Dr. Vigil pleads repeatedly to the Consul in the fractured English that is more telling than it would be if spoken in correct English), for unconsciousness is the only refuge, as Lowry once put it in explaining why he drank, against "the complete baffling sterility of existence as *sold to you.*"[18]

If, then, the Consul is the amalgam of conflicting forces represented by the death-seeking son burning in Moloch-Mexico and by the life-sustaining father come to save him, the novel and its tragic hero stand finally as monuments to the efficacy, despite all the demons, of the Lowry-Aiken symbiosis.

IV *Beyond Borrowing: Emergence of the Consul*

Demarest in Aiken's *Blue Voyage* muses:

> What was this singular mechanism in him that wanted so deliberately, so consciously, to break itself? A strange, a rich, a deep personality he had—it baffled and fascinated him. Everything of course was like this—depth beyond depth, a universe chorally singing, incalculable, obeying tremendous laws, chemical or divine, of which it was able to give its own consciousness not the faintest inkling. . . . A universe that contained everything—all things—yet said only one word: "I."

The passage provides a perfect rendering of Conrad Aiken's obsession with consciousness. Without ever writing in the first person, he is at all times an "I" writer. He neither could nor wished to separate his life from his works. He told me, with a pride undiminished by forty years, that everyone in *Blue Voyage* was drawn from actual life, that everything happened as recorded.

The novelist David Markson, having arranged a reunion after seventeen years between Lowry and Aiken in 1954, writes tellingly of overhearing snatches of their conversation. Lowry tried to summarize the nonexistent plot of a work in progress *(October Ferry to Gabriola),* and finally acknowledged that nothing *happens.* Aiken applauded, adding, "No, no incidents *ever.*"[19] The plots of Aiken's five novels are often uncomplicated to the point of seeming inconsequential. In *Blue Voyage* (1927), there is only one significant outward event, the discovery by the hero, Demarest (the "D." of *Ushant* twenty-five years later), that the woman he wants to marry is traveling on the same ship with him and is already engaged to someone else. In *Great Circle* (1933), again, there is one simple crisis of marital infidelity, and this remains unresolved at the end of the book. *A Heart for the Gods of Mexico* (1939) leads the reader to the death of a girl who is known from the outset to be mortally ill. In *Conversation* (1940), very little happens beyond the bitter wrangling and reconciliation of a rather disagreeable husband and wife. Only in *King Coffin* (1935), perhaps, where Aiken mounts a protagonist who is not a slightly altered version of himself, does he also bring his plot by careful stages to decisive completion.

The temptation of Malcolm Lowry, at 19, to see himself in the image of Demarest was irresistible. He became fascinated, according to John Davenport, who knew both Lowry and Aiken intimately, by Demarest's self-analysis, and was transfixed by such passages as this one:

I am Strindberg. I look at his photograph and a feeling of self-love and self-pity, a profound narcissistic compassion and tenderness, comes over me. Those harassed and noble temples, the tortured deep-seeing eyes, the magnificent head, the small mouth, which is the mouth of the child and of the adder!

(*Blue Voyage*, 77)

Lowry came under similar spells. Margerie Lowry, in a letter to me, recalled her husband's announcement: "I *am* Steppenwolf!" [20] There is a passage early in Hermann Hesse's novel of that title [21] where the narrator recalls his first conversation with Harry Haller.

He called himself the Steppenwolf, and this too estranged and disturbed me a little. What an expression! However, custom did not reconcile me to it, but soon I never thought of him by any other name; nor could I today hit on a better description of him. A wolf of the Steppes that had lost its way and strayed into the towns and life of the herd, a more striking image could not be found for his shy loneliness, his savagery, his restlessness, his homesickness, his homelessness.

(*Steppenwolf*, 17)

From writers ranging from Melville to Hesse, but more especially from Aiken, Lowry learned to convert the surfaces of life into mythologized megalomania. He, like Aiken, sought to penetrate depth beyond depth into consciousness, finding there his own darkness, his personal sense of failure of honesty, integrity, kindness; and, facing them, sought to transcend them in his art. Andrew Cather, in *Great Circle,* proclaims that "life was going to be good. Unexplored, unfathomable, marvelous and terrible. Filthy, and incalculable . . . the wonderful and acceptable nightmare!" (*Great Circle,* 295). Sigbjørn Wilderness in Lowry's posthumous autobiographical novel, *Dark As the Grave Wherein My Friend Is Laid,* muses half-drunkenly: "Yet it seemed to him that if one person had survived such a thing to breathe purer air and love the light that there was hope for the human race. For one man's agony belongs to all men and to God" (*Dark As the Grave,* 124–25). Lowry's and Aiken's writings display a shared obsession to convert "one man's agony" into gain: an agony described by Cather as "the wonderful and acceptable nightmare" and by Dr. Vigil as "throwing away your mind" in alcohol. Their views on art are inseparable from their views of experience: a view which was ultimately messianic.

Andrew Cather, at the end of *Great Circle,* drives toward the scene of the adultery of his mother and uncle (the young Andrew had discovered their bodies in the cabin of his uncle's sunken boat, a fictional analogue for Aiken's own trauma at age eleven over finding the bodies of his mother and father, murder-suicide victims). As he drives, Cather paraphrases a kind of resurrection:

> It would be good to touch, for the last time, that agony, and to expose it—to drown in it derisively, savagely, or even, at last, indifferently. No, not indifferently—at last with acceptance . . . . the strange and exciting mixture of astonishment and suffering with which—at a moment of discovery—one loses oneself in order to create oneself! The end that is still conscious of its beginnings. Birth that remembers death.
> (*Great Circle,* 295)

The "I" of "The Forest Path to the Spring" refuses to resist the life force that is killing him. In fact, "I was in every way delighted that it should, for my whole intention seemed to be to die through it, without dying of course, that I might become reborn" ("Forest Path," 268). The workings of a messianic fervor, combined with those of a guilt complex in a Puritan conscience, run through all of Aiken's fiction, and that spirit coincided providentially with that of the guilt-ridden Malcolm Lowry. Each sees himself as some hideously chosen sojourner in a hell from which, though he cannot emerge alive, he will, Virgil-like, chart circles on the way.

Aiken may have been the first novelist in English to apply Joycean techniques for harnessing flux to his own subjective obsessions. Frederick C. Crews is certainly right when he calls for "the day when Aiken is given credit for his courageous originality as a novelist." [22] To this must be added the hope that literary history will accord Aiken recognition as a major force, the discoverer of, and catalyst for, other talents.

Where Lowry moved beyond his mentor was in his rich conception of the Consul. Anthony Burgess puts the matter bluntly:

The superiority of Lowry's book to any of Aiken's lies . . . in the fact that, where Aiken produced Prufrock figures, small Hamlets, Lowry created in Geoffrey Firmin a giant character whose sloth or accidie ironically suggests the Promethean rebel, whose total alienation from life etches the desired opposite, whose inability to love defines what love is. Firmin is perhaps the last exemplar of one of the forms of Liberal Man.[23]

It is true that the son was a disciple of the father's credo that the extension of consciousness warranted the ultimate sacrifice. Lowry, however, surpasses Aiken in his conception of the Consul as a modern tragic hero who, if he cannot redeem his agony in life, as the Aiken heroes can, will transcend his own monomania in death.

CHAPTER 3

Under the Volcano

> The novel can be read simply as a story which you can skip if you want. It can be read as a story you will get more out of if you don't skip. It can be regarded as a kind of symphony, or in another way as a kind of opera—or even a horse opera. It is hot music, a poem, a song, a tragedy, a comedy, a farce. . . . It is superficial, profound, entertaining and boring, according to taste. It is a prophecy, a political warning, a cryptogram, a preposterous movie, and a writing on the wall. It can even be regarded as a sort of machine: it works too, believe me, as I have found out.
>
> Malcolm Lowry, the Cape Letter

ALTHOUGH *Under the Volcano* has won mention as a "contemporary classic," "the finest and profoundest work of fiction by an Englishman" during the 1940s, and "a masterpiece as rich and humorous as *Ulysses* and far more poetic," the book has been more talked about than read. Admittedly, Lowry is given to *longueurs*—the whole strategy of his book, as will be shown, is circular. He was also a combination of crammer-inner and never-ender. But, for those who will *give* themselves to the *inevitability* of the Consul's fate—an inevitability which eschews any marked line of suspense—the extraordinary *lucidity* of the book will take over. The "story" is always there. While probing to the deepest Dostoevskian level—that aspect of a man he cannot even acknowledge to himself—Lowry never allows the story line to bow to the labyrinthine. I agree with Dale Edmonds that it is on the " 'most immediate level'—the level of people, places, events and circumstances within a fictional world that much resembles our own —that *Volcano* communicates most effectively." [1]

There is no part of this book that is not touched by the shadow of *Volcano*. The next two chapters deal almost exclusively with it. Nowhere, however, do I take up a chapter-by-chapter résumé. The best and the worst of Lowry's books resist any such linear push. This chapter pursues the novel at the "impact level." The less the initial reader thinks about symbols, levels of meaning, and literary allusions, the more he will be able to give himself fully to the impact of this book. The chapter seeks to suggest the nature of addiction—the Consul's full awareness of his condition—and the reasons why this most philosophical of men rejects all offers of human salvation and love. Chapter 4 lays open, largely through analysis of the several versions, the ten-year evolvement of the novel. With Lowry it is what Matthew Corrigan calls the "final expurgatory look" [2] that counts. Even though *Volcano* is Lowry's single major success, few writers of greater quantitative achievement could have brought off a masterpiece under the conditions of Lowry's life in which he, in a sense, fought his genius all the way.

I *Lowry's Overture as Elegy*

The beginning of *Under the Volcano*—a 42-page opening chapter—is such that the word "controversial" may not be inappropriate. Jonathan Cape's reader demanded that Lowry drop it altogether because nothing happens. The fact is, *everything* happens. The chapter has the somberness and beauty of the past recalled in tranquility. It also posts the dread markings—the clues—to the action of exactly one year earlier. If the reader is not caught up in its spirit—if, like the Cape reader, he is bothered by "long initial tedium"—he might wish to reread the first chapter after he had finished the other eleven.

Considered in terms of conventional fiction, then, the opening chapter is all wrong: an epilogue in the place of a prologue; an opening in which the fate of the two main characters is revealed (they are dead, though by means left ambiguous); a chapter which is a series of intricate flashbacks and where Mexican local color, as the Cape reader put it, is "heaped on in shovelfuls." To the objection that the opening is tedious, Lowry replied in a long and justly famous letter.[3] He wrote that readers of like mind might be "conditioned" to accept the slow start if a "preface or

blurb" was appended. This thought led Lowry to a characteristically amusing analogy. A preface, he said, will serve for his
novel as bush for the wine. He could not resist an aside: "I am
not talking of good wine but mescal, and quite apart from the
bush . . . mescal needs salt and lemon to get it down." Then, in
another characteristic ploy, he turned for an ally to an acknowledged classic. He asked if anyone would have ventured into the
drought of *The Waste Land* on his own without some "anterior
knowledge and anticipation of its poetic cases."

When he got down to business, Lowry defended the opening
chapter on the only grounds tenable: its vitality to the "feel"
of the whole novel. He made these claims: (a) Chapter I sets
the mood and tone of the book, (b) it sets the slow melancholy
tragic rhythm of Mexico—its sadness, and, (c) above all, it establishes the book's "terrain," a word Lowry underlined. By "terrain,"
he undoubtedly means many things. It is the physical landscape
of the novel. The reader is introduced to all the talismanic landmarks which Lowry, so profligately in early versions and so
brilliantly in the final, posts: the twin volcanoes, the Malebolgean
barranca, the ruins of the palace where Maximilian and Carlotta,
earlier "empurpled lovers," declared their doomed love, the dark
Dantean wood. The chapter also keys the spiritual landscape. If
the reader is denied the suspense of *impending* tragedy, Lowry
gives him something equally dramatic, something more consonant
with the atmosphere of the book: a sense of dread at what has
already occurred, a thing so shattering that it has left the survivors no peace during the intervening year.

Lowry's Cape letter went on to assert that the opening chapter,
while appearing epilogic, actually prepares the stage for the
book's concerns, which are "the forces in man which cause him to
be terrified of himself . . . the guilt of man . . . his remorse . . .
his ceaseless struggling toward the light under the weight of the
past." [4] The last five words cannot be overstressed, for "the
weight of the past" is what really haunts the book. One sees it
best in the stamp of *former-ness*—pastness—on the characters:
Geoffrey Firmin, dispossessed *former* consul; his half-brother
Hugh, a *former* fighter for the Republic in the Spanish Civil War;
Yvonne, *former* Hollywood child film star and the *former* consul's
former wife; a French *former* film director who is the *former* consul's closest friend and his *former* wife's *former* lover. There is no

escape from the past. Lowry, like Joyce, Proust, and Virginia
Woolf—writers whose major works he insists he did *not* read—
makes the inescapable past hover like a pall. Lowry, it will be
seen, makes a major time shift—one year backward—from Chapter
I to Chapter II. After the explicit shift, time becomes a phantas-
magoria, conditioned by the Consul's "mescalusions."

The novel opens in 1939, in November, near sunset on the
Day of the Dead, in a town in the Mexican interior called
Quauhnahuac. Two tired and sensitive men wail inwardly for a
friend who died exactly a year ago. The death of this man
(Geoffrey Firmin)—once a British consul in a remote Mexican
outpost but more lately a compulsive alcoholic—is never made
explicit, but the feeling of his death is too pervasive in the chapter's lush melancholy ever to be doubted. Dr. Vigil, a Mexican
physician whose name lacks only the "r" to form *Virgil* of the
Inferno whose mosaic this novel unobtrusively follows, has known
the Consul for an evening; Vigil's companion, Jacques Laruelle,
is a French ex-film director who has shared Geoffrey's boyhood
and his wife. They talk over their drinks, and every word pleads
Milton's question to the living about the dead:

> Where were ye Nymphs when the remorseless deep
> Closed o'er the head of your lov'd Lycidas?

Dr. Vigil finally puts the question: "Did you never go to the
church for the bereavèd . . . where is the Virgin for those who
have nobody with?" The question bears that compelling Hispano-
English imperfection of which Lowry was master—an aspect to
be discussed in the next chapter—and it is important as one of
the chapter's closely-packed clues.

The Frenchman finds himself able to laugh over Vigil's syntax,
says good-bye (for M. Laruelle is to leave Mexico the next day),
and walks in the dying light of evening amid landmarks whose
topography is more spiritual than physical. Lowry slowly un-
ravels strands of the story which he will knit again in later chapters. Laruelle pauses by the railroad tracks and recalls a farewell
of a year ago involving himself and Hugh Firmin, the Consul's
half-brother and the third side of the novel's triangle. He looks to
the twin volcanoes, "terrifying in the wild sunset." Laruelle offers

still another farewell—to the Palace of Maximilian—and the chord of tragic love is struck.

. . . he immediately regretted having come. The broken pink pillars, in the half-light, might have been waiting to fall down on him: the pool, covered with green scum, its steps torn away and hanging by one rotting clamp, to close over his head. The shattered, evil-smelling chapel, overgrown with weeds, the crumbling walls, splashed with urine, on which scorpions lurked—wrecked entablature, sad archivolt, slippery stones covered with excreta—this place, where love had once brooded, seemed part of a nightmare.

(*Under the Volcano,* 14)

Laruelle thinks briefly of Maximilian and Carlotta, and almost imperceptibly it is "the Consul's voice, not Maximilian's, M. Laruelle could almost have heard in the Palace." It is not the ancient and historical dead but the recent, still-living dead that haunt Laruelle's memory in this epilogic prologue. He leaves the rotting palace that was haven for two sets of star-crossed lovers in exile for the Calle Nicaragua, the street that a year ago conveyed the Consul to the ravine. Laruelle approaches a bridge over a barranca. He looks down into it. For reasons the reader cannot know unless he has skipped to the last page, the ravine looms as an aftershadow in the position of a foreshadow (". . . here was finality indeed . . . wherever you turned the abyss was waiting. . . . Dormitory for vultures and city Moloch"). The reader does not yet know the dread significance of the barranca in the Consul's tragic history, and the chronicler drops only hints.

Lowry shifts the gears of his time-eclipsing device; by association, the barranca triggers Jacques's thoughts to Hell's Bunker, the lover's knoll on the golf course where the Taskerson boys took their girls. Now with the Taskerson episode, Laruelle is monitoring an earlier past: the boyhood scenes at a Channel resort (Leasowe) when he and Geoffrey Firmin were the guests of the family of an English poet, Abraham Taskerson. From Jacques Laruelle's always shifting focus of consciousness, Lowry creates a surrealistic landscape. The astute Stephen Spender finds Lowry's technique in playing with scenes and language to resemble that of a film cutter.[5] In Chapter I, the film clips are compiled and sorted by Laruelle's memory; in later chapters, they will be filtered through the Consul's mescal-befogged lens.

Jacques remembers the "air of innocence" about the whole business of picking up girls and taking them to Hell's Bunker. He thinks back to the time when he accidentally came upon Geoff scrambling out of the bunker with a girl. Shaken by his unmasking, Geoff takes his friend to a bar and, for the first time in his life, orders a round of whiskeys, which the waiter refuses to serve to the two minors. "Alas" (the foreboding again), "their friendship did not for some reason survive these two sad, though doubtless providential, little frustrations." Lowry has forged an underground connection between events of the distant and the recent pasts.

The trail of clues to later developments is pervasive. The reader is introduced to the horse and rider, whose symbolic and narrative functions will be discussed fully in the next chapter. A drunken man on horseback interrupts Laruelle's reveries by hurtling up the Calle Nicaragua (a riderless horse will be seen near the body of a dying Indian in Chapter VIII; the horse will be the instrument of Yvonne's death in Chapter XI). A movie marquee advertises an old Peter Lorre film, *Las Manos de Orlac.* This film about a man unable to wipe the blood off his hands proves to be the same film that was playing one year earlier, during the novel's main action. A love letter from the Consul to Yvonne, never mailed, falls from the Consul's book of Elizabethan plays, borrowed by Jacques but never returned. The novel, in a sense, becomes an enactment of the dilemma poignantly described in the letter: the knowledge that in love lies the only path upward combined with the failure of desire for that upward path.

As if somehow to exorcise the ghosts of the recent past, Laruelle holds the letter from the dead to a candle whose

flare lit up the whole cantina with a burst of brilliance in which the figures at the bar—that he now saw included besides the little children and the peasants . . . several women in mourning . . . and dark-faced men in dark suits . . . —appearing, for an instant, frozen, a mural. . . .
(*Under the Volcano*, 41–42)

And, for just a moment, Lowry's prose elegy is in stasis. Then the elegiac words are tolled by a bell: *dolente . . . dolore!* The mourning is interrupted in the kaleidoscopic frenzy of a carnival ferris wheel. "Over the town, in the dark, tempestuous night," concludes the chapter, "backwards revolved the luminous wheel . . ." (*Under the Volcano*, 42). But there is one thing more. Like Joyce, Lowry uses the graphic arts—in this case to convey a vital time shift. Thus a single line carries from the last word of Chapter I across the page to Chapter II.

II *The Present Haunted by the Past*

Lowry's lark with time, then, is in the tradition of the finest elegiac writing, a memorializing of the past as a means of returning the dead to life. Calendar time exists as a reminder to us, if we care to acknowledge it, that a world was dying in November, 1939, even as the Mexican dead were being honored.

Lowry plays a similar game with place. Although described in painstaking details from the first word of the novel (the Cape reader's words, "heaped on in shovelfuls," are accurate though wrong-headed), the interior of Mexico really exists only in the green interior of Malcolm Lowry's imagination. In the actual world of November, 1938, British consuls like Geoffrey Firmin had lost their occupation; England had severed diplomatic relations with Mexico over President Cárdenas's expropriation of foreign oil companies in March, 1938, following the refusal of these companies to answer government demands for increasing wages and training native Mexicans for managerial positions. In the world of Lowry's imagination, the dispossessed Consul is the prisoner of a malaise whose interior geography is the main business of the book. When, in the first chapter, Lowry guides the reader on a tour of Quauhnahuac, it is in the interests of forming a correspondence between habitation and humor, between outer and inner geography. Although it was still possible until recently to visit Cuernavaca and walk the Calle Nicaragua where the drunken Consul wandered and to peer down into the barranca where he perished, the facts of place as Lowry assembles them have a different function from the old Fitzpatrick travelogues. The reality that Lowry seeks to evoke in the early pages is hidden and inexpressible until we enter what William H. Gass called Lowry's "conceptual country [where] there are no mere details, nothing is simple happenstance, everything has meaning. . . ." [6]

Lowry starts obliquely. He locates the scene first, not by the symbolic furniture of landscape, but by the precise directions a map maker or navigator would appreciate.

Two mountain chains traverse the republic roughly from north to south, forming between them a number of valleys and plateaus. Overlooking one of these valleys which is dominated by two volcanoes, lies, six thousand feet above sea level, the town of Quauhnahuac. It is situated well south of the Tropic of Cancer, to be exact on the nineteenth parallel, in about the same latitude as the Revillagigedo Islands to the west in the Pacific, or very much further west, the southernmost tip of Hawaii—and as the port of Tzucox to the east on the Atlantic seaboard of Yucatan near the border of British Honduras, or very much further east, the town of Juggernaut, in India, on the Bay of Bengal.

From a navigator's map of Quauhnahuac, Lowry moves to a kind of aerial photograph.

The walls of the town, which is built on a hill, are high, the streets and lanes tortuous and broken, the roads winding. A fine American-style highway leads in from the north but is lost in its narrow streets and comes out a goat track. Quauhnahuac possesses eighteen churches and fifty-seven cantinas. It also boasts a golf course and no less than four hundred swimming pools, public and private, filled with water that ceaselessly pours down from the mountains, and many splendid hotels.

One paragraph later, Lowry narrows his focus still more—to the Hotel Casino de la Selva. Here, for the record, Lowry may be said to have opened his book's bottomless bag of allusions. "Selva means wood," he told Jonathan Cape, "and this strikes the opening chord of the *Inferno*." Much more important is the felt life generated in the scene:

Palatial, a certain air of desolate splendour pervades it. For it is no longer a casino. You may not even dice for drinks in the bar. The ghosts of ruined gamblers haunt it. No one ever seems to swim in the magnificent Olympic pool. The springboards stand empty and mournful. Its jai-alai courts are grass-grown and deserted. Two tennis courts only are kept up in the season.

Like Durrell's Alexandria, Lowry's Quauhnahuac is a mind construct where, as Gass brilliantly notes, "there are no menacing

volcanoes, only menacing phrases, where complex chains of concepts traverse our consciouness. . . ." [7] The tone sought and
achieved is identical to that of the opening sentences of E. M.
Forster's *A Passage to India:*

> Except for the Marabar Caves . . . the city of Chandrapore presents
> nothing extraordinary. Edged rather than washed by the river Ganges,
> it trails for a couple of miles along the bank, scarcely distinguishable
> from the rubbish it deposits so freely. There are no bathing-steps on
> the river front, as the Ganges happens not to be holy here. . . . The
> streets are mean, the temples ineffective, and though a few fine houses
> exist they are hidden away in gardens or down alleys whose filth deters
> all but the invited guest. . . . Houses do fall, people are drowned and
> left rotting, but the general outline of the town persists, swelling there,
> shrinking here, like some low but indestructible form of life.

The tone of both is of unproud decadence, of ruin, of the un-
buried dead. For E. M. Forster, only the Marabar Caves ("the
extraordinary caves") interrupt "the endless expanse." For Lowry,
the two volcanoes, "clear and magnificent," alone can temper
the lush bleakness. Laruelle's hand trembles as it grasps a bottle
of anis "from whose label a florid demon brandished a pitchfork
at him." The king of this realm is alcohol and its crown prince
is the Consul. "I meant to persuade him to go away and get
dealcoholisé." The words are Dr. Vigil's, and the reader, hardly
aware of it, has entered the recollected world at whose center
is the Consul.

> "Sickness is not only in body, but in that part used to be call: soul.
> Poor your friend, he spend his money on earth in such continuous
> tragedies."
>
> (*Volcano,* 5)

Dr. Vigil has touched the elegiac chord, but it is Laruelle who
will orchestrate it.

> What had happened just a year ago to-day seemed already to belong
> in a different age. One would have thought the horrors of the present
> would have swallowed it up like a drop of water. It was not so.
>
> (*Volcano,* 5)

In the Lowry canon, it can never be so. The past always haunts the present. And it is to time past—to time exactly one year past as well as to time in earlier pasts—that Lowry will now turn.

III *The Diffusion of Emotion*

After the long overture-elegy of Chapter I, Lowry gives over the second chapter to Yvonne, the Consul's estranged wife. His choice is logical—he had made a crucial departure from early versions in making Geoffrey and Yvonne husband-wife instead of father-daughter—and, more important, wise fictionally. Yvonne, unbelievably, has returned to Quauhnahuac and to the Consul after almost a year's absence: she and Geoffrey separated in December of 1937; she then returned to the United States where she obtained a divorce. Her reasons for leaving him are painfully clear within a few pages; the reasons for her return are less clear. In fact, her return would not have "worked" at all without the Consul's anguished plea—the epistolary voice in Chapter I of one dead lover to another—which Laruelle finds, unposted and slipped between the pages of the Consul's book of Elizabethan plays.

We meet the Consul, then, through Yvonne's eyes. Theirs is not treated as a conventional reunion of lovers. Lowry's diffusion of emotion saves the scene. Of course, the overt problem from which Yvonne fled a year ago confronts her as she enters the bar.

Then he looked up abruptly and saw her, peering short-sightedly about him before recognizing her, standing there, a little blurred probably because the sunlight was behind her, with one hand thrust through the handle of her scarlet bag resting on her hip, standing there as she knew he must see her, half jaunty, a little diffident.

Still holding the timetable the Consul built himself to his feet as she came forward: "—*Good* God."

(*Volcano*, 46)

But *another* consciousness, operating on the fringes of Yvonne's, draws on the objective world to relieve the subjective. The same group of *borrachos* whose dialogue had earlier intersected Yvonne's chat with a Mexican cabbie now crowd in on the intimacy between her and the Consul. The scene is cinematic. Lowry's technique is exactly the same as that, for example, used

by David Lean, the director of a British film version (1947) of
a Noel Coward story, "Brief Encounter." As the lovers, played
by Celia Johnson and Trevor Howard, say a final good-bye in a
seedy railway station (she will remain with her husband; he will
embark permanently for a medical post in Africa) their precious
last moments together are interrupted by the nonstop chatter of
a woman acquaintance of the heroine. In the blatant face of
the outrage, the lovers can only commune mutely. The horror
of the scene lies in the invasion of privacy, the unknowing destruction of an intimacy the unfulfilled lovers would always have had
in the tranquility of recollection.

Lowry's avoidance of explicit anguish in the reunion is pervasive. Although his aspirations, pleaded in the unmailed letter,
seem possible of fulfillment with her return, Geoffrey can only
make feeble jokes about his cuckoldry, his case of the shakes,
his dismissal from his consular post. When he offers a drink to
the woman who has left him because of his drinking, the poignancy of the moment is suggested by her unspoken words: a
dash enclosed in quotation marks (*Volcano*, 47).

The rest of the chapter can best be described as contrapuntal.
Yvonne's inner dialogue—her memories of the events leading to
their parting a year ago—plays against the Consul's efforts to
be casual (an echo of Laruelle's recollection of the boyhood hikes
and pubs: "The drunker they became, the more sober they should
appear"). Other counterpoint to the dolor of the lovers is provided
by the words of a boxing advertisement and the names of shops
in the square where they walk (*Volcano*, 52). Lowry is always
aware of the effective incongruity of English words that have
never been assimilated into the Spanish.

The chapter's second important disclosure, in fact, appears
between a boxing ad and the marquee words of the talismanic
film, *Las Manos de Orlac*. It comes as the Consul, using his walking stick like a blind man, staggers up the Calle Nicaragua while
Yvonne reviews a tableau that is all too familiar. Geoffrey is not
too intoxicated to point to the villa of the Frenchman Laruelle
("And he's still there too . . . . hasn't budged an inch either,"
Volcano, 58), chidingly remind Yvonne that he has not forgotten
that she cuckolded him with Jacques, and finally drops news of
incalculable significance to her and to the novel:

"Something else, I repeat, very important, that perhaps I ought to tell you."

"Yes. What is it?"

"About Hugh."

Yvonne said at last:

"You've heard from Hugh. How is he?"

"He's staying with me."

—BOX! ARENA TOMALIN. FRENTE. AL JARDIN XICOTAN-CATL. *Domingo 8 de Noviembre de 1938. 4 Emocionantes Peleas.* EL BALON *vs.* EL REDONDILLO.

Las Manos de Orlac. Con Peter Lorre.

"*What!*" Yvonne stopped dead.

(*Volcano*, 60)

Chapter II thus establishes the physical presence of the four protagonists in Quauhnahuac, Mexico, on the Day of the Dead in 1938. Dale Edmonds, writing of the novel "on the immediate level," goes to great lengths to shorten the arm of coincidence. He demonstrates that Lowry has rendered this "confluence of characters" plausible, but he is much more cogent when he notes that "the affairs of these characters have been curiously tangled in the past . . . . [and the] events of the day are more distressing because they bear not upon isolated individuals but upon a closely interwoven group." [8] What interweaves them is that galvanic negative capability which caused Melville's Bartleby *to choose not to* and Camus's Meursault to remain impassive at his mother's funeral. Not since Hemingway brought Jake Barnes and his entourage to the good fishing and bull fights at Pamplona has a group of fictional characters so moved us by their very inability to move.

The Consul is Promethean, he is fallen, and his estrangement from life, as Anthony Burgess wrote in a recent reassessment of the novel, "etches the desired opposite . . . where inability to love defines what love is." [9] *No se puede vivir sin amar* were among the first serious words spoken between Jacques Laruelle and Geoffrey Firman's medical friend, the Mexican Dr. Vigil, in the opening chapter. Moments from death, the Consul will repeat them, adding his own significance: "*No se puede vivir sin amar . . .* which would explain everything." The phrase can be rendered as *one cannot live without love* or, better, *one cannot live without loving*. The book, at the "impact" level, will dramatize this forfeiture of love as being due to various forms of hubris. Certainly the four principals have all tried to live without loving. Their sickness is not only physical, as when the Consul suffers from the d.t.'s, but, in the words of Dr. Vigil, "in that part used to be call: soul." Lowry poses the tortured relationship of the Consul and Yvonne, and, within that greater agony, lesser ones in the abortive liaisons between Yvonne and Jacques and between Yvonne and the Consul's doppelgänger, his half-brother Hugh: all symbolic of the modern malaise. As Dale Edmonds notes, it is not that love has ceased to exist in our world; it is that selfish rather than selfless love is the characteristic form.[10] "Ah," sighs the Consul—it is one of his last coherent reflections—"who knows why man, however beset his chance by lies, has been offered love?"

But hope keeps seeping through: always, for Lowry, the necessary condition, the coexistence, emphasized at the end of his rope by F. Scott Fitzgerald, of aspiration amidst futility. The Consul, reunited with the one person he believed a year before could save him, now attempts to build himself up to meet this threat to oblivion. He is partially successful. Yvonne smiles, "full of thoughts that had already swept her a thousand miles in frantic retreat from all this." She hears the Consul hum; it braces her against her guilt.

Yvonne felt her heart melting. A sense of a shared, a mountain peace seemed to fall between them; it was false, it was a lie, but for a moment it was almost as though they were returning home from marketing in days past. She took his arm, laughing, they fell into step. And now here were the walls again, and their drive sloping down into the street where no one had allayed the dust . . . and now here was their gate, off its hinges and lying just beyond the entrance, as for that matter it always had lain, defiantly, half hidden under the bank of bougainvillea.

"There now, Yvonne. Come along, darling . . . We're almost home!"
"Yes."
"Strange—" the Consul said.
A hideous pariah dog followed them in.

(*Volcano*, 64)

Under the Volcano, in a sense, begins where a book like *The Sun Also Rises* ends. Jake Barnes's war wound is a phantom which will affirm the irony of his last words to Brett who has just asserted her belief in their chances together: "Isn't it pretty to think so?" The Consul's phantom is better explained by psychic than by physical wounds. It is an attendant spirit, a familiar, which will endlessly pace counter to Yvonne's consoling but unwanted shadow. Never to be exorcized by drink and never to respond to Dr. Vigil's appropriately fractured entreaty, "Throw away your mind," Goeffrey Firmin's phantom will live a life of its own on the edge of his tortured consciousness.

IV *Comedian Wearing Tragic Mask*

But there is another Malcolm Lowry which may key best of all with the times: the comedian wearing a tragic mask. Conrad Aiken has said that while Lowry wrote his book in the grip of an unappeasable vision—that while he knew life was an infernal machine tearing him apart—the tragic was only one of Lowry's disguises. To have turned himself into the maker of sad myths was, for Aiken, a deception perhaps without parallel: "It was a great joke: his whole life was a joke: never was there a gayer Shakespearean jester. A fact that I think we must remember when everyone is saying What Gloom, What Despair, What Riddles! Nonsense. He was the merriest of men." [11]

Under the Volcano is also a very funny book. Lowry's humor arises naturally out of a scrupulous observation of life. The comedy is of the Joycean—the domestic—kind: glimpses of human frustration which are both devastatingly true and devoutly compassionate. Lowry's "consular" humor is Pickwickian rather than Black, not *sick* but *wise* laughter arising above the impending tragedy.

In his finely cut tweeds . . . and blue and white striped Chagfordian tie . . . his thick fair hair neatly slicked back, his freshly trimmed brownish greying beard, his stick, his dark glasses, who would say that he was not, unmistakably, a figure of complete respectability?
                                                            (*Volcano*, 127)

And who would know, since the Consul never whined, that his situation was hopeless; that with one side of his mind he sought the volcano's summit while with the other—the dominant, the daemonic, side—he would know surcease only in the barranca?

So, to the tragedy of an addictive Faust, elegized in Chapter I and proclaimed in Chapter II, are added the domestic pitfalls of a Falstaff in Chapters III and V. After a long unpunctuated inner debate between two sides of himself at the start of Chapter III ("But can't you see you cabrón that she is thinking that the first thing you think of after she has arrived home like this is a drink"—*Volcano*, 69), the Consul's guilt-imperative loses out to the drink-imperative. He needs alcohol to support his fragile balance. He runs from the house while Yvonne finishes her bath.

But suddenly the Calle Nicaragua rose up to meet him. The Consul lay face downward on the deserted street.

(*Volcano*, 77)

The Consul's alcoholic haze—a certain Mr. Magoo quality—has taken over. The bibulous inertia of the dipso had probably never been rendered in imaginative literature until Lowry and this novel. The Consul lies face down until given assistance by someone who in his state of diffused attention he imagines to be Hugh.

—Hugh, is that you old chap lending the old boy a hand? Thank you so much. For it is perhaps indeed your turn these days to lend a hand. Not that I haven't always been delighted to help you! I was even delighted in Paris that time you arrived from Aden in a fix over your carte d'identité and the passport you so often seem to prefer travelling without and whose number I remember to this day is 213112. It perhaps gave me all the more pleasure in that it served a while to take my mind from my own tangled affairs. . . . Are you listening, Hugh— do I make myself clear?

A three-page apostrophe to Hugh follows (*Volcano*, 77–79), but Hugh has not heard a word of it. The Consul's rescuer turns out to be a Colonel Blimp type whose possession of a bottle of Irish whiskey is more important to the Consul than his identity. There follows one of the novel's best set pieces, and it provides the first broad humor of the book:

"But damn it all I say you were lying right down in the road there, might have run over you, there must be something wrong, what? No?" The Englishman switched his engine off. "I say, haven't I seen you before or something."

"—"
"—"

"Trinity." The Consul found his own voice becoming involuntarily a little more "English." "Unless—"
"Caius."
"But you're wearing a Trinity tie—" the Consul remarked with a polite note of triumph.
"Trinity?" . . . Yes. It's my cousin's, as a matter of fact." The Englishman peered down his chin at the tie, his red face become a shade redder . . . "Wonderful country this. Pity about all this oil business, isn't it? Bad show.—Are you sure there're no bones broken or anything, old man?"

(*Volcano,* 80)

We can only assume that the combination of the Irish and an in-person reminder of his obligation to the Union Jack has perked up the Consul. Lowry shifts place. The Consul, back at the house ("innocently as a man who has committed a murder while a dummy at bridge"), enters Yvonne's room. His intention is finally to effect a physical reconciliation with his former wife. Drink oozing from every gland, he proves impotent; and, while Yvonne cries in the bedroom, he retires to the veranda, where he drinks himself into insensibility. The booze inflates him, and in his best W. E. Henley style he pontificates: "The will of man is unconquerable. Even God cannot conquer it" (*Volcano,* 93). That authorial consciousness on the borders of Geoffrey's—the one which observed the hideous pariah dog at the end of Chapter II —now perceives "vultures waiting . . . like burnt papers floating from a fire which suddenly are seen to be blowing swiftly upward, rocking." The Consul passes out as the chair under him collapses. Mr. Magoo has given way to Chaplin. As such, the scene is broadly humorous—the would-be lover failing in love, unable even to remain upright. Like a Chaplin film, it contains a spiritual dimension, too; the Consul's impotence is only the outward and visible sign of a much larger spiritual impotence.

Our next direct encounter with Geoffrey comes in Chapter V, the Garden chapter, the most Falstaffian of the book. On the overt level, the Consul is awake again and wandering about in the lushly deteriorating garden behind the house in search of a bottle of tequila he had hidden there days before. He stumbles about and fuzzily ponders a crude sign he notices on the edge of his property. The significance of the words on the sign will be discussed more fully in the next section (¿LE GUSTA ESTE JARDIN?/ ¿QUE ES SUYO?/ ¡EVITE QUE SUS HIJOS LO DESTRUYAN!—*Volcano*, 128). It is enough to note that the Consul both misreads and mistranslates. ("Do you like this garden? It is yours. We evict those who destroy!") But the mis-rendering is the talisman, the key, to the novel's Eden-and-eviction theme. The Consul is a forlorn Adam; his own garden, once beautiful, has become a jungle where he hides liquor bottles; once he even sees a snake there.

It is instructive of Lowry's growth as a novelist to see that, although he evidently had allegorical intentions from the start, he was unable to assimilate the Adamic myth into the dramatic flow. In the earliest version of *Volcano*, he bludgeons the reader with an Adamic conceit and ends with a series of lofty rhetorical questions:

Yes, it was a regular sarpint, as an old bosun he had known used to say, and calling, perhaps, into being some reflection of an eternal dilemma. In what, precisely, now did the *temptation* inhere? Through what medium had the sibilant invitation to partake of the fruit of the tree of knowledge been already accepted, and, in the course of time, passed on to him? And what, if any, was the form of this knowledge?
(*Volcano*, Mexican Version, V, 135)

Here Lowry over-explicitly affirms the Consul's link to Adam. But he might just as well have taken on Milton's task of justifying the ways of God to man for all he accomplishes. The scene bristles with the evidence of contrivance.

In the published version, however, the "ruined" garden appears to the Consul, his senses both heightened and jaded by drink, as lending "an added charm. He liked the exuberance of the un-clipped growth at hand" (*Volcano*, 128). When the familiar keep-off-grass sign rears up, the Consul greets it, not with an im-plausible cosmic despair and the series of unanswerable questions, but with a sense of his precise domestic dilemma.

Words which, perhaps a final judgment on one, were nevertheless un-productive of any emotion whatsoever, unless a kind of colourless cold, a white agony, an agony chill as that iced mescal drunk in the Hotel Canada on the morning of Yvonne's departure.
(*Volcano*, 128–29)

The garden—the world—has all the attributes of an Eden, but, as Lowry told Jonathan Cape, "if you don't want to bother about the symbolism, you needn't." Lowry draws back from conventional symbol-watching no less than he does from conventional tragedy-marking. The Consul, although endowed with some of the qualities of heroes in Greek and Christian mythology, is above all a man in his own right, a product of our own period, and his dilemma, while undoubtedly allegorical, is also immediate.

After pondering the sign, he drinks the tequila and moves on—lurches on—to pleasantries with his neighbor, an American conveniently named Quincey (lacking only the "De" to stand in ironic alignment with one of English literature's most illustrious addicts). Quincey mocks him for his drunkenness. The Consul has hiccups. It is difficult for him to answer his neighbor's surly questions. Instead, we get one of the book's first—perhaps its major—Adamic references—one skillfully and plausibly tailored to the ears of an American tourist like Quincey.

"Perhaps Adam was the first property owner and God, the first agrarian, a kind of Cárdenas, in fact—tee heel—kicked him out. Eh? Yes," the Consul chuckled, aware, moreover, that all this was possibly not so amusing under the existing historical circumstances, "for it's obvious to everyone these days—don't you think so, Quincey?—that the original sin was to be an owner of property."

(*Volcano*, 133)

But Geoffrey's attempts to regain some semblance of sobriety and dignity do not work; for one thing, his fly is still unbuttoned from his abortive sexual advances on Yvonne. When he whistles at Quincey's cat, and the creature's ears twirl in pleased response, he says that "she thinks I'm a tree with a bird in it." "I shouldn't wonder," retorts Quincey (*Volcano*, 134–35).

The kinship of this chapter to Joyce, both in terms of the complex time shifts and the brilliance of the Lowry-*cum*-Aiken puns, has been noted in the first chapter. Quincey's cat, introduced as a foil for the Consul's wordplay, slinks off to allow the intrusion on Geoffrey's blighted consciousness of Yvonne and Hugh. Lowry never breaks narrative stride. He gives us the simultaneity of the Consul's world: a complex that can include a cat playing with a trapped insect as well as paranoid impulses that his wife and brother are talking only about him.

[78]

In this preposterous fashion, the Consul stooping, the cat dancing just out of reach, the insect still flying furiously in the cat's mouth, he approached his porch. Finally the cat extended a preparate paw for the kill, opening her mouth, and the insect, whose wings had never ceased to beat, suddenly and marvelously flew out, as might indeed the human soul from the jaws of death, flew up, up, up, soaring over the trees: and that moment he saw them. They were standing on the porch; Yvonne's arms were full of bougainvillea, which she was arranging in a cobalt ceramic vase. "—but suppose he's absolutely adamant. Suppose he simply won't go . . . careful, Hugh, it's got spikes on it, and you have to look at everything carefully to be sure there're no spiders." "Hi there, Suchiquetall!" the Consul shouted gaily, waving his hand, as the cat with a frigid look over her shoulder that said plainly, "I didn't want it anyway; I meant to let it go," galloped away, humiliated, into the bushes. "Hi there, Hugh, you old snake in the grass."

> (*Volcano*, 140–41)

The imagery of the liberated insect, soaring to freedom, is a foreshadowing perhaps of how the soul of the Consul will ascend to the top of Popo on the last page of the book.

While he takes liberties with time and place in Chapter V, Lowry never leaves the reader marooned. The long single line which connected the two Days of the Dead between Chapters I and II is now repeated, though shortened. Perhaps an hour has elapsed. The Consul has had a blackout. Defoliated, he is back in his bathroom half deliriously trying to sort out what he remembers of the missing interval.

—— Why then should he be sitting in the bathroom? Was he asleep? Dead? Passed out? Was he in the bathroom now or half an hour ago? Was it night? Where were the others. . . . Yet for a moment he could have sworn the house had been full of people; why, it was still this morning, or barely afternoon, only 12:15 in fact by his watch. At eleven he'd been talking to Mr. Quincey. . . .

> (*Volcano*, 141)

What he remembers is couched in those intersecting dialogues Lowry learned from *Blue Voyage*, but, as is not always the case in Aiken's work, they carry the story along. Will they go that afternoon to Guanajuato, a city of life for which Dr. Vigil opts, or to the bull-throwing at Tomalín, which involves Parián (death) and the Farolito (the cantina which Vigil says half-jokingly "es un infierno")?

Dr. Vigil, a character based on a close Mexican friend who shared with Lowry the infernal 1936–38 period, is the one character who can recognize that the Consul, despite his wife's return, is truly one of "those who have nobody them with." Vigil, in fact, almost under his breath issues an exact forecast of the Consul's doom: "But I think if you are very serious about your progresión a ratos you may take a longer journey even than this proposed one" (*Volcano*, 144). The journey to Tomalín will be indeed the longest one of Geoffrey Firmin's life: not in linear time—it will be only a few hours' travel to the Farolito and the barranca—but in the sense of the long day's journey of the soul which has denied love.

For a time the Consul's deliberate alliance with Marlowe's Faustus flying headlong into the gaping earth (see epigraph to novel) is offset by a series of parodies of Prometheus enacted by Leopold Bloom. Chapter V ends with Geoffrey standing in the shower, waiting for the sobering shock of cold water that never came and still clad in his tuxedo trousers. The Consul's push towards self-destruction is never more tragicomically portrayed than in the loop-the-loop scene (Chapter VII) when he becomes trapped, upside down, at the top of the carnival machine as all his possessions fall from his pockets into the hands of the children waiting below. For Geoffrey, the experience with the loop-the-loop is far from funny: he is horrified and sees himself as Ixion, caught forever on a wheel turning in hell (the machine, not so strangely, as Douglas Day reminds us,[12] is named *La Maquina Infernal*—the infernal machine of Cocteau's play, that cruelly and inexorably unwinds, slowly destroying the human lives caught up in it). Yet even in the grips of his own unappeasable passion for self-obliteration, the Consul's obsession is diffused by residual fragments of his Britishness ("This was scarcely a dignified position for an ex-representative of His Majesty's government to find himself in"—(*Volcano*, 222). Although mortally wounded by Mexican Fascists in the book's last scene, he can still manage to tell himself: "This is a dingy way to die."

V *The Consul: Triumphant in His Fall*

Under the Volcano is the dramatic enactment of something Dostoevsky's Underground Man referred to as the "one most advantageous advantage . . . for which, if necessary, a man is ready to act in opposition to all laws . . . in opposition to reason, honor, peace, prosperity. . . ." [13] This advantage beyond advantage, one which induces the Underground Man to speak with savage irony of the Man of Action—is, of course, one's own free unfettered choice, one's own fancy even when worked up to the point of madness. The Consul, with Bartleby, with the Underground Man, with Meursault, simply chooses *not* to—not to act, not to alter his course for love, not to save himself. The Consul's opportunities to requite Yvonne's love raise questions of utmost significance to his existence as a free agent, and it is only by willing his own destruction that he can assert his freedom of choice. "To this end," writes Stanley Jedynak, "it is necessary for the Consul to reject all offers of human salvation . . . they are spurious offers because not in touch with the supreme reality of death and with that sense of chaos . . . at the bottom of everything." [14] Human options pale beside the Consul's battle for the survival of consciousness, which is another way of saying his imperative for preserving his own identity, however harmful to himself are the means.

Lowry's triumph in *Under the Volcano* lies in his making forceful the attempts of the other three principals to save the Consul while making inevitable the Consul's rejection of those attempts. One believes that Yvonne cannot live without loving but that her loving is mainly of herself. Hugh's "indoor Marxmanship" often has the sound of conviction, but it is badly blunted by the Consul, intoxicated as he is, in their bitter dialectical joust at the end of Chapter X. As the Consul observes, Hugh protests too much; his rhetoric has "nothing constructive at bottom, only acceptance really, a piddling contemptible acceptance of the state of affairs that flatters one into feeling thus noble or useful." Jacques Laruelle, the man of many faces, is a purveyor of the *appearance* of reality, a flawed film-maker. It is he, Professor Jedynak reminds us,

who takes on to himself the motto "no se puede vivir sin amar" and makes a mockery of it. It is also he who rightfully accuses the Consul of unnecessary suffering, who denies the greatness of the Consul's battle against death, but who is afraid of the nightmare of life and attempts to hide his fear behind that ironically spurious [for him] inscription at the entrance to his home.[15]

Some readers may believe that Lowry allows the Consul's addiction to mescal to take over. The quality of diffused attention, admittedly, is intensified by drink, but it is also in his drunkest moments that the Consul sees most clearly. His last remembered words to Hugh and Yvonne (Chapter X) before his fatal flight from them are about his verdict for death against life:

"For all you know it's only the knowledge that it most certainly is too late that keeps me alive at all . . . You're all the same, all of you, Yvonne, Jacques, you, Hugh, trying to interfere with other people's lives, . . .

"True, I've been tempted to talk peace. I've been beguiled by your offers of a sober and non-alcoholic Paradise. At least I suppose that's what you've been working around towards all day. But now I've made up my melodramatic little mind. . . ."

(*Volcano*, 312–14)

Actions in the man of sensibility are conditioned by the fateful knowledge of good and evil. The Consul knows the world, and he opts out of it. Beyond that knowledge comes the realm of the deed. It is only here that man's real worth can be assessed. Moralistic knowledge (Hugh's) does not imply strength. Recognition of the need for love is forfeited by romanticizing (Yvonne's). Man is cursed by a constant dilemma: to know and not to be able to act appropriately. Hugh's and Yvonne's indecision in the human matter of the dying Indian (Chapter VIII, to be discussed next chapter) become rationalizations for following the ritual of a bad law, to allow a man to die. The Consul, of course, is no more decisive, drunkenly longing for the bus to stop at the next cantina, but at least he does not assume vain postures.

The Consul, aware that the attempt to act must be made, knows that he cannot make it in a way that is appropriate to his equivalent of the Underground Man's most advantageous advantage: his unconquerable will to assert his own identity. He hovers between the "either" and the "or"—between the illusion of Paradise and the reality of the barranca—but he never really doubts when the test comes what the result will be. He chooses addiction, death, and destruction. He takes the path to Parián; he will meet the ultimate reality. Reality, as Professor Jedynak cogently put it,

is the Farolito, the *barranca* beneath it, Popocatepetl towering above. Man lives under the volcano; he is cleft, like . . . the glacial rock, always crumbling, yet clinging to life like a parasite. He is surrounded by false, unknown authorities who interfere with his probing into the intensity of life, who attempt to foil his choice of death.[16]

The Consul is destroyed, to be sure, but his soul survives, ascending to the volcano's summit, even as his body is hurled into the pit, to lie with offal and dead dogs.

VI *Addiction Untriumphant:* Lunar Caustic

The rendering of the feel of addiction has not been surpassed in the language. Only in one other work has he used the materials of *Under the Volcano*—addiction and madness in the pursuit of transcendence. That work, a novella Lowry labored over under many titles but one which was posthumously published, in English, as *Lunar Caustic*, never satisfied him. Its failure is worth examining briefly in the context of the success of a conceptually parallel work. Lowry began the story, based on his brief commitment in New York's Bellevue Hospital in 1934, a year or so later under the title *The Last Address*. In 1940 he worked, as was always his practice with everything, another version, *Swinging the Maelstrom*, and at his death, reportedly, he was doing a composite of these two versions, *Lunar Caustic*.

David Benham has recently written an exhaustive study of the versions of *Lunar Caustic* in which he places the Bellevue story as the *Purgatorio* to *Under the Volcano's Inferno*, "a kind of median between Heaven and Hell . . . . [where] evil is cauterized from the soul" and "death is the prelude to rebirth." [17] For purposes of this study only the "melded" version of Lowry's multiple reports on the Bellevue experience will be examined. In *Lunar Caustic*, an alcoholic seaman named Bill Plantagenet (one notes Lowry's almost ingenuous use from the earliest fictions of names with allegorical possibilities) commits himself to a New York City community hospital. He remains there for a time, during which he becomes friends with several other patients. Then, when the hospital staff discovers that he is not an American, hence ineligible for charity treatment, he is released to return to his old bibulous life. Lowry's description of Plantagenet's passage through shabby streets is resoundingly reminiscent, as Dale Edmonds notes,[18] of the very early Stephen Crane of *Maggie*. Lowry even gives that name to one of the nurses. The link is viable generally. Both worked naturalistic methods that contrast with the metaphoric richness of their best books, *The Red Badge of Courage* and *Under the Volcano*, respectively.

Lowry keeps turning the environment of the hospital into a ship out of Melville, and the doctor is even named Claggart. Professor Benham investigates thematic analogues to *Billy Budd*, but what I am interested in showing here is Lowry's inability to make us feel, although we see it, Plantagenet's *Angst*. Madness observed from the outside is simply not interesting fictionally. After he is discharged from the hospital, Plantagenet returns to the sailors' tavern he knew. The world of the hospital expunged, "only the world of ghosts coming closer" distracts his concentration on the whiskey. As always with Lowry, drink restores messianism. He remembers the friends he made in the institution; he would now, he believes, free them, "strike his blow for the right." He goes to the washroom, kills the bottle, notices an obscene sketch of a girl chalked on the wall.

For some reason, suddenly enraged, he hurled the bottle against the drawing, and in the instant he drew back to escape the fragments of glass, it seemed to him that he had flung that bottle against all the indecency, the cruelty, the hideousness, the filth and injustice in the world.

(*Lunar Caustic*, 75)

But the tendencies of a Hugh turn into the responses of a Geoffrey. He rejects the world of the tavern, feeling he is being watched, and moves "to the very obscurest corner of the bar, where, curled up like an embryo, he could not be seen at all" (*Lunar Caustic*, 76).

The story leaves one with little but a mild extrinsic indignation over what the world of psychiatrists, nurses, and attendants cannot understand. But, overall, Lowry is unable to impart felt significance to the landscape of waterfront and mental hospital as he would be able to do with a seedy Mexican town and a forest path to the spring. Conrad Knickerbocker tells us in a preface to this long-delayed edition [19] that Lowry went back to *Lunar Caustic* frequently for twenty years, especially during the last period in England. But the purifying metamorphosis of auto-biography into art did not happen. How it did with *Under the Volcano* is the burden of the next chapter.

CHAPTER 4

The Victory of Art Over Life

> You may think that some of this smacks of
> the loyal little wife running to the defense
> of her mate, but I tell you this: that only a
> person whose whole existence *is* his work,
> who has dominated and disciplined the vol-
> cano within him, at what cost of suffering
> even I do not wholly understand, could have
> written such a book.
>
> (Excerpt, letter from
> Margerie Lowry to
> Harold Matson, Aug. 10, 1945) [1]

MALCOLM LOWRY'S reputation rests with one book. To
say this is not to undersell his achievement, which was considerable, but to clear away some of the pettifoggery which in
the fifteen years since his death has delivered him over to the
cultists or the exegetes. Neither path leads to an understanding of
Lowry's extraordinary crucible which may have produced—Alfred
Kazin [2] recently expressed the opinion—the last masterpiece. The
cultists would have one believe that the life and works of writers
like Lowry—the whole labyrinth of the addict—are evidence that
only excess generates art. One of Lowry's misadventurous dis-
ciples, the late Conrad Knickerbocker, went so far as to declare
that the controlled artist provides no clues to the mysteries of the
creative imagination; that only the demonic had interest for him.
Whatever academic claim to Lowry remains has been staked out
by those whom Saul Bellow calls "deep readers of the world."
Their industry was climaxed by Perle Epstein's recent line-by-
line gloss of *Under the Volcano* as a Cabbalistic treasure trove. [3]

Lowry was indeed an alcoholic and a symbolist. Those who
knew him best describe a pathologically shy man in whom drink
evoked a "Shakespearean jester" (Conrad Aiken's words) who

manufactured a tragic myth while laughing at it all.[4] As to Lowry's fervor for symbols, one has to face up to the part of him that lived a life of its own: the part that was spiritual archivist, forever receiving and storing up correspondences out of thin air. The Lowrys came to refer to coincidence-ridden days as signs they were "in the current." A lifelong sense of being haunted, of being a human Leyden jar, produced all those Lowryan personae who live in hell but aspire to heaven; above all, Geoffrey Firmin, the Consul, the single creation for which Lowry will be remembered.

But to understand how Lowry's novel evolved throughout a decade's constant and frustrating revisions from one addict's case history into what Philip Toynbee, coming on the book recently after missing it for fifteen years, calls "one of the great English novels of this century,"[5] it is necessary to leave aside alchemy and addiction, the Cabbala and black and white magicians. It is necessary even to forget Lowry's obsession that he was himself being written. For a decade during which the man knew all the miseries of Job, the artist prospered. Malcolm Lowry struggled with his book, but the struggle was as directive as a sculptor's and as strategic as a film-cutter's.

I *The Making of the Masterpiece*

Even a cursory reading of an epic work, whether of a poem like *Paradise Lost* or of a prose work like *Ulysses*, is likely to make the reader think of the agonizing way huge masses of rock were hauled into place in the Age of the Pyramids. The architects of vast buildings and of epic literary works are alike in depending in considerable measure for their success on simple clarity in the initial massing and division of material. Arthur Barker is especially impressed, in the case of Milton and *Paradise Lost*, with the necessity of hewing out massive blocks of poetical material to gain sculptural control. The effect of balance, always characteristic of any work of art, frequently with Milton

arrives at a mathematical plainness almost suggestive of the counting of lines. We need not suppose that his muse worked quite so mechanically or laid so lowly a burden on herself; but Milton's mind operated at ease only when he perceived in or imposed on his material a precise mathematical division of some sort.[6]

Professor Barker develops with complexity a theory about the direction of the "shifting" structural pattern in *Paradise Lost* as evidenced by Milton's redivision of the epic from ten to twelve books in 1674.

I should like in this chapter to use Professor Barker's "block" concept as a point of departure. I propose to demonstrate that Malcolm Lowry also decided, as his view of his material deepened, upon a blocking-out technique, or something like it, as a way of discovering, exploring, developing his themes, of conveying their meaning, and, finally, of evaluating them. My aim in this chapter is to show, largely by reference to Lowry's successive drafts and expositions, that he also decided upon certain blocks—certain alignments of theme and motif—to serve in a contrapuntal relationship. What Joseph Frank said of Joyce ("The reader is forced to read *Ulysses* in exactly the same manner as he reads poetry—continually fitting fragments together and keeping allusions in mind until, by reflexive reference, he can link them to their complement" [7]) can be said of the author of *Under the Volcano*. Lowry speaks of his first and last chapters as the easterly and westerly towers of a "churrigueresque Mexican cathedral" for

the doleful bells of one tower echo the doleful bells of the other, just as the hopeless letters of Yvonne the Consul finally finds in the last chapter answer the hopeless letter of the Consul M. Laruelle reads precisely a year later in Chapter I.[8]

This is the mosaic. A major theme, dramatized by one of Lowry's symbolic motifs, invariably recurs, usually several times, and is nearly always, as Lowry put it, "repeated with interest" in the final accounting. The toll on the reader who relies on a linear playing out of cause and effect is heavy. Yet Lowry's progress in composition is an evolvement from a profligacy to a clarity of counterpoint: his ability, after excruciating trial and error, to make recurrences serve to crystallize theme while accelerating narrative.

Conrad Aiken recently spoke out after a long silence in an admirable effort to set the record straight; specifically, to prove that Lowry's Mexican phase—the demonic phase—was seminal in the evolvement of the book. He recalled during their memorable reunion in 1937 in Cuernavaca (the Quauhnahuac of the

novel) when, with Lowry virtually *in extremis,* his drinking uncontrolled, his marriage cracking, the younger man showed him

the whole of *Under the Volcano.* The first draft, but complete, and
with a different ending: the horse theme had not then been developed.
. . . In short, that book was going to be rewritten for the next nine
years.[9]

That is the point. Lowry lived his catalytic nightmares in Mexico from 1936 until 1938, where he roughed out the essential Consular report on hell. But he managed, *soberly,* the *writing* of the
great book between 1939 and 1945 in the "northern paradise," in
Canada. It was only there that fictive "truth" evolved—it would
never do so for Lowry again—and it is that progress, traced
through the development of his "horse theme" and the evolving
tableau of *pietà* and *pelado,* that I wish to chart.

II *Lowry's Pietà*

"One day about nine years ago, it was the end of 1936 . . . I took
a bus to go to Chapultepec. . . . There were several people with me,
a person extremely dear to me . . . Senora X my first wife . . . and
two Americans, one of whom was dressed up in cowboy costume. . . .
We were going to a bullthrowing. . . . About halfway there we
stopped beside an Indian who seemed to be dying by the roadside.
We all wanted to help but were prevented from doing so . . . because
we were told it was against the law. All that happened was that in the
end we left him where he was, and, meanwhile, a drunk [a pelado]
on the bus had stolen his money out of his hat, which was lying beside him, on the road. He paid his fare with it, the stolen money, and
we went to the bullthrowing."

(Dark As the Grave, 150)

This quotation describes the kind of experience a controlled
writer might have entered in his notebook to be fleshed out later.
Much of Lowry's later work reads like unfleshed-out notes, fragments fated for the limbo of posthumousness. The above words
appear two-thirds of the way through *Dark As the Grave Wherein
My Friend Is Laid.* They are spoken by Sigbjørn Wilderness, an
unpublished alcoholic novelist who has returned to Mexico with
his second wife in an attempt to exorcise the memory of terrifying

experiences a decade before. But to anyone familiar with *Under the Volcano,* the quotation is a précis of Chapter VIII, an episode which successfully unifies the book's various levels. Wilderness goes on:

"The whole story [of *Under the Volcano*] grew out of that incident. I began it as a short story. . . . There's far more to it of course than that, but out of this . . . came the character of the Consul. . . ."

(*Dark As the Grave,* 151)

For a writer who wrote about nothing that had not happened to him, the incident of the dying Indian had proved galvanic. It remained frozen in Lowry's consciousness like a Hawthorne allegorical tableau. Here Lowry, whose mysticism was inseparable from his messianism, had found his pietà. It became Aiken's "horse theme," a composite of the dying man, his tethered horse with the number Seven [10] branded on its rump, his predator (the pelado, the peeled one), and his witness (the drunken Consul who, unable to act, takes on the guilt for mankind's inaction against inhumanity). Although Lowry had his most important blocks of correlatives, it was not until late in the development of the book that he was able to deploy these elements with classic severity.

Lowry's composition of the short story [11] proved a kind of literary *felix culpa.* It gave him an early opportunity to slide many pieces of his Mexican-Gothic furniture into place. In formation were *Las Manos de Orlac* (the film of Nazi origin about an artist with bloodied hands), the twin volcanoes Popocatepetl and Ixtacihuatl (Lowry's emblem for true lovers), the Consul's overrun garden, which is his life, and the barranca, which will be his tomb. And, of course, the pietà:

The Consul looked back again. No mistake. The man, receding quickly now, lay with his hat over his eyes, his arms stretched out toward a wayside cross. Now they were passing a riderless horse, munching the hedge.

(*Short Story,* 291)

Lowry incorporated the short story into the eighth chapter of the novel by doubling its length and dividing the viewpoint between the Consul and Hugh, but otherwise retaining its exact configuration. In the short story, the Consul is named William

Ames; Yvonne is his daughter; Hugh Fernhead is her fiancé. They continued in this relationship through the version Lowry completed in Mexico. With his overhaul of the manuscript in Canada in the period 1941–45, the Consul (William Ames has become Geoffrey Firmin) and Yvonne became husband and estranged wife, and Hugh became the Consul's half-brother and Yvonne's former lover. From the undramatic relationships of both the short story and the earliest version of the novel, there now emerged a sinister triangle through which Lowry could modulate the book's themes. These he was later to define as "the guilt of man . . . his remorse . . . his ceaseless struggling toward the light under the weight of the past." [12] Lowry's thrust toward dramatic viability led him to narrative viability as well. This double-barreled efficacy can be illustrated by a comparison of early, middle, and final versions.

When he incorporated the short story into Chapter VIII, Lowry wisely allowed the Consul the narrative focus only until he has sighted the dying Indian from the moving bus. Once the bus is stopped and the unaided Indian robbed by the pelado, Lowry needed a clearer awareness than that of the mescal-fogged Consul. Thus he shifts the viewpoint to the sober, idealizing Hugh. The story and Chapter VIII both end with the arrival of the three protagonists at a saloon, ironically named the Todos-Contentos-y-Yo-Tambien. Knowing that the pelado, "stepping high and with a fatuous smile of triumph on his face," has gone in, they linger outside. The door opens slowly; two old peons, in humble contrast to the pelado, struggle out.

Bent double and groaning with the weight, an old, lame Indian was carrying out another Indian, yet older and more decrepit, on his back, by means of a strap clamped to his forehead. He carried the older man and his crutches—he carried both their burdens—
They all stood in the dusk watching the Indian as he disappeared with the old man around a bend in the road, shuffling through the grey white dust in his poor sandals.

(*Short Story*, 300)

Moving as it is, the description at this point distracts the reader's attention from the heart of the story. Lowry came to realize his error, but, never one to discard anything, he worked a transplant.

He moved the two old Indians one chapter further along—from the end of Chapter VIII to the end of Chapter IX:

Bent double, groaning with the weight, an old lame Indian was carrying on his back, by means of a strap looped over his forehead, another poor Indian, yet older and more decrepit than himself. He carried the older man and his crutches, *trembling in every limb under this weight of the past,* he carried both their burdens. . . .

(Published Version, 310)

If we compare the above from the book with the scene as originally written in the short story and then incorporated in Chapter VIII, we note that the words I have italicized mark the only significant change: ". . . trembling in every limb under the weight of the past." In its new setting, the epiphany concludes the relatively lighthearted ninth chapter where Hugh participates, with a kind of serious absurdity, in a bull-throwing at Arena Tomalín, while Geoffrey and Yvonne, for one of the only times in the novel, speak together of reconciliation and rebirth. But the appearance of the aged peons brilliantly undercuts the redemptive mood as "the weight of the past," symbolically portrayed, returns the narrative to its course downhill.

"Downhill," in fact, is the first word of the eighth chapter. Lowry, of course, intends the word in its literal (descent of the bus) and in its metaphoric (the Consul's course toward the abyss) senses. Chapter VII became the tragedy's major peripety. Lowry's skill with "transplant" surgery is the key. Here, side by side, are the endings of Chapter VIII as he blocked them in, respectively, in Mexico and for the final version nearly a decade later:

Ending, VIII (Mexico, 1937)

As the sudden piercing chords of a guitar were struck, Hugh, catching a glance from the Consul, though he understood something of the *real tragedy of Mexico,* which was also the tragedy of the earthly paradise, of Adam and Eve, of Cain and Abel.

And for the first time in his life, Hugh hated Man, whose tragedy it was.

Ending, VIII (1947)

They stared after them [the pelado and the bus driver] as the twin doors of the tavern swung to;—it had a pretty name, the Todos Contentos y Yo Tambien. The Consul said nobly:

"Everybody happy, including me."

And including those, Hugh thought, who effortlessly beautifully, in the blue sky above them,

After a while they saw the driver and the peeled one swagger into a pulqueria, the latter stepping high, upon his face a fatuous smile of triumph.

The three stared after them and at the name of the saloon after the doors had swung shut: the "Todos-Contentos-y-Yo-Tambien."

At a distance the telegraph wires were singing like crickets: "Everybody happy including me."

floated, the vultures—Xopilotes, who wait only for the ratification of death.

I have italicized a phrase whose early use (in the quotation on the left) indicates that Lowry was broadening his Mexican landscape to include analogues to contemporary political situations, not only of Mexico, as here, but of Spain and the entire West. The "loss of the Ebro" is a recurrent correlative for the Spanish Civil War which deeply influenced Hugh and was still being fought even as Lowry wrote. Near the end of the novel, in Chapter X, just before the Consul flees Yvonne and Hugh for the cantina refuge that will lead to his death, he engages in an invective-laden conversation with Hugh.[13] On the political level, the argument is about communism with the Consul lashing out at Hugh's "indoor Marxmanship" and at all those "people's revolutions" that were so much a part of the political climate of the thirties. The early drafts of Chapter VIII indicate that Lowry pushed his newly-found political overtones hard. But what he finally seeks in his climactic chapter is much more: the failure in the principals of charity. He juxtaposes the default of humanity—no one comes to the assistance of the dying man—and the success of inhumanity—the pelado despoils the symbolic saviour. Hugh, to whom the focus of narration is now fully given, makes a characteristically stylized gesture to help, but is warned off by the Consul and other onlookers. They remind him that he could be held responsible by Mexican law for aiding a wounded person. As for Yvonne, she cannot stand the sight of blood.

The published version eschews the singing telegraph wires and, as already noted, becomes a further tribute to Lowry's literary transplanting. He moves the memorable metaphor of

vultures as ratifiers of death from their original place at the end
of Chapter I:

> . . . the obvious vultures . . . hovered and tossed like burnt paper in
> their eternal ritual, fading as the screen grew bright, the lights flooded
> on, and the doors of the theatre were thrown open to the thunder—
> *xopilotes, who wait only for the ratification of death.*
>
> (Mexican Version, 42)

Since the first chapter is an epilogue in the place of a prologue
—an elegy for the Consul precisely one year after his, and
Yvonne's, death—the use of vultures as emblematic of the pall
of death would appear to provide a perfect transition backward.
It may even be that Lowry, who in the word's scientific sense was
a *conductor*, a channel, for other men's works, had been influenced by "The Snows of Kilimanjaro," which appeared in 1936,[14]
the year Lowry arrived in Mexico and began his book. The
Hemingway story is familiar to every freshman, but its myth of
the dying artist could not help but have had impact for the
"dying" Lowry of the Mexican years. Harry, a dissolute writer,
has long since died spiritually; now he is dying physically—of
gangrene. The setting is the plain before Mount Kilimanjaro in
Africa. The "big birds" are Hemingway's major correlative for
impending death.

> The cot the man lay on was in the wide shade of a mimosa tree and
> as he looked out past the shade onto the glare of the plain there were
> three of the big birds squatted obscenely, while in the sky, a dozen
> more sailed, making quick-moving shadows as they passed.

The important thing at this point is that Lowry's shift of symbols
reveals his deepening conception of the whole. He could not end
his elegiac first chapter with a ratification of death but of *life*.
The bright memory of the Consul must be preserved from mortal
oblivion.

In his crucial letter to Jonathan Cape, Lowry stressed that he
came to conceive of his book as "essentially trochal, as a wheel,
the image of which keeps recurring." [15] One could view the
circular movement of *Volcano*—that is, the backward spin in time
which occurs between Chapters I and II—as a great circle voyage

into time whose aim is the understanding of the tragedy of previous Day of the Dead. But to be truly trochal—that is, in the Proustian sense of eclipsing time and death—Lowry needed a more cogent conceit than vultures, what John Woodburn in an early review [16] called "a magnificent sentence of elision":

Over the town, in the dark tempestuous night, backwards revolved the luminous wheel.

(Published Version, 42)

The ferris wheel that bridges the time gap, an innovation relatively late in his revisions, relates to a major theme of the novel, what Lowry's friend, the novelist David Markson, calls the "timeless paradox" of death and rebirth in cyclical repetition. This cycle moves only in relation to the fateful act of the Consul's fall which is linked to the peon's heartless death, hence to mankind's.

"After having written the story about the Indian by the side of the road, and first got the inspiration to make the whole thing a larger novel, I wrote the end of this book. . . ."

(Dark As the Grave, 151)

Lowry goes on in *Dark As the Grave* to recount his decision to have the Consul shot by a bunch of Mexican policemen in a cantina. He reports that the murder of the Consul, by turn tragic and absurd, with the victim unable to undo a simple protective ruse and prove he is not an "espider," was fleshed out from notes he made during a conversation with a group of fellow *borrachones*, they trying to speak English and he, Spanish. Elsewhere Lowry recalled a newspaper story about a man named Eriksen who had been found dead in a barranca; he also recalled that there was a barranca at the bottom of the Lowry garden in Cuernavaca and that the Lowry telephone was on the "Eriksen" exchange.[17]

Here again the Lowry demonology loomed large: his sense of being somehow—the word persists—a *conductor* for human agony. But the artistic fusing of all those currents, this was studied. And nothing illustrates Lowry's controlled operations better than the final metamorphosis of pietà and pelado from figures in an autobiographical fragment to principal icons in an infernal sojourn.

The horse theme—Lowry's pietà and pelado—actually dominates the pivotal first chapter, early version. It turns up eight
times.[18] But since Lowry had not yet settled on the Consul and
Yvonne as estranged husband and wife, it is not surprising that
little is viable. However, Lowry's recovery from the failure of his
original conception is worth examining as an evidence of growth.

The first chapter is related through the lens of a survivor, although a disenchanted one, of the tragic events of the recent past.
The survivor is Jacques Laruelle, the only character whose world
view is comparable in scope to the Consul's, a black melancholiac
who is about to return to France. At this point, Lowry had not
sketched in the abortive love affair between the Frenchman and
Yvonne. Midway through the chapter, Laruelle enters a theater
where *Las Manos de Orlac* is playing, sits down to watch it, and
falls asleep, "drawing down with him the last image he had seen
on the screen, that of Orlac's hands covered with blood and
ceaselessly clutching them over the money, received for the
murder he could not help committing." The dream becomes a
complex and ambiguous state.

Laruelle was sinking down, ever more rapidly downward until the
sensation of sheer falling was paralyzing and then, when he felt that
were it protracted a moment longer he must wake up and save himself,
it was as if he entered, in some mysterious way, into the Consul's
consciousness. . . . And waking from some strange sleep within sleep,
Laruelle was instantly acquainted with all the events of that day of
the dead long past which led up to this conscious moment.

(Mexican Version, 29)

The dream becomes the product of a nebulous state at first called
"some strange sleep within sleep" but twenty words later referred
to as "this conscious moment." One notes Lowry's inability, despite
the high style, to convince the reader that there has been a break-
through of the boundaries between dream and actuality. The
language is self-consciously literary, but the feeling—the key
idea, at this stage—that Jacques is inhabiting, inexplicably and
simultaneously, *two* consciousnesses is missing entirely.

Jacques, however implausibly, is supposed to have *merged* with
the Consul; he has become, in fact, one of the dead man's masks.
He dreams of "plummeting" (a favorite Lowryan word) in pursuit
of Yvonne and Hugh (the unabashed lovers of the first versions),

"obsessed by the necessity of conveying some urgent message to these lovers." (Mexican Version, 30) Although Lowry never gets around to revealing the nature of that message, much else is revealed: notably, his inability to make the parts equal the whole. When the dreamer dreams he hears the young lovers discussing the Indian, they say things that contradict the eighth chapter:

"I wonder what's happened to that peon we had to leave beside the road," he added presently. "Gosh, that was an ugly business."
"Oh, I expect somebody will have taken care of him."
(Mexican Version, 34)

Although he was never noted for his ability to write straight dialogue, surely such "gosh" and "oh" conversations would not have been written if Lowry had any idea of the cogency of their topic. Eventually, Laruelle fades out as Laruelle. Enter Laruelle inside the reincarnated Consul. Consularly, he recalls the bus ride and the pelado:

... and there, waving his arms, was a pelado. ... He had got hold of a melon from somewhere and was approaching with a melancholy gait, swaying, walking straight, yet as if stepping over obstacles, as though the human frame were resentful of harbouring such a will as his and wanted to shake itself clear of it. ...
(Mexican Version, 38)

The pelado boards the bus, stretches himself out on a seat, apparently asleep, but to the still-dreaming Laruelle, "aware of everything that went on." Several pages later, a horse and rider gallop in out of the black. Because Lowry retained a significant section in text and another in concept, it is necessary here to quote in detail:

Once a horseman, crazy with tequila, drew up across the bus's path. The horse stood blinking in the headlights, its rider rolling over the horse, only holding himself on by the reins. The bus hooted nervously and the man rode off before them, almost falling over backwards but somehow saving himself by the pommel as he furiously beat the horse with his machete. Under the moon the sight was evidently frightening to Yvonne and she clutched Hugh, who was looking at her tenderly. Women drew their children into the side of the road as he galloped on, and men stood back against the hedges or into the ditches . . . the sight of the man riding so wildly, whose eyes caught by the headlights were strange as *those soon to be familiar with death,* had been awe-inspiring, and perhaps there was fixed on her mind . . . some picture of *maniacal, uncontrolled, senseless force.* . . .

(Mexican Version, 40)

This discarded passage goes far towards clarifying Lowry's evolving conception. He retained, in essence, everything to the point where Yvonne's reaction is recorded. I have italicized two phrases from the discarded portion. The first is a foreshadowing that Yvonne is intended to survive, for she is one of "those soon to be familiar with death." More importantly, Yvonne's sense of the rearing horse as reflecting "maniacal, uncontrolled, senseless force" became Lowry's, added to the novel's injunction that man must exercise humanity and, above all, love in order to control the life force.

But, even in this earliest stage, Lowry remembers the dying Indian; his sense of pietà is sure. The chapter comes to a virtual end with Laruelle waking at last and realizing that he

was the only one who noticed that it was precisely here where the peon had lain bleeding, and seeing what he did see . . . he began finally to glide out of his sleep. . . .

(Mexican Version, 41)

Only the ratifying vultures remained to close out the epilogic prologue.

The horse theme is never wasted in the published version. Horse and Indian, together or separately, make their appearance during those moments of the novel that are most "loaded." As in the first drafts, a horse, ridden by a drunken man, thunders by Laurelle and interrupts his reverie. The horseman at that early point, wrote Lowry, "is by implication the first appearance of the Consul himself as a symbol of mankind." [19]

The next encounter, their first during the main action after Chapter I, occurs in the fourth chapter as Hugh and Yvonne are crossing a river on their morning ride. They see on the other side a pulqueria, talismanically named La Sepultura (burial place), where

an Indian sat with his back against the wall, his broad hat half down over his face, resting outside in the sunshine. His horse, or a horse, was tethered near him to a tree and Hugh could see from midstream the Number seven branded on its rump.

(Published Version, 109)

The Indian, having been viewed by Hugh and Yvonne, must now be seen by the Consul. This confrontation occurs in Chapter VII, as the Consul and Laruelle walk along the base of the Cortez Palace. They edge into the palace wall to let a man on horseback pass,

a fine-featured Indian of the poorer class, dressed in soiled while loose clothes. The man was singing gaily to himself. But he nodded to them courteously as if to thank them. He seemed about to speak, reining in his little horse—on either side of which chinked two saddlebags, and upon whose rump was branded the Number seven—to a slow walk beside them. . . . But the man, riding slightly in front, did not speak and at the top he suddenly waved his hand and galloped away, singing.

(Published Version, 213–14)

Except for the needless proliferation in Chapter I, all the appearances of the horse and rider were in the manuscript from the start. All, that is, but one. Since Yvonne must die, Lowry hit on the idea of capping her sense of dread at the appearance of the rearing horse (Chapter I, first draft) by making the horse —this time riderless because the Indian lies dead—the instrument for her death in the penultimate—the eleventh—chapter. The tethered animal is released by the doomed Consul at his eleventh hour in the befuddled yet benevolent belief he is doing a last penance to the memory of the dead Indian whose horse his murderers (and they will be the Consul's, too) have stolen.

Thus, symbolically and by cause and effect, Geoffrey and Yvonne are united in death as they could not be in life. At the last, Yvonne visions their home in the "northern paradise" afire, dying like herself. But there is one paragraph more. It is redemptive and suggestive of hope. The dream of the burning house leaves her, and she

felt herself suddenly gathered upwards and borne towards the stars, through eddies of stars scattering aloft with ever widening circlings like rings on water, among which now appeared, like a flock of diamond birds flying softly and steadily towards Orion, the Pleiades.

(Published Version, 366)

As for the Consul, at the same moment (although a chapter later) that Yvonne finds salvation in death, the dying Consul is borne ("born" is closer to the heart of the scene) to the summit of the barranca and flung with a dead dog into its crater. But, like Yvonne's, the Consul's soul survives, ascending to the top of the volcano Popo which, like Hemingway's Kilimanjaro, had always beckoned the mortally doomed artist.

III *Eviction and the Garden*

The above attempt to carry through one major thematic complex is, at best, merely suggestive. What is true of the evolving nature of the horse theme can be applied to others from Lowry's cornucopia of symbols.

It is not until approximately a third of the way into the novel that "the most important theme of the book"—these are Lowry's words to Jonathan Cape—appears. It is found in the words of a sign that rears up before the Consul in Chapter V, the aforementioned Garden Chapter:

¿LE GUSTA ESTE JARDÍN?
¿QUE ES SUYO?
¡EVITE QUE SUS HIJOS LO DESTRUYAN!

(Final Version, 128)

The words as motif bear special significance for this study for they serve as evidence that Lowry did not until late hit on a viable pattern of their recurrence. The words are never mentioned in the short story; they appear, but never galvanically, in the first novel drafts; they form a coherent motif only in the published version where their significance so impressed Lowry that he added them, on a flyleaf by themselves, as a postlude to the novel.

The words, on their face, are merely a rendering, in Spanish, of the familiar injunction to keep off the grass:

DO YOU ENJOY THIS GARDEN
WHICH IS YOURS?
KEEP YOUR CHILDREN FROM DESTROYING IT!

When the Consul first sees the sign, he is under the weather ("an inconceivable anguish of horripilating hangover thunder-clapping about his skull," *Volcano,* 126), and he is looking for the bottle he has hidden in the garden. He sees the sign but, in his frenzy of guilt, reads into it, beyond the words, cosmic doom. He slightly but crucially mistranslates.

YOU LIKE THIS GARDEN?
WHY IS IT YOURS?
WE EVICT THOSE WHO DESTROY!

The Consul has read the first two lines as separate questions and the third as a threat. For him, the misreading works; the words, mistranslated, carry their own rightness. His garden—his life—once beautiful, has become a jungle; he hides bottles in the shrubbery; his garden can never be paradise because it is hell. Lowry carries the mistranslation throughout the Consul's drunken wanderings. Frequently only the first four words are included—LE GUSTA ESTE JARDÍN?—but the use of the interrogation mark indicates the Consul is continuing to read the words as a portent. In the pivotal "dying Indian" section (Chapter VIII) the sign reappears to the Consul from the bus window. This time the words are properly translated—but by the sober Hugh.

In the earliest drafts, Lowry introduced the destroyed-garden motif much earlier—in the Geoffrey-Yvonne reunion chapter (Chapter III in the earlier but finally Chapter II in the published version). Remembering that at this stage the Consul and Yvonne are father and daughter, we encounter them in the first drafts strolling together in the village square. They pass a public letter-writer's open booth:

"Probably writing some odd letter for someone who can't write," the Consul inferred. "I am taking the only way out, semicolon. I am tired of life, full stop. Change of paragraph, change of life, change of worlds."

"You might make use of him one of these days," Yvonne said, "and get him to write to Mother for you." She pointed inquiringly to a tree on which a notice was nailed.

"¿Le Gusta este Jardín? ¿Que es suyo? Evite que sus hijos los destruyan."

"I haven't seen that before," said the Consul. "What does it mean?"

"Roughly speaking, 'Do you like this garden? If so, take care of it. We evict those who destroy."

(Mexican Version, 73)

Significantly, in the clear copy of the Mexican Version, everything is deleted—that is, x-ed out on the typewriter—from the words of the sign on. It is as if Lowry became aware of the potential of this talisman and realized that he needed a more dramatic point at which to introduce it. He found such a place, of course, in the Garden Chapter (*Volcano*, 128).

Having touched on Lowry's non-literal use of language—that is, of his "filtering" process in the case of the efficacious mis-translation—I should like to touch on other aspects of Lowry's "Anglicized" Spanish and his "Hispano" English. If Lowry does not quite creolize language (although "spy" becomes "espider," see, especially, *Volcano*, 371, and "half past six by the clock" becomes "half past sick by the cock," *Volcano*, 352), he certainly renders Mexican English into something that is neither tongue but mightily effective for Lowry as a private hieroglyphic. He will allow long sections in Spanish to stand (as with Dr. Vigil's calling card and physician's shingle, or as with the words of a dire headline, "Es inevitable la muerte del papa," meaning "The Pope Is Dying"), but only when the sound and feel of the Spanish enrich and transmute the material. Lowry's ear is exceptionally sensitive to the way Mexicans speak English. When Dr. Vigil speaks to Laruelle of the truly dispossessed, he refers to them as "those who have nobody them with" (*Volcano*, 6). The addicted, like the Consul, are those who have followed Vigil's entreaty to "throw away your mind" (*Volcano*, 6).

The effect of language exploited in this way is, when Lowry is at his best, galvanic. His way with Spanish is at the opposite pole from that of Ernest Hemingway in *For Whom the Bell Tolls*. In producing a kind of Hispano-English, Hemingway, with a profusion of words like "thee" and "thou," sought to maintain fidelity to the Spanish by a rendering of "translated" English. Lowry's non-literal, his *affective*, use of Spanish evolved as he extended his stay in Mexico. There is little evidence of affective Spanish in the short story. When he quotes cautionary words about passenger safety-ads that run the breadth of the bus over

the window screen—Lowry runs in only the most familiar phrases
and to no dramatic effect (italics below are mine):

> Was it murder? Was it robbery? or both? The peon had ridden
> from the market with more than that four or five pesos, possibly he'd
> been in possession of *mucho dinero*, so that a good way to avoid suspi-
> cion of theft was to leave a little of the money. . . . Perhaps it was
> not robbery at all; he had only been thrown from his horse? The horse
> had kicked him? Possible? Impossible! Had the police been called?
> An ambulance—the *Crux Roja?* . . .
>
> (Short Story, 295)

One notes the arbitrary substitution of only the most obvious
Spanish words and phrases—*mucho, dinero, Crux Roja*. The
same section, reworked to become Chapter VIII of the novel,
bears the Lowryan imprint:

> Perhaps it wasn't robbery at all, he had only been thrown from his
> horse? Posseebly, Imposseebly.
>   Si, hombre, but hadn't the police been called? But clearly somebody
> was already going for help. Chingar.
>
> (Final Version, 245)

The above recital of recurring motifs and lingual devices has
attempted to show how Lowry, in the sense "blocking-out" has
been applied to Milton and *Paradise Lost,* staked out—even
crammed in—a huge residue of symbolic claims. His contrapuntal
methods bring the major themes, with their symbolic correlates,
full circle.

IV *The Consul, a Jungian Prufrock*

My application of Professor Barker's block concept has its
major relevance for Lowry in terms of his arrangement of chapters. If leitmotifs flash like rockets to remind the reader of the
footing of the terrain, the twelve chapters work like a vast check-
and-balance network to condition expectation. The movement
of the book is a concatenation of dark portents, occasionally pen-
etrated by patches of daylight, which transcends any customary
line of suspense. The Consul's fate, implicit from the first page,
is affirmed in every scene, although the gloom is sporadically

shaded by a series of set scenes of Pickwickian and punning humor.[20]

Professor Dale Edmonds was the first to demonstrate that each of the four principals has at least one chapter in which the interplay of thought and action filters through an individual sensibility.[21] The Consul has five chapters (III, V, VII, X, and XII); Yvonne has three (II, IX, XI); Hugh has three (IV, VI, VIII); and Jacques has one (I). Lowry projects a related variation on the Miltonic efficacy of chapter arrangement which is tied to shifting character viewpoints. Where Milton's great poem gravitates between Heaven and Hell but has some of its most powerful scenes in the sublunary realm of the First Couple, *Under the Volcano* teeters between past and future, between despair and hope, and the Yvonne-Hugh shadings of light play like a palimpsest over the Consul's night thoughts.

Lowry likened the architectonic progress of his novel, as earlier noted, to the construction of a cathedral whose east and west towers are the book's first and last chapters. "Doleful bells" in each tower toll their dialogue from the living to the dead and back again to the living. In the ten intervening chapters—a continuum between the towers—Lowry orchestrates contrapuntal theme music: the chords of the three principal players. Yvonne's chords, even at the moment of death, are translunary; Hugh's are redolent of the sea, to whose bosom he speaks of returning; the Consul's are more complex, for he is Promethean. What is perhaps his most moving soliloquy is pitched in the tones of the artist-addict. Shortly before he flees Yvonne and Hugh for his Gethsemane, "oozing alcohol from every pore," the Consul wanders (and wonders) like a Jungian Prufrock:

> How indeed could he hope to find himself, to begin again when, somewhere, perhaps, in one of those lost or broken bottles, in one of those glasses, lay, forever, the solitary clue to his identity? How could he go back and look now, scrabble among the broken glass, under the eternal bars, under the oceans?
>
> (Published Version, 293)

Malcolm Lowry plays the Yvonne-Hugh music as counterpoint to the Consul's solo. The chapters are carefully arranged for the always-sought contrapuntal effect. His aim is to make hope and despair interweave so as to transcend even one's interest in the characters. Since these characters are in one way "Things," as that French philosopher of the absurd fellow has it . . . this hope should be, rather, a transcendent, a universal hope.[22]

What Lowry appears to be saying is that he envisioned his principals as interacting forces, out of whose triumphs and losses a human statement would evolve.

With texture reflecting maelstrom, Lowry has given us a book that is keyed to the contemporary rhythm. Its unrelieved atmosphere of impending disaster is surely mirrored on a less symbolic scale in today's headlines. The vision of the Consul catapulting to the bottom of the barranca, a dead dog tossed in after him, has the same power to numb the mind into despair as the world itself shaking with its own demonic orchestras apparently intent on plunging to its own catastrophe.

Under the Volcano is the story of a possessed man that could only have been written by a possessed man. Yet the always lucid evocation of the Consul's agony is the product of an artist in control of his labyrinth.

CHAPTER 5

Art's Defeat by Life

> For some minutes Lowry endeavored to
> summarize [his] nonexistent plot, after
> which [he said]: "Well, nothing *happens*.
> Nothing should, in a novel." Whereupon
> Aiken: . . . "No. No incidents."
>
> David Markson [1]

I *Skipper Next to God*

AFTER *Under the Volcano* Lowry published nothing in his
lifetime except occasional short stories in little magazines.
The discovery of these became something of an occasion. With
the longer works—at one time he had four novels going—he was
never satisfied. That two of the extended fictions have been published posthumously is due to the dedication of his widow. Lowry,
however, would have been the last to consent to having his work
published in fragmentary form. I agree with Matthew Corrigan
that

when an author dies something happens to his work. It may become
more important for his future reputation that the unfinished work
remain so, rather than be brought to some kind of tentative and
artificial conclusion. I doubt seriously if anyone, even the author's
alter ego, even his muse, has the right to tamper in any way with what
has been left uncompleted.[2]

Professor Corrigan proceeds to an interesting theory that, in
effect, the post-*Volcano* Malcolm Lowry had lost touch with the
novel form; that his hold on life, already made tenuous by alcoholism, was further reduced by his publishers and their failure
to understand that his preoccupations as an artist were taking him
far afield from any rigorous adherence to prescribed forms. "It

is just possible," Corrigan writes, "that he was on his way to discovering something new about literature. . . ." [3]

Unfortunately, an examination of the manuscripts of all the extended work-in-progress gives promise of nothing but frustration. While one can believe that the Consul drank to sustain his battle for the survival of consciousness, one also believes that Lowry came increasingly to write to sustain his battle for the survival of his self-image as ultra-artist. The maker gives way to the autobiographer. Corrigan wishes for a lessening of spiritual distance between Lowry and the New York publishing establishment. The admirer of *Under the Volcano* wishes for an extension in the subsequent long fiction of the distance between Lowry and his material.

Sigbjørn Wilderness, the alter ego Lowry created to be the major repository for autobiographical shavings, sees his torment as that of the damned writer who must "die" that his art can live. In *Dark As the Grave,* Lowry endows Sigbjørn with candor over the dilemma:

It wasn't good art but it was the truth. Anybody more bloody well damned than himself, he considered, it would be next to impossible to find on this planet. What had God been up to in creating such a man and what was his purpose in keeping him alive, if alive he could be said to be? Was He so kindly that He would do it for his wife? Yet what strange power was it in him, strange, and it could not be but evil—Yet, was he not good, were they not good, had they not sacrificed their own house, their work, to the forest, for others' good—he had forgotten this, this was something else again—was this a power that was wasted on writing and that God had determined must in some sense serve chaos.

(*Grave,* 122)

Such a passage is a characteristic evocation of Lowry's messianic view of art. A kind of desperate animism defines his creative life. The sound of a ship's engine during a voyage through the Panama becomes a portent of doom. A visit to the house in Rome where Keats died links him to all the possessed artists who have ever lived. As Sigbjørn Wilderness, Lowry acknowledges that

his agonies must be far from unique, yet it seemed to him that if one person had survived such a thing to breathe purer air and love the light that there was hope for the human race. For one man's agony belongs to all men and to God.

(*Grave*, 124–25)

All his life Lowry sought to convert "one man's agony" into gain. The pain of Malebolge and hellfire would be redeemed by what he could report back. Lowry's answer to the Cape reader who criticized his shortcomings in character drawing ("There are a thousand writers who can draw adequate characters . . . for one who can tell you anything new about hell fire" [5]) carries, in practice, pitfalls. If an imaginative writer comes to see as his first —increasingly, in Lowry's case—his *only*—duty the endless analyzing of himself, the results are likely to be like the vain scratchings a beetle makes inside a box where it is trapped.

No one has perceived the dangers to the artist of introspection unaccompanied by projection better than the critic John Wain. He finds that what is ruinous in the modern situation generally and in Lowry particularly is that "for the first time the artist is content to gather his evidence from the self and *leave it at that*." [6] Wain goes on—mistakenly, I believe—to decry Lowry's "process of elaboration" in *Under the Volcano*. It is, as I have tried to show (Chapter 4), that very "elaboration," entailing a rigorous selection of imaginative reference, that enabled Lowry to transcend monomania and, in *Volcano*, to make a statement of universal dimension.

With notable exceptions, to be discussed in the next chapter, Lowry's prose work after *Volcano* reads like the extended entries a captain might place in his ship's log provided he was sure he was—to borrow the title of a Broadway play—"skipper next to God."

II "Through the Panama"

From the mass of material Lowry thought he was working into a vast pilgrim's progress of the rootless soul seeking harbor, the most self-contained units were assembled by Margerie Lowry in *Hear Us O Lord from Heaven Thy Dwelling Place*. The book contains seven stories, all refined into completion or near-completion in Dollarton, British Columbia, during the 1950s.

Three of the stories, "The Bravest Boat," "Gin and Goldenrod," and "The Forest Path to the Spring," are wholly about Canada. "The Forest Path" is really a novella, fully successful on its own terms and bearing promise of a new spirit in Lowry, a reconciliation between man and nature. These three stories will be discussed in their proper place, Chapter 6, the Canada section.

Two of the others serve in the retrospect of Lowry's last decade as a gloss of the obsessions of the artist marooned in an alien world. Although Lowry adopted many masks, the messianic voice ultimately dominates. The most persistent of these deceptions is the persona of the man of supreme sensibility who is trapped in a phase of history of whose ethos he claims ignorance.

Thus, in "Through the Panama," Lowry, in Wilderness's journal, records that he is

capable of conceiving of a writer today, even intrinsically a first-rate writer, who *simply cannot understand,* and never has been able to understand, what his fellow writers are driving at, and have been driving at, and who has always been too shy to ask.

("Panama," 84)

This writer, we are not surprised to learn, is the main character of the novel Sigbjørn is working on. His name is Martin Trumbaugh (a namesake, perhaps, of Frankie Trumbauer, one of Lowry's jazz idols), and he is caught in a characteristically Lowryan dilemma: he is enmeshed in the plot of the novel he has written. Shades, one senses, of another book on which Lowry was working at the time *(Dark As the Grave).* And sure enough, a few lines later, Sigbjørn tells us that Martin's novel is to bear that title. The sticky fact emerges that Lowry was allowing himself to become obsessed by writers writing about writers writing about books in which they are the main characters.

The preoccupation is not in itself disabling. The Consul, it may also be remembered, was also a writer working on a book. Lowry never allowed the motif to take over *Under the Volcano.* Firmin's book, never seen or quoted from, became a part of the consular mystery, a muted product of the Consul's malaise. In "Through the Panama," once the reader accustoms himself to the shifting narrative focus that is necessitated by a story within a story, the chronicle succeeds. No other single work, page for page, tells us so much directly about Malcolm Lowry. At this level, the story is as confessional as F. Scott Fitzgerald's *The Crack-Up*. Lowry even has Martin thinking that Fitzgerald "would have been saved by life in our shack." When Sigbjørn breaks in with a digression on drink, Lowry provides us with the best capsule explanation of his own excesses to be found anywhere in his writings:

Everything written about drink is incidentally absurd. Have to do it all over again, what about conflict, appalling sadness that can lead equally to participation in the tragic human condition, self-knowledge, discipline. Conflict is all-important. Gin and orange juice best cure for alcoholism, real cause of which is ugliness and complete baffling sterility of existence as *sold* to you. . . .

("Panama," 44)

The real protagonists of "Panama," however, are neither Sigbjørn nor his double Martin—not even men at all—but man's consciousness—and, in the void, the unconscious. It is Aiken's *Blue Voyage* all over again: the juxtaposing of inside and outside narratives. It is the consciousness of the apprentice-artist, Dana Hilliot, the cabin boy of *Ultramarine*, grown up to become that of Sigbjørn Wilderness whose voyage aboard the good ship solipsism has become a one-way passage. Where, at the end of *Ultramarine*, the nineteen-year-old Dana can forget the horrors aboard the *Oedipus Tyrannus*, believing his return to England and his beloved Janet is a return to spiritual port, too (". . . no factors wrongly co-ordinated, no loose tangled ends," *Ultramarine*, 170), Sigbjørn, at thirty-seven, sees himself as Saul in the process of becoming Paul. Life for him will be a never-ending road to Damascus.

. . . when the scales drop from his eyes, he will be given the grace to understand the heroic strivings of other artists too. Meantime he must slug it out, as they say, in darkness, that being his penance.

("Panama," 85–86)

It will be penance, too, for admirers of *Under the Volcano*. For Lowry, there will be no return to port on the good ship solipsism.

It soon becomes clear that Lowry's portrait of the artist out of time in "Panama" is but a mask for his fondest self-image. Far from being a humble anachronism, he is the deliberately isolated spokesman for humanity. His voice is not that of the artist in any contemporary sense—the modern artist, for Lowry, having forfeited his links to mankind—but that of a kind of Steppenwolf figure whose look goes to the heart of all humanity, bespeaking the despair of one who knows the meaning of life. Sigbjørn inserts in a note that Martin often resisted his own perceptions as extra-human.

> He could not find his vision of the world in any books. He had never succeeded in discovering more than a superficial aspect of his sufferings or his aspirations. And though he had got into the habit of pretending that he thought like other people, this was not the case.
> ("Panama," 86)

It deserves to be noted that Lowry's messianic urge does not prevent him from providing "Through the Panama" at least the appearance of dramatic movement. Sigbjørn is after all aboard a real ship which is subject to real gales. The *Diderot* almost capsizes in a storm, and Lowry gives us an electrifying description of how the French seamen work through the night placing a *ceinture* (a belt) around the ship to keep it together. Lowry dashes motifs, familiar to readers of *Under the Volcano,* together like billiard balls. These excerpts from the last two pages will illustrate:

> Prayer to the Virgin for those who have nobody them with.
> For she is the Virgin for those who have nobody them with.
> And for mariners on the sea.
> And to the Saint of Desperate and Dangerous Causes . . .
> Plight of an Englishman who is a Scotchman who is Norwegian who is Canadian who is a Negro at heart from Dahomey who is married to an American who is on a French ship in distress which has been built by Americans and who finds at last that he is a Mexican dreaming of the White Cliffs of Dover. . . .
> Sonnez les matines!
> Sonnez les matines!
> ¿Le gusta esta jardin? ¿Que es suyo? . . .
> S.O.S. going on next door. Battement de tambours! . . .
> Martin swore that if he survived he would never willingly do another injurious action . . .
> —Wish old Charon was here . . .

*The whole is an assembly of apparently incongruous parts, slipping
past one another—*
Great God—we seem to be steering again. . . .
Dawn, and an albatross, bird of heaven, gliding astern. . . .
("Panama," 96–98)

As in *Volcano,* Lowry uses the graphics of the printed page.
He indents the main text to accommodate literary and subliterary
material ranging from Coleridge's *Ancient Mariner* to a book on
the history of the Panama Canal given Sigbjørn by the third mate.
If the test of fictional experimentation lies in whether the devices
heighten an effect or tauten the dramatic line, Lowry's typo-
graphical games do not much enhance the story. Lowry was always a perhaps too willing slave to the Jamesian mandate that
there be depths.

Thus, even so successful a story as "Through the Panama"
charts Lowry's unhappy course as a creative writer. Where once
he could write that rarest of contemporary fictions, an authentic
modern tragedy, he would now, except for a precious instance or
two, apply himself to the literature of exhortation. His single
creation during the last ten years of his life would be himself,
convinced as he was that he belonged in the vision-plagued company of the damned who live in hell but dream of heaven.

III   *The Game of Literary Immortality*

In "Strange Comfort Afforded by the Profession" Lowry uses
some of the same literary materials as in "Panama," but the story,
less than a quarter as long, is more self-contained. Nowhere, outside the pages of *Under the Volcano,* does Lowry so effectively
control his symbols while endowing them with a life of their own.
"Strange Comfort" is an underground prose version of Stephen
Spender's "I Think of Those Who Were Truly Great" and a tour
de force on the tension between life and art.

Sigbjørn Wilderness, in Rome on a Guggenheim Fellowship,
pauses before the house where Keats died in 1821 at the age of
26. He dutifully records in his notebook everything that is written
there, even to the drawing of the lyre which appeared on the
house between the Italian and its translation. He feels like an
interloper, partly because in true Lowryan style he fears being

taken for a spy and partly because of an awareness that he is invading private domain. He moves to a glass case containing "remnants of aromatic gums used by Trelawny when cremating the body of Shelley," then to another containing letters from Keats's friend Severn describing the poet's death throes. Sigbjørn records Severn's words, *"On Saturday a gentleman came to cast his hand and foot,"* and adds, "that is the most sinister line to me. Who is this gentleman?" ("Strange Comfort," 101)

Within three pages, we have moved from the tidy world of Guggenheim researching into Lowry's world of portents disguised, in this case, as tourist information. It does not surprise us that Sigbjørn moves quickly from Keats's house to a bar. The third grappa triggers in Sigbjørn a series of literary associations, all tinged in black humor: Byron's desire to appropriate Shelley's skull for a goblet; Trelawny's having snatched Shelley's heart from the flames; Sigbjørn's remembrance of Proust's remembrance that the heart was interred in London. Sigbjørn glances idly at previous entries in his notebook, comes across notes made two years ago—but never subsequently used—during a visit to Poe's shrine in Richmond, Virginia. Time shifts. Sigbjørn is touring, notebook in hand, on the other side of the Atlantic. Seeing again, among Poe's relics, coats belonging to George Washington's dentist, he is brought back to the present with thoughts of Shelley's gums. Sigbjørn's consciousness installs a space-time continuum between the three poets who died too young. Assisted by a fourth grappa, he senses a fearful irony between the lot of tortured poets who leave behind crematory gums, salvaged hearts, and letters pleading for help and the exploitation of them by such as he.

And the despair in the glass case, all private correspondence carefully destroyed, yet destined to become ten thousand times more public than ever, viewed through the great glass case of art, was now transmuted into hieroglyphics, masterly compressions, obscurities to be deciphered by experts—yes, and poets—like Sigbjørn Wilderness.

("Strange Comfort," 109)

A wave of horror passes over him, but he knows pity for his literary kinsmen will not keep him from using "these mummified and naked cries of agony . . . thus exposed to human view in permanent incorruption, as if embalmed evermore in their separate eternal funeral parlors" ("Strange Comfort," 110).

Lack of space in his notebook prevents Sigbjørn from expanding on the idea that suffering, as nothing else, unites artists of every era. He pulls a larger notebook from his pocket, finds a letter, never mailed, dating back to a youthful crucible of his own, an epistolary S.O.S.:

. . . Literally I am dying in this macabre hole and I appeal to you to send me, out of the money that is after all mine, enough that I may return. Surely I am not the only writer, there have been others in history whose ways have been misconstrued and who have failed. . . .
("Strange Comfort," 112)

It is of some interest that the letter is a fragment of autobiography. It parallels, with only the names changed, Lowry's own bitter appeals in 1939–41 to a Los Angeles attorney charged by his father with doling out money to the prodigal son. Of more signficance is Lowry's identification with the great dead writers. This community of spirit is evidenced by the manner of Sigbjørn Wilderness's response to rereading his old letter. He does a triple-take. He resists an impulse to tear out the letter because it might ruin the notebook, decides instead to scratch out the words line by line. He then comes to a mordant realization of why he kept the letter in the first place. He might be able to use it in a story; be able, should he become as famous as Edgar Allan Poe, to leave behind a remnant from his suffering for some future Guggenheim fellow. The story ends with Sigbjørn, fortified by a fifth grappa, breaking into belly laughter which changed into "something more respectable . . . a prolonged—though on the whole relatively pleasurable—fit of coughing . . ." ("Strange Comfort," 113).

Why does Sigbjørn laugh? I believe that Lowry intends the laughter as cosmic, not immediate, and that whatever "pleasure" is in it stems from Lowry's honesty in recognizing a complicity between suffering writers and succeeding generations in the game of literary immortality. It is a game Lowry plays to the hilt.

IV "Voyage Along the Knife Edge of Paranoia"

Midway through *Dark As the Grave*, Lowry's first full-length work of fiction to be published after his death, the ubiquitous Sigbjørn Wilderness, an unpublished alcoholic novelist, arrives with Primrose, his second wife, in Cuernavaca, Mexico, where they spend the night in the same bedroom tower that almost ten years before had witnessed the crack-up of his first marriage. The infernal scenes and themes call up the original material that Wilderness had worked into a much rejected novel about Mexico entitled *The Valley of the Shadow of Death*. While his wife sleeps nearby, Sigbjørn is seized by a hangover which evolves into a torturing metamorphosis. He imagines himself inhabiting—unaccountably and simultaneously—several spheres. While thinking they are merely the sounds of last night's revelry, he hears a clarinet soar into the strains of his first wife's favorite song followed by the "infernal din" of a ragtime version of the Mexican Raspa ("debombditty bombditty bombditty bomb de bomb!"), compounded by howls from the always present Lowryan pariah dogs.

Although Sigbjørn has convinced Primrose that their trip to Mexico is an exorcism to overcome a massive writing block, he mournfully recognizes anew that every hangover brings nothing but the memory of a hangover, a dread cycle, and that he has sunk to becoming his own "character." But this despair is coupled with the delicious awareness that he is undergoing a unique experience; that the demons who are the conductors of human agony are orchestrating pandemonium and that he must not miss a note.

Dark As the Grave Wherein My Friend Is Laid was hemstitched together by his widow and his biographer into something looking like a novel, but the work is other things before it is fiction. Three aspects, each interrelated to the others, invite a more fruitful inquiry than any attempt to channel the book as a novel, withal an embryonic novel. First, it is a companion—a gloss—to *Under the Volcano*, and cannot be read intelligibly without first having read its predecessor. The place of *Dark As the Grave* on the modest shelf of Lowry's writings is to the right of *Volcano;* to the left should be Lowry's letter to Jonathan Cape justifying the major novel. Second, *Grave* is the extended—and best—statement we have of Lowry's unformulated ideas about the relationship of art to life. Lowry conceived of art and life as in necessary but imperfect correspondence. His job for as long as he lived was to perfect that correspondence. To that task of transcendence he would marshal addiction in the service of the eidetic, solipsism charged with a messianic current, and, above all, the notion that he, a writer, was himself being *written*. Third, the book is about what takes place in the mind of a writer while he is writing. "Through the Panama" provided a short trip, via a spiritual voyager's journal, through the stormy crucible of lost identity to recovered balance. *Dark As the Grave*, in the words of Elizabeth Janeway, is "a voyage along the knife edge of paranoia." [7] Sigbjørn Wilderness, the ultra writer who cannot write, seeks to align the forces that block writing with the forces that darken life. For Malcolm Lowry, if he is to be saved, it is all a single jeopardy: salvation in life is inseparable from salvation in art.

V *Flawed Equations of Life and Art*

In Chapter VII of *Dark As the Grave, Sigbjørn* recounts to two drunken acquaintances the story behind the autobiographical novel he has written but cannot get published. Its title, *The Valley of the Shadow of Death*, not surprisingly was Lowry's original title for *Under the Volcano*. When I traced the evolution of that book in Chapter 4, I drew on Sigbjørn's words to prove that everything in the earliest versions of *Volcano* had some exact equivalence in Lowry's Mexican experience. At this level, *Dark As the Grave* has no other value than to show how exhaustively Lowry projected his art beyond life, and wrote a masterpiece.

Lowry made no attempt to cover his tracks from the earlier book. His general tendency bears a resemblance to that of the writer with whom he is most compared. Joyce's *Portrait of the Artist* often makes assumptions which are based on incidents and epiphanies found only in his previous work, the unpublished apprentice novel *Stephen Hero*. Much of what Sigbjørn narrates in *Dark As the Grave* misfires unless related to the original book. For example, the principal link between Sigbjørn's unpublished book and the Wildernesses' pilgrimage to Mexico is his desire to find a Mexican named Juan Fernando Martinez. This is a man we never encounter directly in the book and, as we shall see, for the best of reasons. We know that he shared infernal experiences with Sigbjørn who recalls his constant entreaty to "throw away your mind, old maker of tragedies." However, it is only when we recall that Dr. Vigil's calling-card creolism to the Consul is to "throw away your mind" and that in the elegiac opening chapter Vigil spoke to Laruelle about their dead friend "who lived such continuous tragedies"—it is only with reference to the earlier book—that we gain the right *feel* about Sigbjørn's compañero, his good angel. For, as Douglas Day notes in his necessary preface to *Grave*

> Juan Fernando is really the key to Sigbjørn Wilderness, and to this book, in spite of the fact that he never appears: for Sigbjørn comes ultimately to realize . . . that, though he has all these years thought of Juan Fernando as a symbol for life and vitality, he actually is equally symbolic of *death,* in its most attractive forms.
>
> (Grave, Preface, xviii)

It will be recalled that Lowry's most persistent symbol for death is the horse-and-rider tableau in *Under the Volcano.* We learn early in *Dark As the Grave* (Chapter IV) that Juan Fernando has been a messenger for a benevolent credit arm of the Cárdenas government (called, in both books, the Banco de Crédito y Ejidal) and that he delivers payments on horseback into the interior. Hugh's friend, Juan Cerillo, like Juan Fernando a heroic but offstage presence, is such a messenger, and so, implicitly, was the murdered peon.

The cross-reference ties between the two books are limitless. Someday someone will program them on a computer. In passages that must be tedious for anyone unacquainted with the earlier book, Sigbjørn gives Primrose a *Volcano*-revisited tour of his Mexican landscape. When he talks of his last memories of Juan Fernando Martinez—and, for the record, there was a Juan Fernando *Marquez* in Lowry's life, 1936–38—it is of his friend's fictional echoes that he thinks:

> . . . I went with Fernando to deliver money for the Ejidal to . . . two other villages . . . that were fighting each other across the ravine . . . [not] far from Parian, where Fernando and I had to say goodbye.

Or Doctor Vigil and I [or] Juan Cerillo and I, just as you like to call him.

(*Grave,* 146)

Fictionally, Dr. Vigil was the Consul's good angel whose ministrations ("throw away your mind") failed to save him from the volcanic pyre. Juan Cerillo was Hugh's hero of whom that "indoor Marxman" strove to be worthy. In the mystical equation by which Malcolm Lowry related life and art, the search for Juan Fernando is a quest to relive, in all its agony, the past, and the death of Juan Fernando provides Sigbjørn a kind of absolution.

The climax of *Dark As the Grave Wherein My Friend Is Laid* does not work fictionally. The scene in the penultimate chapter—like *Volcano,* the book has twelve chapters, and the eleventh in each is a "death" chapter—is one of the most contrived in all of Lowry's works. Sigbjørn and Primrose are told by the credit agency that "Don Fernando has—how you say—murió." They take it to mean he has moved, and it takes more than a page for "murió" to become "muerto." He was murdered years before while drunk in a cantina. Since *Dark As the Grave* is not a novel anyway, perhaps the failure of the climax does not matter. The death of Juan Fernando had already been *written,* not only in words but in the haunting predilection of Lowry's life and art to follow one another.

VI *Esthetic of the Writer Being Written*

Lowry thought of *Dark As the Grave* as " a sort of *Under Under the Volcano*" and "ten times more terrible." [8] In the years after *Volcano,* he simply made no distinction between the ordeals of living and of writing. Life would *write him,* and he would record what his life wrote. What is fascinating about *Dark As the Grave* is that Lowry's transcribings—the endless self-absorption which destroys it as a novel—also characterized *Under the Volcano* in its preliminary stages. With every page of the later book, the triumph of *Volcano* looms larger. Literary transmutation saved *Volcano.* Alchemical transmutation ruined *Dark As the Grave.*

Standing with Primrose in a queue to board the Los Angeles-Mexico City plane, Sigbjørn allows his consciousness free play.

It ranges from an excessive self-pity over a book called *Drunkard's Rigadoon* by Jack Charleson (an undisguised reference to Charles Jackson's *Lost Weekend* which was a best seller in 1945 when the Lowrys went to Mexico), whose enormous popularity Sigbjørn sees as wrecking his own unpublished book's chances, to a recent fire which destroyed their beach cabin and the manuscript of an early book (the Lowrys did indeed lose their first cabin in a fire on June 7, 1944, and the notes of *Ballast to the White Sea* went up with it). Sigbjørn recognizes that his writing is like his life "a form of prolonged concentrated debauch" but with the major difference that you can lie in life but had to tell the truth in writing.

Suddenly Sigbjørn is ecstatic. "Every man his own Laocoon!" he exults to himself. And how much better, he muses, if that Everyman be a writer, capable of making a pattern of life's "maze of complicated suffering and interrelated nonsense!" His suffering—his willingness, even eagerness, to be a conductor for every conceivable kind of agony—transforms

into something else, a feeling almost of having been brought to the brink of discovery: it was more even than that, he had suddenly a glimpse of a flowing like an eternal river; he seemed to see how life flowed into art: how art gives life a form and meaning and flows on into life, yet life has not stood still; that was what was always forgotten: how life transformed by art sought further meaning through art transformed by life; and now it was as if this flowing, this river, changed, without appearing to change, became a flowing of consciousness, of mind, so that it seemed that . . . just beyond that barrier, lay some meaning, or the key to a mystery that would give some meaning . . . the brink of an illumination. . . .

(*Grave,* 43)

There is nothing wrong with this statement as a position on life and art. Unformulated though it is, it makes sense. The artist has always harnessed individuality to the fathoming of life's most troubling mysteries. Dostoevsky, supremely, believed that one could rank people in a descending line according to thickness of inner wilderness, the number of sunken boats they will not —cannot—permit to surface. Introspection, as far as it will go, gives the artist his best divining rod.

What shipwrecks this book is clear. Lowry drives it aground

from first to last on rocky coastline: his obsessive concern for nothing and no one apart from himself. Sigbjørn is always proclaiming himself "merely a drunk" and proving himself right by getting tight. What is missing is an antagonist to put Sigbjørn's negative capability to a test of strength. In *Under the Volcano*, one viewed the Consul's drinking as more than life-sized. Drink, he told Laruelle, was his weapon in the battle for the survival of consciousness. It is a world, as Hugh told Yvonne, which would die of remorse on the third day after two days of sobering up. Missing is a coeval force to play against Sigbjørn as, say, Dostoevsky allows the elder Karamazov to play against Dmitri. Here the lecherous father makes public accusation against his son for lechery. While it produces Dmitri's confession of depravity, that confession is glorified by the companion assertion that within him lives a saint, hidden and inviolate, that is of more account than the outer sinner.

It is not only that Sigbjørn Wilderness protests too much but that he does so in a self-enclosed world from which give-and-take is barred. Sigbjørn ventures beyond the provincialism of self only in his solicitude for Primrose and his concern for finding Juan Fernando. In neither case does he project any imaginative concern for the other or any ability to experience the world through a persona different from his own.

Sigbjørn's solicitude for Primrose is the excessive uxoriousness one is likely to find in an alcoholic writer whose helpmate not only controls his drinking but believes in his writings. But Lowry was not the only important contemporary who cannot portray women plausibly. His failure to make viable the memory of Juan Fernando—hence his failure to make a climax of Juan Fernando's death—stands as a more severe charge against this book.

Lowry's failure, in part, is his inability to make introspective retrospection dramatic. This problem combines with Lowry's over-reliance on the reader's knowledge of the earlier book. Sigbjørn's thoughts flash back to his first meeting with Juan Fernando—unsurprisingly—in a pub. Expectedly, too, the first words he hears are ". . . if you don't mind, throw away your mind." For anyone who has read *Volcano*, the words have their own built-in place in the mythic world of Malcolm Lowry. But it is to another phrase of Juan Fernando's that Lowry now builds with a passion he has heretofore reserved for Sigbjørn's Promethean posturing. What Juan Fernando answered to Sigbjørn's question about his identity was

> so beautifully [spoken] in such mournful accents and with such a dying melancholy fall, with all the music that there is in the word Oaxaqueñan or desconsolado, pronounced, or sung, as only the Oaxaqueñan can, that to this day Sigbjørn could not be persuaded—there were perhaps other reasons for thinking so—that his friend had not said something profound and great. . . .
>
> (*Grave*, 223)

Juan Fernando's words, remembered with all the passion of Proust's madeleine, were these: "I am a drunk." What Sigbjørn really remembers about the friend whom he had all through all the intervening years "talked up" to Primrose and himself as his symbol for charisma is that they were tragic jesters together in the court of King Alcohol.

For just a moment Lowry's meditative rhapsody has been improvised into sounding a true note. The single most plausible revelation in a book crammed with self-indulgent longueurs is that what Sigbjørn and Juan Fernando had most in common was spirits rather than spiritual. That the relationship will not bear up under the weight of the dying-artist mythology charged to its account is revealed by a sudden breakdown in style immediately following Sigbjørn's recollection of the meeting with his friend.

> Sigbjørn Wilderness's loyalty was, he told himself, *terrific*. The few friends he had made he cherished and would have died for at the *drop of a hat*. But he had few friends left.
>
> (*Grave*, 224)

I have italicized "terrific" and "drop of a hat" to show that, at the very point where it is crucial for Lowry to get at the heart of Sigbjørn's *need* to find his friend, he can only manage a vulgarism and a cliché. Sigbjørn goes on to a characteristic—and by now, tiresome—flood of self-pity. He concludes that if he is loved at all it is for the wrong reasons ("the saying had got around that even to meet him was disaster"), that he is the thorniest of thorns in God's side ("perhaps he was an experiment of God's"), and that he was a failure ("merely a drunk and an unsuccessful writer").

The triumph of *Under the Volcano* was the Consul's transcendence over easy relegation to the trash heap of the addict.
The victory of Lowry's art over his life enables him, even in the
Consul's fall, to apotheosize him. The failure of *Dark As the
Grave* is that Lowry would not—or could not—let the artist be
stronger than the man. We do not believe that the tie between
Sigbjørn and Juan Fernando is more than alcoholic or that by his
friend having been laid in his dark grave, the threat to Sigbjørn
is also buried, the demon exorcised.

By Chapter X, the Wildernesses have arrived at Oaxaca, not
only the city of Juan Fernando's birth but Dr. Vigil's destination
in *Under the Volcano,* the *locus* of life and health, as contrasted
to Parián, the place of death towards which the Consul inexorably
moved. In a hotel dining room, Sigbjørn is shocked to see a man
from his past.

Stanford was hangovers; Stanford was lies; Stanford was the prescience of disaster and its coefficient. . . . Stanford was an accomplice
. . . the past and the difficulty of transcending it: and here he sat—
the sorrow of his life, together with all its evil, everything . . . he
thought so miraculously transcended.

(*Grave,* 219)

Sigbjørn avoids Stanford, but the latter's presence temporarily
changes his plans. He tells Primrose that the search is futile, that
"even if we did see Fernando, it would mean only another
bender." For once, Primrose demurs. Given one of the few opportunities for a healthy intrusion by an antagonist for Sigbjørn
other than himself, Lowry again drowns the scene in literary
posturing:

". . . I am damned. And when I say that I am damned I mean that
I am still burning. My soul is not a soul, it is a conflagration."
"Oh, pile on the faggots, Jeeves," Primrose said disgustedly, wrap-
ping herself up in the blanket on the far side of the bed, while
Sigbjørn wondered what Henry James would have done with such
a conversation.
"Perhaps I have not got a soul. . . ."

(*Grave,* 222)

Such passages as this reveal Lowry's blind obedience to an
esthetic once formulated by D. H. Lawrence: "One sheds one's

sickness in books, repeats and presents again one's emotions to be master of them." But to do what Lowry has done in *Dark As the Grave*—merely to repeat one's emotions, merely to look into one's heart and write, is also, in the absence of some "distancing" perspective, to make backbreaking the load of emotional baggage.

CHAPTER *6*

Lowry in Canada

> Though we like this place quite a lot, please don't think we have abandoned Dollarton, we have not, and think of it constantly, and of yourself, and miss the old times, but it seems better for reasons of health to stay where we are just at the moment, though the beach will always be home.
>
> Malcolm Lowry
> Excerpt from letter
> to Jimmy Craige, Manx
> boatbuilder, from Lowry
> in Sussex, England,
> April, 1956 [1]

I *Eridanus and the Styx*

ONE errs if he tries in any way to make Malcolm Lowry into a regional writer. His relationship to Canada, as in all things, was cosmic. Even at the other extreme of North America, he is never far, spiritually, from his earlier home under the volcano. The great Cordilleras loom in his view as the "northern cousins" of Popocatepetl. No habitation had any meaning for him except as a station in his soul's itinerary.

Canada is never viewed, except in the letters, in Commonwealth terms. Its fictional identity is that of the "Northern Paradise," the refuge dreamed of but never achieved by the doomed Geoffrey and Yvonne in *Under the Volcano*. The Consul and his wife are resurrected by Lowry in a series of couples in his Canadian fiction from Sigurd and Astrid, the young newlyweds of "The Bravest Boat" (written in the early 1950s) to the evicted pilgrims Ethan and Jacqueline of the work destined to be Lowry's last, *October Ferry to Gabriola* (published posthumously in 1970).

Lowry changes the Canadian names to enable them to bear mythological significance for the legend he fervently believed he and Margerie were living. Thus Dollarton, a squatters' beach across Burrard Inlet from Vancouver, becomes Eridanus, a condemned community, perpetually under the shadow of eviction. To the ancients, Eridanus was known both as the River of Life and of Death. What really appealed to Lowry about Eridanus is that it is also the Styx. The narrator of his magnificent Canadian novella "The Forest Path to the Spring" tells of the oil refinery across the bay from Eridanus. The company put up a sign, it was to be SHELL, "but for weeks they never got around to the S, so that it was left HELL. And yet, my own imagination could not have dreamt anything fairer than the heaven from which we perceived this." Lowry's vision of Canada is always that of the still possible but about-to-be-despoiled Northern Paradise, and his metaphors of human loss and eviction made him, at one level, an early prophet (the late 1940s and throughout the 1950s until his death in 1957) of what humanity faces ecologically in the 1970s.

Lowry ought not to be taken, except in a secondary way, as a serious conservationist any more than the Thoreau of *Walden* ought be taken seriously as an economist. Both, as will be seen later in this chapter, had more important fish to fry. Lowry seeks to transmute the atmosphere of the Dollarton years into a theme of redemption—of paradise regained—after infernal life under the volcano.

The early manuscripts of *Under the Volcano*—those I have lumped together as the Mexican Version—make no mention of a haven for the Consul. Lowry filled in the Northern Paradise motif at a relatively advanced stage in his revisions and did so from his regenerative experiences on the beach at Dollarton. The three major protagonists of *Volcano* each envisioned the paradise. The Consul reveals his dream in the elegiac first chapter, in the unmailed letter to Yvonne:

. . . right through hell there is a path . . . and though I may not take it, sometimes lately in dreams I have been able to see it. . . . I seem to see now, between mescals, this path, and beyond it strange vistas, like visions of a new life together we might somewhere lead. I seem to see us living in some northern country, of mountains and hills and blue water; our house is built on an inlet and one evening we are standing, happy in one another, on the balcony of this house, looking over the water.

(*Volcano*, 36–37)

Lowry used the letter, as he used the first chapter, as an epilogue. The Consul, his will paralyzed by drink and his descent to the abyss irreversible, never spoke of the water-girded retreat. In Chapter IV, however, Yvonne and Hugh, who had been lovers, discussed the Consul's drinking. Yvonne suggested that she and the Consul might "get away" to British Columbia where the Consul owned some property. At first Hugh was skeptical but soon warmed to her plan's redemptive possibilities. Hugh's words were the first real suggestions of those strong veins of hope, of *Paradiso*, that abound in the Canadian works.

"The thing to do," he went on [to Yvonne], "is to get out of Vancouver as fast as possible. Go down one of the inlets to some fishing village and buy a shack slap spang on the sea, with only foreshore rights, for, say, a hundred dollars. Then live on it this winter. . . . No phone. No rent. . . . Be a squatter. Call on your pioneer ancestors. Water from the well. Chop your own wood. . . . you can have your stars and the sense of the seasons again. . . . And get to know the real people: the seine fishermen, the old boatbuilders, the trappers. . . .

. . . .

"I can see your shack now. It's between the forest and the sea and you've got a pier down to the water over rough stones . . . covered with barnacles and sea anemones and starfish. You'll have to go through the woods to the store. . . ."

(*Volcano*, 121–22)

Hugh's conceptions corresponded, line for line, to the reality of the Lowrys' way of life on the beach.

Yvonne's vision of the Northern Paradise included even more details which were like those of the life the Lowrys lived throughout the 1940s and early 1950s. In Chapter IX she visualized a pier which she and the Consul would build—much as Lowry, his wife, and their neighbors built a pier at Dollarton. She sees their dwelling as "small and made of silvery weathered shingles, it had a red door, and casement windows open to the sun"—a fairly close description of the actual Lowry dwelling.

[126]

II *Canadian by Accident of Geography*

Lowry's inclusion in the Canadian portion of this series can be justified on the basis that his best writing was done during his fifteen years on Canadian soil. George Woodcock, the prolific Canadian author, has stated that *Under the Volcano* is the finest work of fiction ever written in Canada.[2] On this point, Lowry was fond of quoting from the *Encyclopaedia Britannica Yearbook* for 1948: ". . . But the year [1947] produced no new voice as commanding as that of the Canadian, Malcolm Lowry, in *Under the Volcano*, to presage a major movement among younger writers of fiction." The tribute appears under a section headed "American Literature." He could write to his older brother Stuart Lowry in the fall of 1950: "I have done more for Canadian literature than any living Canadian. . . ."[3] He could add in the same letter, echoing Robert Frost, that he and Margerie "now consider Canada and their fisherman's shack home which is the place where, when they have to, they take you in."[4] But this letter like all those he wrote to his family had a formula: convince them that he was becoming famous while needing money desperately.

To his friends, Lowry was inclined to anguish over Canada's indifference to him. He complained to an enthusiastic reader of *Volcano* "that the sales in Canada from the end of 1947–49 were precisely 2 copies. The Vancouver *Sun* published only a few syndicated lines that called it a turgid novel of self-destruction, not for the discerning (or something) reader."[5] No plaque marks the place where the Lowrys lived for the most part of fourteen years; no civic recognition has been awarded him in Vancouver or elsewhere. Judging from the dearth of response his name invokes, except in academic circles, in Vancouver, Malcolm Lowry passed his fourteen years phantom-like in the Northern Paradise.

Lowry was, in fact, a Canadian only by an accident of geography. Aged thirty and with a Cambridge education and a novel *Ultramarine* behind him, he came to Vancouver in wartime (1939) via Mexico, Los Angeles, and Hollywood. In Southern California, dying by the glass at the Brown Derby, he was "rescued" by Margerie Bonner, a writer, former actress, and at the time of their meeting the private secretary of filmdom's "Blondie," Penny Singleton. Visa problems had led to his emigration to Canada. He sent for Margerie Bonner promptly. She entered Canada illegally and—characteristic Lowryan dilemma—feared deportation. Together they lived in secrecy in a city which to them looked little better than their boarding house. At first Lowry found Vancouver depressing and paralyzing. He drank almost as heavily as in Mexico, writing desperate letters to Conrad Aiken begging him to help generally and, specifically, to get "the old man" to appoint Aiken, as he had done in the 1930s, chancellor of the Lowry exchequer; that is, "trustee of my income and my guardian." [6]

His initial despair was understandable "in a strange and, believe me, damned hostile and ugly country with no place to go and no friends." The "abominable climate" was to remind him again and again of London. He obtained a divorce from his first wife, and on December 2, 1940, he married Margerie. They left Vancouver the following year to become Dollarton squatters. In their tiny cabin Lowry worked and reworked the novel he had begun five years before in Mexico while Margerie wrote mystery stories, two of which were eventually issued at about the same time as *Under the Volcano*.

Life went well until June 7, 1944, when, in a kind of apocalyptic event, never to be forgotten by Lowry in life or in his fiction, their cabin burned down. They left Vancouver for a short stay with a Cambridge classmate (the Canadian radio and, later, TV producer, Gerald Noxon), in Niagara-on-the-Lake, Ontario, but in February of 1945 returned to Dollarton to begin anew. With lumber from a sawmill they built another house, a cabin on piles in the inlet with the forest behind in a quiet idyllic location, the exact like of which is described as the "Northern Paradise" in *Volcano*. This period is dramatized through the nightmares of Ethan Llewelyn in *October Ferry to Gabriola*.

The eventual completion of his epic novel and its concomitant success have been described elsewhere in these pages. Although literary success had come—it would never come again for Lowry —he and Margerie had no wish to give up their simple home. But, as Anthony Kilgallin puts it in a recent article, "Dollarton was soon to become Dolortown, the sad town, for envious taxpayers wanted the rent-free squatters evicted, dispossessed of their Paradise." [7]

The winter of 1951–52 was one of the worst in human memory as "the flooding inlet with gales at the January high tides almost swept the house away altogether." That winter was apparently the one described in "The Forest Path to the Spring." Since the cabin had only cardboard inside walls, and was equipped with a small cookstove out of the Gold Rush but no heater, they were driven each winter to renting a room in Vancouver.

Although each spring found them back on the beach, time was running out. By 1952, the village which still consisted of fishermen's huts, mostly abandoned, was falling to pieces. Along the granite-strewn shore there remained only four other diehard inhabitants to enjoy the forest primeval. In the last pages of *October Ferry*, the Llewelyns read in a newspaper that the threat of eviction had been lifted—at least temporarily. Life in reality was not so kind. Lowry was drinking sporadically. His Consular bouts are described by his friend David Markson in a poignant memoir:

The man could not shave himself. In lieu of a belt, he knotted a rope or a discarded necktie around his waist. Mornings, he needed two or three ounces of gin in his orange juice if he was to steady his hand to eat the breakfast that would very likely prove his only meal of the day. . . .

Yet what one remembers is less the excess than Lowry's own attitude toward it, an incredible impression he conveyed that he could never take any of it quite seriously. He had an acute sense of his own dissolution, eternally chagrined at being a nuisance, apologizing hourly for small disasters, but what he sensed equally was the underlying absurdity of it all: the very idea, a grown man and that is the third burning cigarette I have misplaced tonight.[8]

The Lowrys settled in England in 1954. Although letters continued to promise a return to Dollarton, there was to be none. The White Cottage, Village of Ripe, Sussex, was to be the scene of his unexpected death on June 27, 1957, "by misadventure," a death which went virtually unreported in the American press.[9] In and out of hospitals almost from the time he left North America, Malcolm—with Margerie—went on a walking tour of the Lake Country in the late spring. Although his being on the wagon had been a precarious perch since his teens, Lowry had not had a drop for some weeks. However, during a stroll back to the cottage, they had made a stop at the Yew Tree, described to me by Mrs. Lowry as "a charming thatched roof pub where often when walking we stopped for a beer." He had been writing a poem to Margerie, remembering the nest they had built for themselves in Canada. Lowry, unknown to his wife, obtained a bottle of gin. Later, a struggle ensued, there was a shattering of glass, and Margerie fled in fear of her life to their landlady's—a Mrs. Mason's—cottage. The last night of Lowry's life was one of the few times, apart from hospital stays, when they had been separated. "I should have gone back," she wrote me, "and I'll never forgive myself for not doing so." The next morning, Margerie found him face down on the floor, dead. He had taken, she learned upon finding the empty bottle, 60 capsules of sodium amytol (20 of the three-grain sedatives given him by his doctor to induce sleep). The coroner's verdict was "death by misadventure."

Thus the man who had gone to the extremes of the North American continent to escape the "English death" had at last come full circle. Even in death, the figure is poetically appropriate for the artist who saw life and art, with Thoreau, as "great-circle sailing."

III *Three Canadian Stories*

Three of the stories in the posthumous collection, *Hear Us O Lord from Heaven Thy Dwelling Place,* have a Canadian setting. Each is self-contained, further proof that Lowry never lost the storyteller's art which first brought him to the attention of American readers in Whit Burnett's famous magazine of the best in short fiction, *Story.* Each of these three stories contains a metaphor that dramatizes poetically the tension between the promised land of *Under the Volcano*—the "Northern Paradise"—and the threat of eviction in the wake of what Lowry called in one of the stories the "suburban dementia."

Like everything he wrote, the stories are autobiographical, dealing with day-to-day slices from the Lowrys' life in their squatters' cottage on the beach near Dollarton. They stand apart in more than setting from stories like "Through the Panama" and "Strange Comfort Afforded by the Profession." Lowry is able to subsume the anguish of the artist into the more universal anguish of good people who try to hold onto their humanity despite sprawling encroachments of industrial civilization.

"The Bravest Boat" was suggested to Lowry by a story he read in a Vancouver newspaper about that much-repeated but never tiresome feature writer's staple, the bottle set adrift with a note in it. Lowry expands on the bare bones, develops the idea with his own mythology of the rootless voyager, and ends with a story that is considered a minor classic in France where it was first published.

"Gin and Goldenrod" is Lowry's most successful anecdotal story. The protagonists are the same as those in "Through the Panama," but here the similarity ends. In place of Sigbjørn Wilderness's desperate search for himself through the creation of a masking fictional persona, we have an almost light-hearted yarn, the barest suggestion of the Shakespearean jester in Lowry. The title effectively juxtaposes gin—addiction as a refuge against the numbing sterility of urban litter—and goldenrod which is symbolic of the benison that nature offers, an antidote to the poison of addiction.

The best story in *Hear Us O Lord*—the purest expression of Lowry's redemptive thrust to a *Paradiso*—is "The Forest Path to the Spring." The story is the antiphon to the demonic voices, "the inconceivable pandemonium," that accompanied the Consul in his fall. It is not by accident that the story is the final of the seven in *Hear Us O Lord*. For, as Margerie Lowry wrote in an unsigned "publisher's note," "The Forest Path" foreshadowed the climactic book of the Proustian sequence Lowry had always planned: "It seems significant that Lowry should have placed this short novel, which is concerned with human happiness and ends on a note of fulfillment and resolution, at the end of what was destined to be a posthumous volume." [11]

A "The Bravest Boat"

"The Bravest Boat" is a love lyric. Its tone is that of one of Lowry's earliest published stories, "Hotel Room in Chartres" (published in *Story* in 1934 when Lowry was 24), a story that was discussed in another connection in the first chapter. The newlyweds of the earlier story—the heroine is Lowry's romantic projection of his first wife—have been quarreling. He has given up the sea for her and he misses it. She feels his resentment. They board a train for Brest, via Chartres (where they had spent their honeymoon), barely communicating as he joins the flow of wine and song with a group of French sailors. They are happy, he assumes, because they will join their ship at Brest, and he is envious. The implicit twin threats to the marriage of drink and male camaraderie loom large. Their marriage, a series of domestic crises, drives him to wish "to join some lousy old ship . . . a rotten life reeling from filthy port to filthy port . . . but . . . better than this ceaseless quarreling. . . ." Upon learning that the sailors are homeward bound, the lovers recognize that it is a spiritual port—symbolized by a hotel room in Chartres—that they too seek

in the only room in the world [where] they were folded together in each other's arms crying with joy that they had found each other once more.

"The Bravest Boat" is a companion story to "Chartres" although written almost two decades later. That the story is Lowry's most anthologized is a tribute to the poignancy of its theme. A side of the reader's credulity is strained by Lowry's *donnée*, a toy boat, set adrift with a child's note, has found haven years later, found by a girl (Astrid) who, though not yet born when the boy (Sigurd) released his boat, would grow up to become his bride. Lowry wisely devotes his story to the couple's recollection of the precipitating circumstances.

The sea maintains its regal place in Lowry's iconography. "Chartres" ended with two contrasting metaphors, both marine: the railroad station, the potential instrument for separation, becomes for the lovers an ugly presence "like a huge ship being dismantled"; the great cathedral takes on a regenerative aspect, "the configuration of a green wave, falling along the tall rock of the spire, the blue and white sea of the cool sky rushing behind. . . ." In "The Bravest Boat" the metaphoric polarities are more obvious: the beauty of a public park, "seagirt . . . wisely left in places to the original wilderness . . ."; the squalor of the neon-festooned metropolis at the park's back seeming to squeeze it into the sea.

The city is Enochville, but as Anthony Kilgallin alertly observes, Lowry has used a satirical pseudonym for Vancouver.[12] Enoch was the son of Cain. Lowry may have been thinking of Cowley's statement that "God the first garden made, and the first city Cain." The land of Cain is described in a three-page paragraph whose imagery will recur in all of Lowry's Canadian fiction:

"dilapidated half-skycrapers," "new beer parlors crawling with verminous light even in mid-afternoon," "modern apartment buildings and other soulless behemoths." The only relief is provided by a "few lowly self-built shacks and floathouses . . . driven out of the city altogether, down to the water's edge into the sea itself, where they stood on piles, like fishermen's huts. . . ." Here, Lowry might have been describing his own dwelling at Dollarton, but what is more important is that he once more casts the sea in a germinative role, as he had done in his earliest writings.

It is toward Lost Lagoon that the two lovers of "Bravest Boat" stroll. It is a day in June, an anniversary of the miniature boat-launching which united them. As they recall ritualistically the pure chance which brought them together, they approach a cage containing two Canadian lynxes, "demonic creatures . . . . in which seemed to be embodied in animal form all the pure ferocity of nature." Watching the desperate animal couple, the truly damned, they see again "that tiny boat, battling with the seas, at the mercy of a wilder ferocity yet, all those years before [she] was born."

For a time what passes between the lovers is rote. They remind themselves that the origins of their life together lay in the limbo of unknowable dates: unknowable for Astrid because he launched the boat five years before she was born. Another twelve years had to pass before the seven-year-old girl, playing on another beach, would find the boat and its message. More years would have to elapse before Sigurd and Astrid could marry— seven years ago.

But Lowry brushes lightly over the chronology of his love lyric. Ritual becomes incantation. A circumstantial story rises to a kind of pantheism that few other modern writers could manage. Their walk, by now a pilgrimage, takes them at last to the very edge of the water, a driftwood-littered wasteland of the entrails of marine life in wasteful burial amidst fishermen's discards. But the desolation is appearance only; the lovers feel the stir of life in a cosmic sense:

. . . beneath the flotsam, under the very shells they crunched, within the trickling overflows of winterbournes they jumped over, down at the tide margin, existed, just as in the forest, a stirring and stretching of life, a seething of spring.

("Bravest Boat," 26)

[133]

Life is a continuum, throbbing in the midst of death. The lovers, like their little boat, have braved the imponderables of time and place. The boat safe in harbor—their coming together—is a poem of God's mercy. The lovers, renewed by the example of their bravest boat, have come to see life—all human destiny—as all one with the chaos that destroys and the faith that nurtures.

And it was to this shore, through that chaos, by those currents, that their little boat with its innocent message had been brought out of the past finally to safety and a home.
But ah, the storms they had come through!
("Bravest Boat," 27)

There is a poignant footnote to the publication of "The Bravest Boat," one of the two stories in *Hear Us O Lord* ("Strange Comfort" is the other) which Lowry lived to see published in English. A little more than a year before his death, Lowry wrote to David Markson asking him to send the June 1954 issue of *Partisan Review*. Seeing it in print for the first time, he wrote to Markson: "I'm very fond of the old 'Bravest Boat' though I have never managed to ascertain what anyone thought of it, if anything, in the U.S." [13] Like a number of his shorter pieces, "Bravest Boat" was first published in France. Lowry lived to know that the story was listed among "Distinctive Short Stories in American Magazines . . . Foreign Authors . . . 1954," appended to *Best American Short Stories 1954*, edited by Martha Foley.

The story merits its honors. That it and the other fine stories collected in *Hear Us O Lord* were not published in those American magazines which paid commercial rates is an ironic footnote to Lowry's lifelong financial miseries. In the Lowry canon, a story like "The Bravest Boat" is vital because it indicates that Lowry was working in his life and art to a reconciliation that promised to put at bay the demons that threatened to overwhelm him.

B *"Gin and Goldenrod"*

Even when plunged to the depths of despair by their two-edged sword of Damocles—addiction and eviction—the Lowrys could always write "cheer keeps breaking in." The second Canadian story in *Hear Us O Lord*, "Gin and Goldenrod," dramatizes one such moment. What adds an extra dimension to the story is that, in terms of what is known about Lowry's latter years in Canada, the story is a kind of whistling in the dark. The congeniality of the surface adumbrates the shadows underneath.

The hero is Sigbjørn Wilderness whom we have already met in "Through the Panama" and *Dark As the Grave*. It is difficult to relate the underground man at the heart of these works to the bird watcher on a woodland trek with his wife in search of the place where he had got drunk and contracted a debt with bootleggers. Perhaps the tie between the inner-obsessed outsider and the outside-obsessed insider is that both are troubled by T. S. Eliot's need to prepare a face. Another look at "Panama" on top of a reading of "Gin and Goldenrod" reveals that the difference is only a matter of degree.

Perhaps, as Dale Edmonds suggests,[14] the Sigbjørn of "Gin and Goldenrod" is the outer side of the inner sojourner who has lost his bearings in a maze of personae; the mask-creation of the introverted Sigbjørn, the man he has named Martin Trumbaugh,

disinterested in literature, uncultured, incredibly unobservant, in many respects ignorant, without faith in himself, and lacking nearly all the qualities you normally associate with a novelist or writer. . . . he sees practically nothing at all, save through his wife's eyes.

("Panama," 84)

What Lowry recaptures in this story is the diffusion of attention that was characteristic of the Consul when, for example, his concentration on the inhuman treatment accorded to the dying Indian in Chapter VIII vies with his concern about the next drink. While Sigbjørn is ashamed over having lost money to a bootlegger, he seems to be paying some implied penance to his wife and anxious to get home for a bracer.

Although Professor Edmonds is probably right in placing the story with "The Bravest Boat" in tracing the theme of civilization's encroachment upon nature, it fails on those terms. Sigbjørn's alcoholism—or, better, Lowry's—gets in the way. Wilderness tries to make a scapegoat of civilization. He recalls the time when "there hadn't been any bootleggers . . . to sell you firewater on Sunday, or, come to that, any reason for drinking it." Thus, the Rousseauvian romantic speaking, but a few sentences later, the alcoholic—half fighting his problem and half resenting sobriety in the wilderness:

> The bootlegger, in times of prohibition, in great cities, has one function. The bootlegger, in times of partial prohibition, has another. The bootlegger, on Sundays, where there is Sunday prohibition, is a secular savior. The bootlegger, in rural places, is as fundamental as the prostitute in the city—
>
> ("Gin and Goldenrod," 212)

The story almost but not quite drones off into the kind of sycophantic chatter that marred *Dark As the Grave* and will threaten *October Ferry*. They find the house where Sigbjørn got drunk. He makes out a cheque for his part of the bootleg gin. They exchange apologies. He spots a pippit and she some goldenrod. As the story ends, Primrose confesses that she has kept the last bottle of gin, the bottle he thought he had lost in the forest. They walk back to the cabin, happy in the thought that they can now mix martinis. The final sentence carries an ironic note for anyone familiar with the penalty to the alcoholic of the quick bracer back at the cabin: "In the cool silver rainy twilight of the forest a kind of hope began to bloom again." But hope for what? Salvation for their life in the woods or for the resumption of controlled drinking unassisted by bootleggers?

The story is important as one of the few Lowry left behind which deal, without the introspective longueurs, with what day-to-day life in Dollarton was like. It is only when one approaches the last and best story in *Hear Us O Lord* that he truly learns.

C *"The Forest Path to the Spring"*

Early in "Through the Panama," which appears like a kind of opening movement in the symphonic *Hear Us O Lord*, Sigbjørn Wilderness interrupts one of his inner monologues with the question, "Who *am* I?" He grapples to no decision with that problem throughout the rest of the novella. "The Forest Path to the Spring," which concludes the collection, certainly can be regarded as the answer. But if Lowry intended this seventy-page novella as an answer to Sigbjørn's identity quest, why did he resort to the first-person narrator? Lowry learned from Aiken to believe in Henry James's injunction against using the first person, "the cursed fluidity of self-revelation." [15] Their subjective esthetic was better served by posting another consciousness like a movie camera on the outer boundaries of Demarest's and Firmin's to record internal and external movements, in tandem, as they developed. In "The Forest Path," Lowry has eschewed all ambiguity of viewpoint—all those shifting personae—for a unity of narrative stance that is absolutely without precedent in his fiction.

Although he employs the "I," Lowry appears reluctant to limit his narrator to a precise identity. He is never given a name. For once, here is no writer writing about the writer. To be sure, Lowry tells us that his narrator has been a jazz musician but one who has given up his old life of the night.

> . . . How far away that seemed now, my life in which my only stars were neon lights! I must have stumbled into a thousand alcoholic dawns, but drunk in the rumble seat I passed them by. . . . Never had I really looked at a sunrise till now.
>
> ("The Forest Path," 248)

But this curriculum vitae appears halfway into the story. No disquisition on drink takes over. There is a brief tribute to jazz musicians like Venuti, Satchmo, and the Duke, who have for him "the aspects of a very real glory," but no detailed digression. Lowry's thrust at all points is toward control of his materials and away from the self-indulgent ruminations that wrecked a work like *Dark As the Grave*.

What gives Lowry supreme control in "Forest Path" is that he has subjected the *felt* life of the protagonist to a *created* structure which elevates it to art. That structure is much more than chronology—specifically, the cycle of the seasons around which its eight sections swing. What really unifies these sections is that Lowry has waived his usual subjective strategies for those of a kind of narrative pastoral, a poem.

To call this story a poem could lead to inter-genre problems that are outside the scope of this study. I am neither suggesting extraction of the best passages from "Forest Path" for stanzaic rearrangement nor calling it a "prose poem," that hybrid term I resisted earlier in discussing the love-sonnet "feel" of the Consul's unposted letter to Yvonne. What I am suggesting is the need for a technique for reading this story, which is Malcolm Lowry's finest achievement after *Under the Volcano*.

The book with which "Forest Path" has most in common is *Walden*.[16] I have never seen anywhere in Lowry's notes or letters a single mention of either Thoreau or his masterpiece.[17] The kinship between the two is accidental but pervasive, a matter that transcends any commonality of circumstances. Certainly, Thoreau and Lowry, a century apart, were searching for solitude and rejecting an economy of abundance in favor of a simple natural life. The real theme of both is the search for perfection, for a life of holiness, and for a way to endure what Thoreau called his "several more lives" away from Walden Pond and what Lowry feared would be his life after eviction from Eridanus.

Charles R. Anderson presents a persuasive case in *The Magic Circle of Walden* for thinking of the book as poetry rather than prose, if one does not insist on the mechanical distinction of verse as opposed to paragraph form. Wit and metaphor, he writes,

serve Thoreau as the negative and positive means of his quest. These set up the direction of the book and open out its multiple contrasts. Not only are society and solitude juxtaposed but the civilized and the primitive, complexity and simplicity; also matter and spirit, animal faculties and the higher laws, earth and heaven, nature and God. Man cannot achieve his high aims by rejecting the one and leaping into the other, but must work his way up from the sty of materialism to the perfection he seeks.[18]

This is true of *Walden* and, as will be shown, it is true of "The Forest Path to the Spring." The goals in both works and the journey toward them are rendered in a deceptively simple series of image clusters: animal, water, rain and shelter, the imagery of time, the quest or journey, the self reborn even as the ice thaws and the land becomes green again. Lowry's novella is as poetic as Thoreau's and the presence of *another*—wife, helpmate, guide —renders Lowry's counsels more outgoingly human, less cranky, than Thoreau's.

The novella is dedicated, in fact, "To Margerie, my wife." If Thoreau went to Walden Pond "to transact some private business with the fewest obstacles," Lowry makes it clear that retreat to the Canadian Northwest wilderness could only work as a partnership. Life became "a continual awakening . . . . until I knew her I had lived my whole life in darkness" ("Forest Path," 234).

The couple arrived at Eridanus on Labor Day at the beginning of the war, intending to combine a delayed honeymoon with a last summer holiday. For a time, "the garishness and strangeness of . . . the sun . . . to me, long used to the night and sleeping fitfully . . . . [brought] the quality of a nightmare" ("Forest Path," 226). But metamorphosis soon takes place, a curious giving in to benevolent nature, a sense of their $12-a-month cabin as part of "eternal flux and change" which on the arms of the tides seemed alternately to lower and elevate "like a strange huge cave where some amphibious animal might have lived" ("Forest Path," 232). Fall gives way to the first frosts, and they are still there. In an epiphanic moment one winter's night, the poet knows why:

> . . . coming across the porch from the woodshed with a lantern in one hand and a load of wood under the other arm, I saw my shadow, gigantic, the logs of wood as big as a coffin, and this shadow seemed for a moment the glowering embodiment of all that threatened us; yes, even a projection of that dark chaotic side of myself, my ferocious destructive ignorance.
>
> ("Forest Path," 233)

Lowry's real subject in "The Forest Path" is the war which Nature wins over nature, the triumph of the discovered correspondence between elemental forces and man's abiding but muted selflessness. Just as Thoreau's arguments against the railroads are among the pretended subjects of *Walden,* Lowry's diatribe against the oil refinery across the bay is a diversionary tactic against another antagonist altogether. Tonally, Thoreau's strategy is directly hortatory: go ye and do likewise. When he lashes out at the railroads, Thoreau explodes into wit and metaphor that are aimed at the rescue of time from the deception of speed. Men live life too fast, thinking

> it is essential that the *Nation* have commerce, and export ice, and talk through a telegraph, and ride thirty miles an hour . . . but whether we should live like baboons or like men, is a little uncertain. If we do not get out sleepers, and forge rails, and devote days and nights to the work, but go to tinkering upon our *lives* to improve them, who will build railroads? And if railroads are not built, how shall we get to Heaven in season? . . . We do not ride upon the railroad; it rides upon us.
>
> (*Walden,* 75)

From this point in "What I Lived For" to the end of the section, Thoreau opens each paragraph on a cautionary note against being taken in by the lures of technology. The essence of time, he declares, is not changed by the post office or by the telegraph or by newspapers. Rather "Time is but the stream I go a-fishing in. I drink at it; but while I drink I see the sandy bottom and detect how shallow it is. Its thin current slides away, but eternity remains" (*Walden,* 80).

Malcolm Lowry's way is much more directly confessional. His entire thrust in "The Forest Path" is summed up by one of Thoreau's relatively rare acknowledgments that his life before Walden had been sham. He went to the woods so as not, "when I came to die, discover that I had not lived" (*Walden,* 74). Near the end of "Forest Path" Lowry apologizes for the "mere heroics" and "vain gestures" that have characterized his life. Yet he—Everyman—must "go beyond remorse, beyond even contrition . . . pass beyond the pride I felt in my accomplishment, and to accept myself as a fool again" ("Forest Path," 280). Eridanus, finally for Lowry, is out of time altogether. The narrator gladly accepts his previous life as a necessary hell, a *felix culpa.* He and his wife have transcended the passions of the moment and their attendant fears—even the hellish fear of losing their third little house—for "now the joy and happiness of what we had known would go with us wherever we went or God sent us and would not die" ("Forest Path," 281).

The real antagonist is the world which Thoreau and Lowry would banish in the interests of discovering the self. The purpose of their experiments is now clear: to withdraw from the life of civilization so that they can merge with the life of nature, to leave the artificial for the real. But the lives at Walden and Eridanus are means, not ends. *Walden* and "Forest Path to the Spring" are the records of quests for the buried life of the soul.

In the midst of writing "The Forest Path," Lowry wrote to Harold Matson that his book, as far as he knew, was "the only short novel of its type that brings the kind of majesty usually reserved for tragedy (God this sounds pompous) to bear on human integration. . . ."[19] The last is the important word. Not only is his story a raging toward self-integration, but its poetic technique at all points a working toward an integration of man's primal urges and fears with the false buffers civilization builds against them. Like Thoreau an inveterate punster, Lowry devotes much of the first section of "Forest Path" to a play on the names of the beach cottages, a practice which he sees as a human's rebellion in day when "streets and houses are mere soulless numbers . . . a survival of some instinct of unique identity in regard to one's home . . . for identity itself." He concludes the section with a discussion of Eridanus, named for a wrecked steamer which still lies nearby. To show how brilliantly Lowry plays with wit and metaphor, always in the interests of discovering, in Thoreau fashion, higher laws, it is necessary to quote at some length:

We poor folk were also Eridanus, a condemned community, perpetually under the shadow of eviction. And like Eridanus itself, in its eternal flux and flow, was the inlet. For in the heavens at night, as my wife first taught me, dark and wandering beneath blazing Orion, flowed the starry constellation Eridanus, known both as the River of Death and the River of Life, and placed there by Jupiter in remembrance of Phaethon, who once had the splendid illusion that he could guide the fiery steeds of the sun as well as his father Phoebus.

Legend merely states that Jupiter, sensing the danger to the world, shot a thunderbolt which, striking Phaethon, hurled him, his world on fire, into the River Po, then that, in addition to creating the constellation in Phaethon's honor, in pity he changed Phaethon's sisters into poplar trees, that they might always be near and protect their brother. But that he went to all this trouble suggests that he, even as Phoebus, was impressed by the attempt, and must have given the whole matter some thought. Recently our local paper, showing a sudden interest in classical mythology, has claimed to see something insulting in the name of our town of a political, even an international nature, or as denoting foreign influences, as a result of which there has been some agitation, on the part of some distant rate-payers, with I know not what motives, to change its name to Shellvue. And undoubtedly the view in that specified direction is very fine. with the red votive candle of the burning oil wastes flickering ceaselessly all night before the gleaming open cathedral of the oil refinery—

("The Forest Path," 226)

One notes Lowry's ability—it was Thoreau's, eminently—to synthesize the mythological and the quotidian. Jupiter had to save the world from Phaethon's "splendid illusion," but made a protective garden of the place where he died. The Shell refinery is emblematic of waste in the guise of industrial progress, but no Jupiter destroys it (although today's ecologists might find a prophetic irony in Lowry's metaphor). Rather, "distant rate-payers" consecrate the refinery as an open cathedral.

Lowry establishes a series of polarities to warn of man's fate: squatters' shacks on one side of the bay, the refinery on the other; the finding of paradise against the threat of eviction; God's sovereignty against man-made laws; the good fishermen and boatbuilders against the real estate people and the tourists; the achievement of oneness with nature against the fatuities of progress. All are one tension, of course, and Lowry represents their reconciliation in one magnificent metaphor: the daily act of redemption in walking, at dusk, through the forest to the spring for water.

In a later chapter, I shall summarize the workings of the archetypal and mutually compensatory themes of fire and water throughout Malcolm Lowry's life and work. It is enough for now to recall that his early voyages to sea—the "out-Mobying of Melville"—gave Lowry his first congenial persona and that the burning of their shack—the loss of irreplaceable manuscripts to the fire—almost destroyed him as a writer. The Consul, it will be recalled, aspired to a water-wreathed Northern Paradise but fell to his death "through the blazing of ten million burning bodies" under the volcano. "The Forest Path to the Spring" in effect resurrects the Consul, his demons purged.

Lowry's handling of the water-as-rebirth motif is pervasive but never intrusive in the story. The sheer logistics of obtaining water in the wilds—getting a boat, maneuvering it to a spring, returning a distance of miles to their house—led to frustrations and bitter resolves to return to the city. One afternoon late in the fall, everything about the water having gone wrong, he sees a ship's cannister on the beach left by the receding tide. They recover it. A light rain begins to fall. Their bitter despair forgotten, she explains with "inexpressible wonder" that "rain itself is water from the sea, raised to heaven by the sun, transformed into clouds and falling again into the sea." He, who has been a ship's fireman, relives the story behind the discarded cannister. It does not matter that the story he tells his wife while cleaning the cannister is unlikely to have happened. What matters is that they have recharged each other's flagging spirits. One of their boatbuilder friends then shows them a spring, its running delayed by the long Indian summer, less than a hundred yards from their house.

His first walk down the path to the spring takes the form of a ten-page central section. It is an ode to recovery from life's *Sturm und Drang;* to a man's recoil from the dreadful Wendigo, the man-hating spirit of the wilderness. He sees his hatred and suffering as like a forest fire (a figure that will return with compound interest in *October Ferry to Gabriola*), "a perversion of the movement of the inlet." The fire was his hatred, turning back on himself, self-devouring.

Always standing as a counter-force to his torment is his wife, who had lived in the country as a child and who "somehow turned our limited and humble fare into works of art." She is no better characterized than other Lowry women. Failure to realize Primrose as a person was one of the many shortcomings of *Dark As the Grave*, just as a similar failure to individualize Jacqueline will be a defect in the admirable *October Ferry*. In a story like "Forest Path," however, the idealizing of the wife is a kind of imperative. Hers is the role of a vital human station in the pilgrim's progress. She and the old Manx boatbuilder Quaggan and his friend Kristbjorg become archetypal of everything that is right in the felt life at Eridanus just as in *Walden* the Irish bog farmer is archetypal of everything that is wrong in life without spirit.

The onset of winter leads to contrasting strategies by Thoreau and Lowry. Thoreau's winter at the pond never threatens, is only a time for deeper reflection. "Why is it," he asks, "that a bucket of water soon becomes putrid, but frozen remains sweet forever?" Thoreau's answer is wittily metaphoric: "It is commonly said that this is the difference between the affections and the intellect." Lowry's winter at Eridanus shakes all their resolves with cosmic terror: ". . . we would lose all hope . . . the rending branches, the tumult of the sea, the sound of ruination under the house, so that we clung to one another like two little arboreal animals in some midnight jungle . . ." ("Forest Path, 253). But both winter sojourners conclude their songs on notes of apotheosis. Thoreau bathes his intellect in the Bhagavad-Gita. He lays down his book, "so remote is its sublimity from our conceptions," and goes to the well for water finding the pure Walden water mingled with the sacred water of the Ganges. Lowry's actual path to the spring is made impassable by the winter, but he still walks it in imagination "as if eternally through a series of dissolving dusks." He thinks of Renan's Isle of Delight,

where the lamps light of themselves for the offices of religion, and never burn out for they shine with a spiritual light, and where an absolute stillness reigns, and everyone knows precisely the hour of his death, and one feels neither cold nor heat nor sadness nor sickness of body or soul. . . . And then I thought to myself, stopping in the path: what if we should lose it? And with this thought of all-consuming anxiety I would always pause with a sigh. And then came the season of spring and I forgot this anxiety too.

("Forest Path," 256–57)

Nothing in "The Forest Path" can compare to Thoreau's rejuvenation at the sight of the spring thaw on Walden Pond. He sees man molecularly, as but a mass of thawing clay where

one hillside illustrated the principle of all the operations of Nature. The Maker of this earth but patented a leaf. What Champollion will decipher this hieroglyphic for us, that we may turn over a new leaf at last?

(*Walden*, 257)

But Lowry's ecstasy ascends the same pantheistic empyrean. "My God," he asks while looking at the full moon blazing clear of the pines behind the mountain, "why have you given this to us?" The remainder of the spring section is a poem to man's unworthiness. Encounters with a mountain lion and the sheer difficulty of the upward return climb take their toll until by a kind of twelve labors of Hercules he is able to face "those nameless somnambulisms, guilts, ghouls of past delirium, wounds, souls and lives, ghosts of actions approximating to murder" which threaten to destroy everything.

Thoreau's great book concludes with a chapter whose main business seems to be a series of exhortations: to explore one's "private sea"; to advance in the direction of dreams; to simplify; to step to the music one hears; to love one's life poor as it is. But the real theme of the chapter—of the whole work—is embodied in a single sentence near the beginning of the chapter: "Our voyaging is only great circle sailing." Thoreau's plea is to transcend human limitations which allow the present to be a mere replay of the past.

. . . . mere lapse of time can never make to dawn. The light which puts out our eyes is darkness to us. Only that day dawns to which we are awake. There is more day to dawn. The sun is but a morning star.
(*Walden*, 278)

Thoreau's imprecation for transcendence of time and place is echoed at the end of "The Forest Path" by Lowry's rage against giving in to the tyranny of the past:

. . . It was my duty to transcend [the past] in the present. . . . Sometimes I had the feeling I was attacking the past rationally as with a clawbar and hammer, while trying to make it into something else for a supernatural end.
("Forest Path," 280)

He must transcend the hubris that has driven him to read mystic portents in every passing moment; must return to a state of acceptance of himself as innocent of such perceptions. The story concludes in a bucolic kaleidoscope—a pastoral celebration— and, at last, a "great circle sailing" back to the regenerative fount, on the forest path to the spring.

CHAPTER 7

Eviction from Paradise

> New lines are wreathed on old lines half-
> erased,
> And those on older still; and so forever.
> The old shines through the new and colors
> it.
> What's new? What's old? All things have
> double meanings.
>
> Conrad Aiken
> *Palimpsest*

I   *A Paradise Teetering Toward Hell*

LOWRY'S "The Forest Path to the Spring" was a triumph of com-
pression. Its strength lay in his uncharacteristic shying away
from the provincialism of self, the "special" subjectivism of his
later fiction. For all those unretouched photographs of *Dark As the
Grave*, he substituted a series of universal metaphors for renewal.
The "I" who speaks in the novella is only in small part the man
who burrowed beyond recovery for the persona of his own species
of ultra writer. That persona became assimilated in a fictive
character—unnamed and unnameable—who threw off the masks
of the tortured artist for the celebrations of the man reborn.

October Ferry to Gabriola goes beyond the cameo of renewal
to a rich prose lode he had not mined since *Under the Volcano*.
One of the failures of *Dark As the Grave* was its hollow echoing
of themes Lowry had struck so galvanically in *Under the Volcano*.
While *October Ferry* sounds the "Forest Path" note—the quest
for Eridanus—it goes beyond to the place where the Northern
Paradise teeters toward hell. It chronicles what befalls the tran-
scendent spirit when the threat of eviction, first posed in "Forest
Path," jars the delicate balance between ecstasy and damnation.
Although sadly unfinished and fated for a kind of posthumous

limbo, this is the one book which shows evidence that Lowry could consolidate the gains of *Under the Volcano* and go on to new ones.

If *October Ferry* is not quite the *Paradiso* to Lowry's *Inferno*, it is at least antiphonal to it. In place of the Consul and his estranged though loving wife moving toward violent death in Mexico, Ethan and Jacqueline Llewelyn are about to be evicted from their British Columbia beach cabin. Lowry intended the fear of eviction to overlie this book as he intended the Consul's addiction to underlie *Volcano*. He managed the threat of eviction in "Forest Path" much more deftly than he does its actuality here. The artistic problem is twofold: Llewelyn is a flawed figure from the start. He has been fleeing ghosts, real and imagined, all his life. The real business of the book is the charting of inner flights.

Ethan Llewelyn clearly qualifies as a Lowryan persona. Dispossessed of his Thoreauvian retreat, he has given up a lucrative law practice upon learning that the man he saved from the scaffold is indeed a murderer. The overt action of *October Ferry*, like that of *Under the Volcano*, takes place on a single day. It opens on an October morning. Ethan and Jacqueline are heading northward by Greyhound bus from Victoria toward Nanaimo, where they will catch a ferry to Gabriola Island. The novel ends with the couple sighting the lights of Gabriola, the dreamed-of harbor apparently theirs.

Mrs. Lowry, who edited this book and whose care for nearly twenty years undoubtedly extended the life of her catastrophe-prone husband, writes that the novel grew out of a trip taken by the Lowrys in the fall of 1946.[1] Lowry has moved the time ahead to October, 1949, possibly to gain a postwar perspective. But for more than two-thirds of the novel, the bus trip provides the flimsiest of narrative coverings for the extraordinary play of Lowry's preternatural imagination.

Mrs. Lowry told me in conversation that the publisher of *October Ferry* was willing to issue the novel without cuts. This is regrettable. The book consists of several novella-length experiences which, if they could have been unified by Lowry, would have produced a major work. But, as Matthew Corrigan has noted, its unevenness juxtaposes the banal with the profound.[2] It is the novella-length experience within this mound of prose that one must look for. Each of these experiences is capped by what Joyce called an "epiphany," and each relates to the inner world of Ethan Llewelyn.

The first and most important of these is fire. One cannot resist the impulse to trace fire as Lowry's archetypal symbol, both in his life and in the life of his fiction. His letters are full of references to the fires that dogged him all his life. A fire of ambiguous origin destroyed the first shack he and Margerie had taken at Dollarton. Lost in the flames was the manuscript of *In Ballast to the White Sea,* a massive novel written before *Volcano.* A bizarre charred fragment survives in the Lowry Collection, University of British Columbia.

The Wildernesses fled to Mexico in *Dark As the Grave* partly to escape the memory of their house going up in flames at Eridanus. The narrator of "The Forest Path to the Spring" had composed a symphony which was lost beyond recapture in a fire. He had gone on to compose an opera by that title, a chronicle of "human happiness in terms of . . . high seriousness usually reserved for catastrophe and tragedy."

Lowry's most concentrated use of fire occurs in *October Ferry.* Fire of a cause never determined (Lowry fires never have a natural cause) destroyed their first house in Eastern Canada, at Oakville, across from Niagara-on-the-Lake. That tragedy left Ethan with a tangible-intangible feeling he was being punished. For Jacqueline, it was

the beginning of Ethan's real obsession with signs, portents, and coincidences, which from that period forward were so rooted in some ground of primitive logic in his brain that, he sometimes thought, he seldom questioned that the fire had been occasioned by other than a "supernatural" agency.

(*October Ferry,* 94–95)

Four chapters, almost the exact center of the novel, were excerpted by Mrs. Lowry and published by *Show* magazine in 1964. They are vintage Lowry and the best part of the book. Ethan describes a bizarre chain of coincidences involving burning, including fires by the dozen that hounded his family. There is also a cabbalistic series of correspondences, the most chilling of which is a childhood recollection of posters for a play portraying a Jew burning and a reference in a book to a victim of fire. The names of the playwright and the burned person prove identical. Maddened

by visions of actual and spiritual fires, Llewelyn prays. His words
mock him: "Our fire which art in fear. . . ." He concludes that
the mind is a haunted house and the devil a relentless pyromaniac
who invades the mind, evoking

long-forgotten hatreds of schoolmates who'd persecuted him about
his eyes at school; hatred of the day that ever gave him birth to be
the suffering creature he was, hatred where your house burned down
with no reason, hatred of himself, and out of all this hatred did not
grow sleep.

(October Ferry, 124)

Llewelyn recoils from fire, obsessed by it as the correlative of
all his agonies. Lowry's own blindness as a youth may also be
connected to his tormented vision. The above passage is an interesting one, vital as a connective from Ethan Llewelyn to the
Consul. This link can be clearly demonstrated. Throughout most
of the later novel, it seems that redemption is no more possible
for Ethan than for Geoffrey. The Llewelyns flee the fires. However, approaching the other side of the continent, at Vancouver,
they see "from the train window on their right . . . a fisherman's
shack, built on piles, burning. . . ."

The vision is identical with Yvonne's last conscious impulse
as she dies under the rearing horse's hooves during a storm in
the Dantean forest de la selva:

And she must escape, through the friendly forest to their home, their
little home by the sea. But the house was on fire . . . everything was
burning, the dream was burning, the house was burning . . . Geoffrey's
. . . book was burning, the pages were burning . . . whirling up from
the fire they were scattered, burning along the beach, and now it was
growing darker and the tide coming in . . . the pleasure boats that
had ferried song upstream sailed home silently over the dark waters
of Eridanus. Their house was dying, only an agony went there now.

(Volcano, 336)

And with the Consul's last vision: "The world itself was bursting,
bursting into black spouts of villages catapulted into space, with
himself falling through it all, through the inconceivable pandemonium of a million tanks, through the blazing of ten million
bodies, falling into a forest, falling—" *(Volcano, 375)*.

If the fires were visible element of the satanic deity which hunted him down even in paradise, Ethan's horror of himself as a murderer is the invisible. His is not deliberate but a kind of *de-facto* murder, and he an Ivan Karamazov figure whose crime was a failure to act to forestall a violent deed. As with the intellectual Karamazov, guilt takes the form of a fever—acute with Ivan, chronic with Ethan—which leads to a series of set scenes that are comparable in their grisly humor with Ivan's dialogue with the devil near the end of *The Brothers Karamazov*.

Ethan feels a deep guilt over his part in the suicide of Peter Cordwainer while the two were at college twenty years ago. Advertisements for "Mother Gettle's Kettle-Simmered Soup" crop up throughout the Llewelyns' day-long journey as reminders of the incident. Several carry a picture of Cordwainer as a boy— the soup is made by the Cordwainer family. Although Ethan has been able to forget Cordwainer for months at a time, lately he has been haunted again. The details are never entirely clear, but it appears that Ethan believes himself responsible for his class-mate's suicide. Cordwainer was in the habit of making theatrical threats of suicide. One night, exasperated, Ethan told Cordwainer, in effect, to make good his threats, never expecting to be taken at his word. Ethan is plagued by a belief that, in neglecting Peter Cordwainer, he has "failed in both my duty to God and man."

Ethan's specific guilt, as with the Consul's, becomes emblematic of man's universal guilt. Lowry almost carries it off. Chapter 27 ("Useful Knots and How to Untie Them") is, except for the central chapters on the fires, the most brilliant set piece of the book. Ethan realizes that he and Jacqueline are traveling to Gabriola on the very day—October 7—that is the twentieth an-niversary of Peter's death. The guilt nearly overwhelms him as one billboard after another rears up at him:

STOP! LOOK! LISTEN!
Mother Gettle's Kettle-Simmered Soup. M'mm, Good!

It must have been there all the time of course, the advertisement staring him in the face; perhaps the mist had obscured it, or the high-piled timber on the open cars trundling by, while now there were some curiously meaningless cars that he could see right over; but it had been in his mind anyhow, all the time, he had been ex-pecting it sometime or another all morning, but not *this* one, not the one with Cordwainer himself on it, not this comparatively rare one, showing a twenty times life-size cartoon of Peter, a lively, handsome, grinning youth of fifteen, gulping a great bowl of steaming soup and saying, "M'mm, Good!"

(October Ferry, 208–209)

No writer since Joyce has Lowry's ability to merge the graphics of the roadside—billboards, cautionary signs, driver warnings—with the mnemonics that sound combinations evoke. In his fevered consciousness, the *swish* and *clack* of the bus's windshield wipers unite with the trundling sound of the logger caravan on rails. Both combine in the measured cacophony of *Mother——Gettle's——Kettle——Simmered——Soup——M'mm——Good!* The chapter builds to a crescendo of self-condemnation whose ending is as predictable as it is powerful:

Suddenly he saw his whole life had been like one long malignant disease since Peter's death, ever since he'd forgotten it, forgotten it deliberately like a man who assures himself, after it begins to disappear, that the first lesion of syphilis is simply impetigo. . . . The face in the mirror, a half face, a mask, looked at him approvingly, smiling, but with a kind of half terror. Its lips silently formed the one word:
Murderer!

(October Ferry, 216)

The trouble with the novel as published is that it lacks "the final expurgatory look" which required in its predecessor a decade to evolve. Lowry keeps stockpiling portents. Ethan remembers that October 7 is not only the anniversary of Peter's death but the centennial of Edgar Allan Poe's. He simply had not been able at the time of his death to control embellishment, not drawn the circle tight enough, to produce that sense of inevitability which distinguished every segment of *Under the Volcano*.

Again and again, the material almost works as a novel. Lowry sought to relate Ethan's guilt as a man over the suicide of Cordwainer with his grief as a lawyer at the approaching hanging of a fifteen-year-old boy in the rape-slaying of a school companion. Whether Ethan has ever been directly involved in the case is never made clear, but he has prepared a brief for the public defense of the boy. The defense takes for its argument a passage from Hermann Hesse's *Demian*. Moving as that excerpt is— Hesse's signaling of youth as the one time of passage where the

[151]

terms of life are truly glimpsed—it is unconvincing as the crux
of a capital-crime defense plea.

The consuming shame of the man and that of the lawyer never
unite in one statement on universal guilt. Lowry tries valiantly
to produce from the man of good will and justice the cogent
metaphor. But Malcolm Lowry, ultra writer, cannot *think* in another language. A legal analogy like the following goes right
back to the tensions between life and art which haunted Sigbjørn
Wilderness in "Through the Panama" and *Dark As the Grave:*

Ethan's method of thinking . . . involved a process akin to composition:
not as though he had been composing a brief, exactly, but had been
loosely composing a mental dossier, preparatory to making a brief
on behalf of an accused he proposed to defend. But the actual and
frightening and certain knowledge at this moment that he had been
consciously deceiving himself all morning, actually suppressing and
misrepresenting the very events of his life for the sake of making them
fit into a bearable pattern, came with the force of a revelation. If the
first consciousness was the counsel for the defense, this second was the
counsel for the prosecution.

(*October Ferry,* 210)

Despite continual justification for indulging his obsession with
the writer writing about a writer writing, Lowry evidently ac-
ceded in *October Ferry* to his mentors' criticisms.[3] Ethan Llew-
eyln is nominally a lawyer. But in passages like the above—
Ethan's wrestlings with conflicting fragments of his personae—
the mind is ascetic not legal—a spiritualist's, a phenomenologist's.

Ethan Llewelyn, whose creator knew the Cabbala intimately,
is a mystic, and the book his attempt to locate himself "in the
current." Lowry's protagonist moves through a haze of disguises,
alter-egos, poltergeists, hermetic correspondences, but each disguise is nothing other than a new level of consciousness. To this
extent, as Matthew Corrigan was the first to stress, *October Ferry
to Gabriola* has nothing to do with fiction.

Conflict . . . . is never dramatized, never fictionalized. It transpires
in the mind of the book as in the mind of the author. The work becomes a treatise on writing . . . with what was to him the staggering
realization that literature had not yet caught up with the calamity of
modern civilization. . . .[4]

[152]

Sensitive as this assessment of Lowry as non-novelist writing novels is, it ought not to overlook how close he was to a created work that was worthy to be paired with *Under the Volcano*. Ethan Llewelyn's musings might have been functional if Lowry had done something with the potentially compelling character of Angus McCandless, Jacqueline's father and a cabbalist, a "white magician" with a Falstaffian side. McCandless possessed the fictive charisma to have provided a kind of Consular anchor for the book, a consciousness as encompassing as Geoffrey Firmin's and one which might have provided, through indirection, a deepening of Ethan's. But McCandless drops quickly out of sight. Mrs. Lowry apologizes in a postscript [5] for this and other lapses, but lapses they remain.

The book also fails at the narrative level because Jacqueline is little more than a sycophant for Ethan. Long passages of dialogue between Ethan and Jacqueline about his retreat from law and life and about her Scottish ancestors are impossible to defend. Ethan recalls the circumstances of their first meeting— at a cinema—and that memory stirs fond recollections of a D. W. Griffith film as

so much more poignant than anything he had ever experienced in fact . . . like deducing the real from the unreal . . . by the transpiercing beauty of the manner in which it was perceived and photographed [giving] . . . life itself . . . a new reality. . . .
(*October Ferry,* 16)

Lowry's unfinished last book cannot succeed where Griffith's film —all art—succeeds. The *real* in *October Ferry*—the outpouring of autobiography—only occasionally evokes the fictive *unreal,* that is, what Louis Rubin calls "the lie that tells the truth." The conversations between Ethan and Jacqueline are too special, too much like the chatting of family among outsiders. Unassimilated autobiography in fiction is the truth that tells lies.

Of course, the final lines of *October Ferry* are redemptive, an answer to Ethan's pleas for a sign that he is saved:

And now through the twilight . . . [they] distinguished the outlines of a sheltered valley that sloped down to a silent, calm harbor. Deep in the dark forest behind was the glow of a fire with red sparks ascend-

ing like a fiery fountain. . . . A voice called out, clear . . . lights . . .
gleamed in the dusk.

(*October Ferry*, 333)

A few pages earlier, the Llewelyns had read in the newspaper
that they and the other squatters at Eridanus had been reprieved;
the plans for a park had been put aside. The book ends in a
deluge of maritime imagery, presumably suggestive of the compensating force to fire: water. As the ferry makes for Gabriola,
Ethan and Jacqueline stand arm in arm on the deck. A lonely
lighthouse blinks, silver breakers crash against the rocky shore,
the "primeval island" heaves into view. The apparent resolution is
achieved stylistically, but it is as false to life as the tinkle of a toy
train at Christmas.

Although the fragments of Malcolm Lowry's confession are
present in *October Ferry*, the eviction theme has not been the tie
that binds. It failed both as motif and dialectic. Lowry, whose
preoccupation with the forces within a man that are bent on
destroying him had no equal in modern literature, could galvanize
his vision but once.

CHAPTER 8

The Jungian Conductor

> Hilliot [in *Ultramarine*] is a man who admittedly lives in "introverted comas" and that is part of his trouble, however typical it may be: his is a vicariousness beyond a statement of vicariousness because it is unobjectifiable, he is never sure that any emotion is his own, and he quite genuinely is "cuckoo," he is a poet who can't write and may never be able to. . . . [U]nder the reign of Bloom and Sweeney, a greater freedom seems to be permitted, these are being absorbed into the racial consciousness.
>
> Malcolm Lowry
> Excerpt from unpublished, undated letter to Conrad Aiken [1]

I   *Life in "Introverted Comas"*

DOUGLAS DAY has said that the problem with Lowry lies in the impossibility of separating his life from his works. "He was incapable of distinguishing himself from his characters, from people he was writing about. So in order to understand his protagonist one must understand Lowry." [2]

This is mercilessly true, more so with Lowry than any writer I can think of. Yet one diminishes Lowry as creative artist by pushing for exact equations; by insisting that the alcoholic Consul, the tragic hero of *Under the Volcano*, equals Malcolm Lowry, the alcoholic author of the novel. Certainly there are crucial elements of Malcolm Lowry's character in Geoffrey Firmin. Both drink compulsively, and both live their lives, as Lowry once said of the hero of *Ultramarine*, in "introverted comas." While both

are endlessly introspective, each burrowing deeper into his consciousness than any reader or listener could follow, the Consul is
a fictional artifact, triumphant in his fall, and Lowry, the man,
died an alcoholic's death, his torments unresolved.

The Consul tells Laruelle, at the close of an argument in which
the Frenchman blames the Consul's alcoholism for Yvonne's infidelity (Chap. VII):

"You are interfering with my great battle. . . . I have to have a
drink or two now, myself . . . else I shall become confused, like your-
self.

"—the truth is, I suppose, that sometimes when you've calculated
the amount exactly, you do see more clearly," M. Laruelle was ad-
mitting a minute later.

"Against death." The Consul sank back easily in his chair. "My
battle for the survival of the human consciousness."

It would be easy to take the Consul, or Lowry, or both, as ironic.
Near the end of his life, Lowry wrote David Markson, apropos
of Aiken's *Ushant:* ". . . it never occurred to me that consciousness
itself could be of any aid, quite the contrary, and let alone a
goal. . . ." [3] I believe the Consul and Lowry here reflect a crucial
distinction between art and life. The Consul, approaching death
in the Farolito, has nothing left but his messianic impulses. Even
under the influence of mescal—that is, even when living on the
boundaries between the conscious and the unconscious—he sees
himself as a survivor of an era and a sensibility, both corrupted
in a time of dying peons and bloodied hands: Liberal Man. In
life, Lowry came—finally—to see what he once called "the good
ship Solipsism" [4] as a wreck. As he found to his great sorrow
during the ten years remaining to him after the long-delayed
publication of *Volcano,* the infernal machine that ground out his
life carried no guarantee of grinding out, in its self-destroying
course, major fiction.

Conrad Aiken told me in conversation that he represented for
Lowry the part of the Consul that still sought deliverance in
a quest for Eridanus but that Lowry himself was the self-destructive element that sought the barranca. "Malc really wished for
the unconscious—the womb, if you will, and nothing any of us
could do for him changed that." [5] Lowry's Cambridge University
classmate—the late critic John Davenport—made the same point,

only stronger, to Conrad Knickerbocker: ". . . I finally decided what it was about Malcolm. It was simply that he hadn't wanted to be born at all. . . ." [6] Is it laboring the obvious to say that no one but Lowry, who was *not* the Consul, could have created him?

What, really, was Malcolm Lowry? Douglas Day, who as Lowry's official biographer, has had to wrestle with the multiple Lowryan personae, concludes that his man "was not really a novelist, except by accident," and acknowledges "that it is difficult to know what to call him: diarist, compulsive notetaker, poet manqué, alcoholic philosophizing rambler—any of these would do for a start, but only for a start." When Day finds a category, it is the expected one: autobiographer. We are back at the point where this chapter began: Lowry the writer whose only topic is Malcolm Lowry.

In his unfinished novel, *The Ordeal of Sigbjørn Wilderness,* Lowry has Wilderness assess himself as a creator of character: ". . . the truth was that he had unusual difficulty in seeing anybody, of forming the slightest impression: particularly this was true of women. . . . It was odious to think . . . that he [ever studied] a friend simply to put him in a book." [8] John Wain finds Lowry "a strange writer, tremendously developed in some respects and entirely undeveloped in others. Of the necessary equipment of the novelist, he had about half, and his fatal tendency was to work too hard with the half he did have." [9]

Wain's statement is useful—as far as it goes. However, it implies that Lowry ought to have lopped off some of what Day calls his "layer upon layer . . . that tremendously complicated network of correspondences" [10] and should have brought in fuller characterization and fuller imaginative concern for people other than the single protagonist who is Malcolm Lowry under another name. Lowry's dilemma as a craftsman is not to be solved by a balancing of assets and liabilities. He possessed the virtues of his defects; without the flaws, the undeniable powers might have been diminished.

This chapter is a tentative coda—at best, an incomplete attempt to deal with the extra-literary Lowry, the spiritual archivist who was forever receiving and storing up mystical correspondences out of thin air. Lowry was a *conductor* of what one unsympathetic reviewer called "mescalusions" [11] but which really come close to being in Carl G. Jung's terms "archetypal fragments" or "primordial images." These visions—I shall define their Jungian equivalents shortly—obsessed Lowry to the point that their incidence outpaced his ability to assimilate them into artistic fiction.

Except for *Under the Volcano,* a handful of short stories, and several fragments of *October Ferry to Gabriola,* all of Lowry's prose boils down to being a catalogue of one protagonist's inner visions and lacking "the final expurgatory look." If we did not have the evidence of *Volcano,* it would be easy to conclude that Lowry was incapable of transmuting vision into viable fiction.

II *Jung-Lowry: A Shock of Recognition?*

One of the keys to understanding Malcolm Lowry as conductor of mystic impulses may come less from literature than from modern psychology—the writings and theories of Jung in particular. A Canadian Broadcasting Company documentary on Lowry's life notes that he once considered going into psychoanalysis.[12] The film reports that he decided against it on similar grounds to those which Ernest Hemingway raised in protesting to Philip Young his (Young's) intention to publish a book whose thesis was that the Hemingway heroes all showed the psychic effects of the wounds the actual Hemingway suffered on the Italian Front in World War I. To tell a writer he has a neurosis, Hemingway wrote Young, is as bad as telling him he has cancer: you can put a writer permanently out of business this way.[13] The Lowry documentary film concludes with a paraphrase of Hemingway's well-known remark that his typewriter was his analyst. Analysis might effect a cure, but the patient—the artist—would die.

Mrs. Lowry presents a somewhat different version. In a letter to me, she notes that in 1948 Carl G. Jung, although in retirement, had invited Malcolm Lowry to come to see him in Switzerland for treatment, and that her husband had really wanted to go. "Malcolm had read Jung and considered him the best—at least for the artist. . . . I sent Jung the *Volcano* and he was so impressed he offered to treat Malcolm himself." She adds that she went to England—the Lowrys were abroad at the time (1948)—to see Malcolm's brothers to finance the trip. "It would have been peanuts to them but so horrified were they by the thought of mental illness (sweep the skeleton into the closet, quick!) they flatly refused to help." [14] What is significant—what may in the last analysis point to a major loss to anyone seeking to probe to the roots of the creative process—is that Jung, according to Mrs. Lowry, knew nothing about her husband yet expressed the desire to treat him on no other basis than a reading of *Under the Volcano*.

It is beyond the scope of this book to investigate ramifications of the likelihood that Jung recognized the Consul—and hence, recognized Malcolm Lowry—as a monitor of archetypal images. My only aim in this section is to suggest aspects of Lowry's works which, given Jung's concepts, could have provided a shock of recognition.

Lewis Mumford has written that for Carl G. Jung dreams were more gripping than wakeful life. [15] He often felt himself living simultaneously in two different ages and being two different persons. This feeling of double life, which persisted to the very end of Jung's life, haunted Lowry daily. In his earliest fiction, dream was a favored narrative device. Lowry conceived of dream as bearing the same relationship to the dreamer as film to the viewer.

This idea can best be illustrated by reference to an early and little-known story, "The Bulls of the Resurrection," rescued from Lowry's effects and published several years ago by his friend, the poet Earle Birney, in *Prism International*,[16] the literary magazine of the University of British Columbia. Two Cambridge undergraduates, Rysdale and Sam, stand at a bar in Granada, Spain. Like all the names of places in Lowry's writings, the designation of the tavern is significant. It is Café Fray Diego de León. A girl named Terry, their companion on the trek to Spain, has deserted them for a third young man, Smith. The resentment of Rysdale, the girl's original lover, spills over as he recounts to Sam his dream of the death of Terry and of the execution by beheading of Smith. The scene is characteristically Lowryan, Jungian: the hero's youth and early manhood are merged. The dream takes place in a prison where Rysdale and Smith are simultaneously inmates and pupils; the setting is concurrently Spain (the present) and Dartmoor (the past), where the two men had played as children. Sam asks if the dream might not have been evoked by a haunting El Greco original they had seen. Rysdale explains that it was like El Greco gone mad. No, I'll tell you what it was like. It was as though a moving picture had been projected onto a Greco instead of onto a screen. There was this fixed, timeless, haunted background, but this was not part of what was going on, this was only the relief against which it could be seen, the means by which it became visible.

("Bulls of Resurrection," 8)

Here, in an apprentice story, Lowry provides in capsule his concept, not then refined, of the interplay between linear time-space and flux; that is, between place frozen in time and movement and change that are continuous.

By the time of *October Ferry to Gabriola*, Lowry had refined the literary apparatus by which Ethan Llewelyn's visions could be made viable in fiction. At the end of the extraordinarily rich "fire" sequence at the heart of the book, Ethan sits alone in a hotel beer parlor. He has had a quarrel with Jacqueline over the series of fires which, coupled with reverberations and correspondences in his current reading, have placed him "in the current," at the threshold of consciousness transcended. He becomes aware of something which Freud described, writing of the epilepsy of Dostoevsky, as a "mind explosion."

. . . something more frightening yet taking place in his mind. It was a feeling that permeated the high ill-lit yellow walls . . . , the long dim corridor between the two beer parlours, on which the door now seemed to be opened by an invisible hand. . . .

(*October Ferry*, 145)

Ethan finds this collective mental image held unwaveringly if instantaneously "on the screen of his mind." The unconscious, hiding place of demons, has not only been opened (". . . the home also of more conscious mental abortions and aberrations; of disastrous yet unfinished thoughts, half hopes and half intentions . . . where precepts, long abandoned, stumbled on") but become the province where a peak at Creation is vouchsafed (". . . why, then, should he have rushed to the conclusion that . . . this collision of contingencies, was in its final essence diabolical, or fearful, or meaningless? . . . Mightn't he equally well consider that he'd been vouchsafed . . . a glimpse into the very workings of creation itself . . . ").

Lowry wisely undercuts the messianic thrust of the vision by allowing it to happen while Ethan is downing one beer after another. Nevertheless, the juxtaposing of motifs from one of his earliest stories and his last book reveals that Lowry never ceased in the quest to pin down "the constant irrelevant relevancies of life—the 'thinginess' of life—impinging on us, expanding, diminishing, falling away . . . as mind moves through landscape, or landscape through mind (it is all one)." [17] But if mind and landscape indeed are all one, it took Lowry a lifetime of trial-and-error, revision-on-revision, to dissolve the false boundaries erected by every novelist until Sterne and most of those following Sterne until the arrival of Joyce and Proust.

III *Life as Archetypal*

It is necessary here to try to summarize those aspects of Jungian psychology which have pertinence in being linked to Malcolm Lowry's life and works. In general, Jung's stress on the manifestations in art of unconscious *ex*pression over Freud's concern with the morbid effects of unconscious *re*pression make his findings of enormous relevance to so tireless a collector of the residue of the unconscious as Lowry. Jung's impulse was that he had located in the unconscious "the matrix of a mythopeic imagination that has vanished from our rational age." Lowry, through the Consul, felt himself a survivor of a sensibility that has disappeared in this century. The heroes of "The Forest Path" and *October Ferry* live visionary lives dreaming that they have found an earthly paradise out of time and place.

In company with Freud, Jung suggests that dreams serve the purpose of compensation by transmitting unconscious reactions or spontaneous impulses to consciousness. Jung acknowledged that thus far—he was writing in 1961, the year of his death—nobody could say anything against Freud's theory of repression and wish fulfillment as apparent causes of dream symbolism. Jung breaks with Freud on this point only in denying the Master's insistence that sexual repression was the sole source of neurotic symptoms. He was far more ready than Freud to admit that burdens and calamities having nothing to do with sex might be responsible for disorders and the dreams they evoke.

Jung departs from Freud in his belief that it is not necessary to use a dream as *the* point of departure for the process of "free association." For Jung, the dream was no more and no less useful than any other possible starting point. Dreams, though, have a particular significance, even though they often arise from an emotional upset in which the habitual complexes—the tender spots of the psyche—are also involved. Jung says he came increasingly to disagree with "free" association as Freud first employed it.

I wanted to keep as close as possible to the dream itself, and to exclude all the irrelevant ideas and associations that it might evoke. True, these could lead one toward the complexes of a patient, but I had a more far-reaching purpose in mind than the discovery of complexes that cause neurotic disturbances.[18]

When dreaming becomes obsessive and dreams highly charged, the personal associations produced by the dreamer do not usually suffice for a satisfactory interpretation. Elements often occur, according to Jung, that are *not* individual and that cannot be derived from the dreamer's experiences. Their presence cannot be explained by anything in the individual's own life: they seem to be aboriginal, innate, and inherited shapes of the human mind. Jung calls them "archetypes" or "primordial images." "The archetype," he writes, "is a tendency to form . . . representations of a motif—representations that can vary a great deal in detail without losing their basic pattern."

I do not believe it an oversimplification to say that Malcolm Lowry's life was itself an archetype. And, because all of his fiction except for *Volcano,* duplicated his life, the fiction, too, is archetypal in the Jungian sense: representational of a motif. What, then, is the motif, the archetype?

Throughout his life, Lowry retained as the title for the whole under which all the fictional parts would eventually be grouped, *The Voyage That Never Ends.* He saw life in a series of compensatory metaphors that recur in his fiction: water and fire, the river and the ravine, the volcano as emblematic of life and death. The dramatic tension, symbolized by these metaphors, was always the possibility of salvation, the chance for rebirth. When Jung read *Under the Volcano* in 1948, did he recognize the Consul as a collector of—a conductor for—archetypes and *Under the Volcano* as an epic built around an archetypal motif?

In the previous chapter, I discussed fire as a major archetype of all of Lowry's long fiction. In his last book, Jung recounts two dreams—one ancient, the other modern, having to do with fire. In the ancient one, quoted by Artemodorous of Daldis, second century A.D., a man dreamed that he saw his father die in the flames of a house on fire. Not long afterward, he himself died in a phlegmone (fire or high fever), perhaps pneumonia. In the modern one, a colleague of Jung's was suffering from a deadly gangrenous fever—a phlegmone. A former patient of his, who had no knowledge of the nature of his doctor's illness, dreamed that the doctor died in a great fire. At that time the doctor had just entered a hospital and the disease was only beginning. The dreamer knew nothing but the bare fact that his doctor was ill and in a hospital. Three weeks later, the doctor died. For Jung, dreams could have a prognostic effect.

The Consul's visions run a vertically cyclical path—from the snowy peak of Himavat and the summits of the twin volcanoes to life under the volcano, the depths of the barranca "through the blazing of ten million burning bodies falling. . . ." The volcano, at once infernal and redemptive, provides the book's title and its most insistent symbol. The path is both an ascent and a descent: an ascent from fire to light—Yvonne's death vision—and a descent from light to fire—the Consul's.

The Consul's obsessive thoughts of fire always produce the compensating image, the opposite symbol of water. One cannot help but note the water imagery of the Consul's vision in the Garden Chapter (V) just before he flees to his overrun flowers seeking the bottle he has hidden among them. He imagines himself on Mount Himavat, pausing in his ascent to slake his thirst:

Whereupon the lake was lapping . . . the waterfalls were playing . . . and still he was thirsty. . . . Then the lake was blowing, the snow was blowing, the waterfalls were blowing . . . the seasons were blowing—blowing away— he was blowing away himself, whirled by a storm of blossoms into the mountains, where now the rain was falling. . . . He was standing, among cattle, in a stream. He was resting with some ponies, knee-deep beside him in the cool marshes. He was lying face downward drinking from a lake that reflected the white-capped ranges, the clouds piled five miles high behind the mighty mountain Himavat. . . .

(*Volcano*, 125)

The profusion of language suggestive of regenerative water is unmistakable. Finally, in his vision, the Consul realizes that he is drinking not water but "certainty of brightness." The scene represents the Consul's loftiest aspiration until the final pages: the closest he comes to salvation. At the last, seven chapters—perhaps seven hours, but, in terms of *rendered time*, a lifetime—later, the Consul's ears pick up "the distant clamour of a waterfall and what sounded like the cries of love" (*Volcano*, 374). But the dream of Eridanus—the life-renewing river that legend says received the dead Phaethon—gives way as the Consul, dying, is borne to the edge of the barranca to the accompaniment of "the noise of foisting lava in his ears . . ." (*Volcano*, 375).

But it remains to try to formulate in a phrase a motif, galvanic in Jung's terms, to describe Malcolm Lowry's ethos. Once again, an anecdote related by Jung gives a clue. In analyzing the relevant motifs from twelve dreams of a ten-year-old girl which she had written up into a booklet she presented as a Christmas present to her father (a psychiatrist), Jung deduces that the motifs were everywhere suggestive of impending disaster. The child died of an infectious disease about a year after that Christmas. Her dreams, Jung writes, "open up a new and rather terrifying aspect of life and death. . . . Experience shows that the unknown approach of death casts an . . . anticipatory shadow over the life and dreams of the victim. Even the altar in Christian churches represents, on the one hand, a tomb and, on the other, a place of resurrection—the transformation of death into eternal life." [19]

Jung concludes with an analogy that is of astounding pertinence to Lowry and *Under the Volcano*. Writing of the child's recourse to a kind of psychic memory originating outside historical tradition, he observes: "It was as if future events were casting their shadow back by arousing in the child certain thought forms that, though normally dormant, describe or accompany the approach of a fatal issue." If one were to substitute the consciousness of Jacques Laruelle (the central intelligence of Chapter I) for that of the child, Jung's analogy can be considered an exact description of the circular progress—the "infernal machine" aspect—of *Under the Volcano*. The events and landmarks touched on by Laruelle in the epilogic opening of *Volcano* cast their shadows backwards with the luminous wheel by arousing in Laruelle the memory of the fateful happenings that signaled the "approach of a fatal issue," the tragic death of the Consul.

It is not too much, then, to assume that Carl G. Jung would have been deeply moved by a novel that is, in his terms, a representation of an archetypal motif, a novel whose hero, like Jung's colleague's child, is haunted by visions portending doom. Jung believed that archetypal forms are never static patterns but dynamic factors that manifest themselves in impulses.[20] Close friends of Lowry's, like John Davenport and David Markson, watched him go into what Davenport called "Malcolmspells" and Markson termed his "private recitals." During all those convoluted monologues—in periods of drunkenness, too—Lowry experienced his Jungian impulses, apparently as spontaneously as those physiological urges, perceived by the senses and called "instincts." Jung from his youth on was quite apt to surrender to the unconscious and immersed himself in all its fantastic presentations —poltergeists, ghosts, thought transference, clairvoyance, and prophecy. Far from scoffing at Lowry's visions, as refracted in the Consul, the man who has written cogently of occultism and prescience (". . . just as our conscious thoughts often occupy themselves with the future . . . , so do the unconscious and its dreams. . . ." [21]) could not have been other than attentive and receptive to *Under the Volcano*.

Jung wrote that the psychologist cannot do without a "comparative anatomy of the psyche." He "must not only have a sufficient experience of dream and other products of unconscious activity, but also of mythology. . . ." [22] Lowry, who lived a kind of megalomaniacal mythology, did not casually apply to his aspired-to paradise the name Eridanus. As I have noted earlier, Eridanus is the River of Life and also the Styx, and it is connected with the legend of Phaethon. The latter borrowed the chariot of the sun for one day and drove it so dangerously close to earth that Zeus struck him down with a thunderbolt to save the world from catching fire. The mysterious river Eridanus, never seen by mortal eyes, received the burning Phaethon, put out the flames, and cooled the body. The naiads, in compassion, buried him, with this epitaph carved on the tomb:

> Here Phaethon lies who drove the Sun-god's car.
> Greatly he failed, but he had greatly dared.[23]

Phaethon's mourning sisters, the Heliades, were turned into poplars, on the bank of Eridanus, where they wept into the stream forever.

The legend, with its suggestions of death and rebirth, must have appealed to Lowry whose fondest hope was that he, like Orpheus, would soar from—transcend—the ashes of his fiery life. Life as a wheel continuously turning forward and backward on itself—life as a river (Eridanus and Styx alike) that contains at once the beauty of flow and the murk of stagnation: these are the major motifs in Lowry's working in life and art of an archetype to which now can be applied this name: the Pilgrim's Everlasting Return. Or—better—the Everlasting Voyager. For, as Ethan Llewelyn muses near the end of *October Ferry*, everybody was on the homeward-outward-bound voyage. He sits with Jacqueline in the bar of the Ocean Spray Inn, looking toward Gabriola on the horizon, and *the* archetypal metaphor for his life looms before him. The sea is transfixed, looking like

a luminosity between two darknesses, a space between two immensities . . . . [everybody] was on such a voyage, to the junction of the two infinities, where it would set out on its way again, had already set out, toward the infinitely small, itself already expanding before you had thought of it, to replenish the limitless light of Chaos—

(*October Ferry*, 252)

Moments later, aboard the ferry for Gabriola, Ethan Llewelyn—or Sigbjørn Wilderness or Malcolm Lowry, for they are all one—experiences a characteristic distillation of time, place, and experience. As Gabriola draws nearer, and their beach house that much more distant, it is as if "Eridanus and the little cabin drew nearer. . . ."

IV   *The Failure of Archetype as Art*

"It is quite within the bounds of possibility for a man to recognize the relative evil of his nature," Jung declares, "but it is a rare and shattering experience for him to gaze into the face of absolute evil." [24] The Consul looks on the dark side of his nature with an intensity that is rare in modern literature. *Under the Volcano* is the story of a possessed man that could only have been written by a possessed man. Yet the always lucid evocation of the Consul's madness is the product of an artist who was in control of his Jungian labyrinth. The contrapuntal resonances by which Lowry built his symphonic novel echo only occasionally in the inner monologues of Sigbjørn Wilderness, Ethan Llewelyn, and all the Lowryan personae of the subsequent fiction. After a novel in which nearly everything—at last—worked, nothing really worked again. For what is perhaps the most cogent statement ever made on why art must fail if it echoes neuroses without transcending them, one again turns to Jung. Should anyone claim that an analysis of neurosis accounts for the work of art itself, a categorical denial, Jung asserts, is called for.

The personal idiosyncrasies that creep into a work of art are not essential; in fact, the more we have to cope with these peculiarities, the less it is a question of art. What is essential in a work of art is that it should rise far above the realm of personal life and speak from the spirit and heart of mankind. The personal aspect is a limitation—and even a sin—in the realm of art. When a form of "art" is primarily personal it deserves to be treated as if it were a neurosis.[25]

So one hand of the master, in a sense, strikes down what the other has built. In life, Lowry enacted daily Jung's concepts of the Unconscious. In art, Lowry's attempts to metamorphose Jung-like impulses failed and eventually overwhelmed him.

CHAPTER *9*

Malcolm Lowry and the
Addictions of an Era

> For many of our writers—the Elias Canetti
> of *Auto da Fé, the* Malcolm Lowry of
> *Under the Volcano,* the Camus of *The
> Stranger* . . . have made us feel that the
> world for them was very nearly a kind of
> nightmare—as Henry James phrased it in
> his last years, "a nightmare from which there
> is no waking save by sleep."
>
> Nathan A. Scott Jr.
> *The Broken Center*

LOWRY wrote Jonathan Cape in that mock apologetic way of
his that since his defects were those of a poet trying to write
a novel with the strategy of a long poem, his "deformities" might
be forgiven.[1] Conrad Knickerbocker learned that Lowry once
told a London psychiatrist that he wished to remain obscure so
that his plagiarisms would not be discovered.[2] Although he had
no need to excuse himself on either count, the confessions are
vintage Lowry. He never made the novelist's leap into the skins
of other people. His only character was the outsider who prospered artistically by negative capability; the masquerader who,
as one of Lowry's poems has it,

> . . . plays the piano with a razor,
> The concertina with a pair of scissors;
> A rigadoon for all his customers,
> He is the Sweeny Tod of improvisors!
> Though all men fear this poor relation,
> His keener music gives a strange sensation . . .
>
> ("The Comedian," *Selected Poems*)

Lowry put all his weakness into the Consul of *Under the Volcano:* he is closer to Joyce Cary's Gulley Jimson than to Lawrence Durrell's Pursewarden, but he is more likeable than either of these Promethean modern artist-heroes. Geoffrey Firmin had to be a character of extraordinary shading and possibility to provide a repository for Lowry's megalomania: the man he was, added to the man he would like to have been; the messianic figure suffering his long day's dying to be able to report back the weathers of hell.

Lowry's poet-gods were the Elizabethan sonneteers and the Romantics of the last century, especially Shelley and Coleridge. He used *Alastor* and *Rime of the Ancient Mariner* as accompanying music, respectively, in a discarded draft of *Volcano* and in the novella "Through the Panama." In a sense, *Under the Volcano* belongs most closely to the allegorical and transcendental world of the great nineteenth-century Americans, to Melville and Hawthorne. The seascapes of Conrad and O'Neill were the modern prose works he most admired until he read *Blue Voyage* in 1928 and arranged a meeting with its creator the following year. While he received a transfusion of Joyce through the veins of Aiken, he always remained, like those other myth-makers Joyce and Faulkner, the poet manqué. When he turned to prose, he overlaid it with a heavily allusive texture, replete with borrowings from, even parodies of, the classical poets.

Aiken says that Lowry worked on his novel as one would on a patchwork quilt. "Every snippet of colour or serendipity out-of-the-way knowledge that he found in his reading (he was always wanting me to send him old copies of *The Dial* and *Criterion*) was tucked in to enrich it, whether or not pertinent." [3] Thus Lowry borrowed arcane information and adjusted the Consul's visions to Faustian and Dantesque leitmotifs. From Aiken, he learned word-spinning, inspired punning, and the controlling device of great-circling. He also, as he confessed almost too freely to his mentor-friend, felt himself sometimes dispossessed, a specter of Aiken's own discarded ideas. "Malc had this way of being admiringly predatory in the using of other men's writing and contrite about it at the same time," Aiken told me in conversation, not without bitterness. [4]

But what Lowry invested in his novel, during his decade-long trials-by-fire at the extremes of the North American continent, was derivative of no one. The terrible intensity of the book, every-thing—line by line, image by image—transfigured, was only his to give. Texture evolved into symbolic structure, an accomplish-ment usually of only the great poems. One remembers the elegiac sadness long after the incidents have retreated from the mind. If, as George Steiner has said, *Under the Volcano* "endures by virtue of excess" and is overwritten and "overfelt," the true rich-ness of the book emerges in the rereading—its coherency and its control.

The two extremes which are the technical dangers of this kind of novel are, as Robert B. Heilman pointed out in the first ap-preciation of *Volcano* by a major critic,

the tightly bound allegory, in which a system of abstract equivalents for all the concrete materials of the story constricts the imaginative experience, and a loose impressionism, in which a mass of suggestive enterprises sets off so many associations, echoes, and conjectures that the imaginative experience becomes crowded and finally diffuse.[5]

But, while wishing for a more ordered synthesis of the parts, Professor Heilman declares he "would never want a diminution of the power of Lowry's possessed art." [6] Few young writers—for, although Lowry was thirty-seven when *Volcano* was pub-lished, he began it at age twenty-six, with only an unsuccessful apprentice novel behind him—have been able at the start of their careers to make so masterful a statement of so unique a vision of life.

Conrad Aiken, a survivor of the small company who watched Lowry dying by the glass in Cuernavaca but also preserving at least a stillborn version of the giant work that would surface a decade later, has publicly called *Volcano* "inspired melodrama" [7] and, privately, a "literary accident." [8] The book is both. In being melodrama and a kind of masterpiece-by-accident, the book, two decades after its original publication, sheds a distinctive shadow across our landscape.

Jung has said that every period has its psychic ailment requir-ing a compensatory adjustment. This, he believed, is effected by a poet-leader. Such a man allows himself to be guided by the unexpressed desire of his times and shows the way to the attain-ment of that which everyone blindly expects—whether this attainment results in good or evil, the healing of an epoch or its destruction.[9] How much of this function is assignable to Lowry?

Under the Volcano appeared at a time when the world was emerging from the most punishing war of the century. Its essential drafts were written late in the interwar years when the ominous notes of exile and doom were being sounded. Neither the malaise of alienation nor the Bartlebyan prerogative that now carries the label "existentialism" was yet large enough a subject for either melodrama or for general consternation, except in France. When, in 1947, the Consul emerged, he was commonly passed over as an already out-of-vogue kinsman of Don Birnam, the drunken hero of Charles Jackson's tour de force, *Lost Weekend*, published three years before. It is unlikely, despite Lowry's often expressed feeling that the earlier book spoiled the psychological moment for his own,[10] that the mass of readers who made a best seller of an alcoholic's monumental binge on Third Avenue would (or could) do much with a drunken, disgraced British ex-consul staggering through the streets of a seedy Mexican town, called Quauhnahuac, quoting Dante and Marlowe. The "first" book (Lowry's composition of the early drafts of *Volcano* preceded Jackson by five years) made a peripety of a Jewish holiday which kept pawnshops closed and Birnam sober; *Volcano* made the Mexican Day of the Dead an archetypal holiday standing for humanity's dying. For, as Hugh puts it in Chapter IV, while discussing with Yvonne the problem of the Consul's drinking: "What's the good? Just sobering him up for a day or two's not going to help. Good God, if our civilization were to sober up for a couple of days it'd die of remorse on the third—."

If, as the anthropologist Kluckhohn believed, our mid-century has been a time, especially in the United States, when a sense of *sin* is rare but feelings of *guilt* are common,[11] *Under the Volcano* touches on a mainspring. The Consul turns to alcohol at least partly to assuage his feelings of personal guilt. His sensibilities are racked by the past. There is, for one thing, his obscure sexual guilt arising from the Hell Bunker episode at Leasowe, described by Jacques in Chapter I. That the Consul has not forgotten this disquieting incident is clear from a passage in Chapter VII. On the catwalk at Jacques's house the Consul peers through the binoculars at the countryside, and thinks, "It was as if they were standing on a lofty golf-tee somewhere. What a beautiful hole this would make." After the childhood incident at the bunker, the Consul inevitably associated feelings of embarrassment and guilt with sex. The Consul's inability to consummate the sexual act with the unexpectedly returned Yvonne in Chapter III and his pleasureless fornication with the whore Maria in the last chapter combine to touch on another of mid-century's reversals: the male loss of sexual identity giving rise to the twin themes of emasculation and homosexuality.

Geoffrey Firmin also appears to drink out of a hypersensitivity to the guilt and shame that all men share for the human condition. Lowry uses the Consul's alcoholism as a symbol of the sickness which afflicts the whole of mankind. This general guilt is felt strongly by the Consul on the literal level. Perhaps among the last exemplars of Liberal Man, Firmin is civilized, sensitive, ideal-istic, and he cannot bear to think of the world of the barranca, dominated by the bloody hands of Orlac. He therefore seeks consolation in alcohol.

The Consul imbibes for positive reasons, too. His rationale is especially *au courant* for the 1970s. Drinking is a means of mystical release, of the sort of induced transcendental flights that are so commonly taken today. In Chapter VII, Jacques refers to the trouble the Consul's drinking causes, while "what is mystical in you is being released, or whatever it is you imagine is being released." The Consul took his trip thirty years before the era of psychedelic drugs. But his drinking may have been a prophecy. Mescaline is a hallucinogenic obtained from peyote, one of the species of mescal which is the Consul's favorite drink.

One of Lowry's central concerns in the novel is what John McCormick has called "the nature of love in a fragmented so-ciety." [12] The phrase is forbidding, but it provides a statement of a main theme of contemporary novelists. Meursault, the anti-hero of Albert Camus's *The Stranger*, announces in the first sentence of the novel that "mother died today." He opts out of—and is martyred by—a world that seeks to catalogue the responses of love in a neat series of equations. "In the town there were two mutes, and they were always together." Thus does Carson Mc-Cullers on the opening page of her first novel announce her career's preoccupation with the failure of humans to reach each other on any conscious level.

The main tension of *Under the Volcano* is between the necessity of love and the terrible difficulty of love; between the Consul's aspiration to love and his forfeiture of that aspiration. His alienation from life, as Anthony Burgess says, "etches the desired opposite [in the Promethean anti-hero] whose inability to love defines what love is." [13] Certainly the four principals have all tried to live without loving. Their sickness is not only physical, as when the Consul suffers from delirium tremens; but, in the talismanic words of Dr. Vigil, "in that part used to be call: soul."

The plots of hundreds of contemporary novels testify to the failure of marriage. In terms of the mid-century *Zeitgeist*, this pattern for estrangement may comprise the most tragic failure of all. The Malcolm Lowry who confessed in "Through the Panama" that he could not understand what his contemporaries were writing about still manages to follow their lead. He poses the tortured relationship of the Consul and Yvonne, and, within that greater agony, lesser ones in the abortive liaisons between Yvonne and Jacques and between Yvonne and Hugh: all symbolic of the modern malaise. As Dale Edmonds notes, it is not that love has ceased to exist in our world; it is that selfish rather than selfless love is the characteristic form.[14]

"Ah," sighs the Consul—it is one of his last coherent reflections —"who knows why man, however beset his chance by lies, has been offered love." The Consul's anguished cry for Yvonne's love issued in his unposted letter read by Laruelle in the epilogic first chapter is not answered until the last, just before his death. Love and the counterfeits of love bound the novel at all points.

The novel, as Aiken said, is melodrama—melodrama in the Graham Greene sense. We hear that the Consul has been suspected of being an English "espider." He suffers from the mania of persecution, like Greene's guilt-ridden colonial, Scobie, or his self-destructive adulterer, Bendrix.[15] Yet the Consul, whose attention is invariably diffused, is less aware of being followed by the "man in dark glasses," the "counter-espider," than the reader is aware of being *himself* haunted by the forces that crowd in on the Consul and finally, in the Farolito-Gethsemane, trap him.

Lowry sought in his one major achievement to follow Cyril Connolly's dictum that "the true function of a writer is to produce a masterpiece and . . . no other task is of any consequence." But "masterpiece" is too generic a term, applying equally to *War and*

Peace and to *Rasselas*. Lowry did not live to see a profusion of doctoral theses, all trying, like Prufrock's enemies, to formulate him and his book in a phrase. But he seems to have known what was coming, for he wrote, in a special preface to the readers who have most valued him, the French:

The novel can be read simply as a story during which you may—if you wish—skip whole passages, but from which you will get far more if you skip nothing at all. It can be regarded as a kind of symphony or opera, or even as something like a cowboy film. I wanted to make of it a jam session, a poem, a song, a tragedy, a comedy or a farce. It is superficial, profound, entertaining, boring according to one's taste. It is a prophecy, a political warning, a cryptogram, a crazy film, an absurdity, a writing on the wall. It can be thought of as a kind of machine: it works, you may be sure, for I have discovered that to my own expense. And in case you should think that I have made of it everything except a novel, I shall answer that in the last resort it is a real novel that I have intended to write, and even a damnably serious novel.[16]

The totality of Malcolm Lowry's one great statement—the achievement which moved Alfred Kazin to call it the last authentic masterpiece—carried the defects of its virtues. Lowry found it impossible to give his career a second act. He appears to have become obsessed with the necessity of claiming for all the unfinished work of the last ten years the Proustian rage that the whole subsume the parts. So obsessed by the whole that he was never able to devote himself to any part, he tried unsuccessfully to find a Maxwell Perkins who would understand what he was up to.

Living on a lonely beach near Vancouver, a place where he could conceptualize the possibilities of a water-garlanded paradise exorcising the consuming fires of the Moloch he had known, he tried to renew the excess of feeling which galvanized *Volcano*. He managed it only occasionally: in that ecstatic, lyrical prose poem to rebirth, "The Forest Path to the Spring"; in "Through the Panama," his wholly original evocation of the writer as a juggler of masks in a precarious holding action against self-exposure; in the hellish portions of his *Paradiso* novel of Canada, *October Ferry to Gabriola*, where the protagonist seems to have contained the fires and reversed even his own tendency to marshal forces towards his own destruction.

Lowry set himself a grim task, the commitment to meet his own standards. Judging from his unwillingness to consider any of his long fiction after *Volcano* publishable, he never left the confinement of his own single success. In Matthew Corrigan's view, which I believe is the right one, Lowry dropped altogether from the ranks of novelists and slipped into the loosely kept annals of another tradition altogether, "a spoiled mystic who tried to bridge all mystical and esoteric traditions at once . . . . a writer . . . anomalous, unless lumped in some loose tradition which includes Plotinus, Cabbalism, Boehme, Swedenborg, Blake, Poe, Hesse; visionaries Lowry imagined kept the Creator on his toes." [17]

Under the Volcano is simply—or complexly—*sui generis* and just as well left unclassified. It belongs in a distinguished line of hybrid fictions stretching from *Tristam Shandy* through *Ulysses* and the works of Nabokov. Dr. Johnson predicted no future for *Shandy,* but a century and a half later Joyce, in an aside to Eugene Jolas, apropos of *Ulysses,* knew better: "I am trying to build up many planes of narrative, with a single aesthetic purpose. . . . Did you ever read Laurence Sterne?" [18] Maybe in the twenty-first century, if books are still written and read, an unorthodox writer will explain his technique with an aside: "Did you ever read Malcolm Lowry?"

Notes and References

Introduction

1. For a writer who thought of his equipment as "better . . . for a certain kind of poet than a novelist," Malcolm Lowry has, at present writing, no standing as a poet. An anticipated omnibus edition of Lowry's poems by Earle Birney may undo whatever injustice has been perpetrated by the relegation of the poems to limbo as vagrant echoes of his prose. It is almost a commonplace to say that Lowry's best fiction—*Volcano,* "The Forest Path," segments of *October Ferry*—evokes something of the esthetic response of poetry rather than what is normally felt toward a conventional novel. In *Volcano,* as I sought to show in Chaps. 1, 3, and 4, the continual switching in and out of Consular fantasy and the pivoting of the story on enormous symbols take the book out of the domain of the documentary-realistic novel of which Lowry despaired all his life.

The main problem with Lowry as a *maker* of poems is that, as a couplet from one of his posthumously published pieces has it,

> . . . one flying line among such fragments
> soar[s] on forever like the Bird of Paradise.
> > (excerpt, "One Flying Line,"
> > *Epoch,* Vol. 11, No. 3,
> > Fall, 1961, 157)

Rarely does there emerge a poem whose parts synthesize the whole. His best effects are achieved, as with his prose, through rhythm, verbal shock and strangeness, and the intricate repetition and passionate development of very personal symbols. If, as Earle Birney has declared, Lowry's voice in the poems "was seldom fully in control," the by-product of a man's inner agony openly evoked is instant pain. To modern readers, especially the young, artistic control is often less compelling than maelstrom—emotion directly felt and directly transmitted.

In 1962, *Selected Poems of Malcolm Lowry,* edited by Birney with the assistance of Mrs. Lowry, was published. This tiny paperback, from the start a best seller in Lawrence Ferlinghetti's City Lights Pocket Poets Series, contains more than seventy poems which, according to Birney, comprise about a quarter of the poems Lowry completed. As yet this is the only collection of Lowry's verse. It contains most of his better poems; those that have appeared in periodicals since its publication—more than a hundred—are of inferior quality.

The groupings in *Selected Poems* are the same as Lowry himself had made for a full edition he planned, *The Lighthouse Invites the Storm.* This was a collection he mentions as early as 1938 in a letter to Nordahl Grieg. Four of the subtitles were his own: The Roar of the Sea and the Darkness, The Cantinas, The Comedian, and Songs from the Beach: Eridanus.

The first group—"Roar of the Sea and the Darkness"—echoes *Ultramarine,* his apprentice novel about a galleyboy on a British freighter. It images life as a voyage that has no beginning and can have no end. The literal voyage has been disenchantment:

> I had expected the roar of the sea,
> and of tempest,
> not this sullen unremitting calm, . . .
> ("The Days Like Smitten Cymbals of Brass,"
> from *Selected Poems,* 21)

But the voyage as the human condition, that is something else:

> Is that star wormwood out
> Among love's stars? This freighter eternity?
> Where are we going? Life save us all.
> ("The Ship Is Turning Homeward," 17)

"Thunder Beyond Popocatepetl," the second section, contains the poems Lowry began during the period of the early drafts of *Volcano,* Mexico: 1936–38. The most powerful poem of the group, "For *Under the Volcano,*" is everywhere redolent of the novel that was then in embryo. Earle Birney astutely terms it "not so much an echo of that novel as a powerful rhythmic prelude to it, a moving lyrical cry of the man behind the book, in fear 'of his sick life.'" There is hardly an image that is not "compounded with interest" in the novel. The vision of vultures—xopilotes, ratifiers of death—which closes Chapter VIII (see my Chapter 4) become crucial emblems in the poem "For the Love of Dying":

[178]

The tortures of hell are stern, their fires burn fiercely.
Yet vultures turn against the air more beautifully
than seagulls float down wind in cool sunlight,
or fans in asylums spin a loom of fate
for hope which never ventured up so high
as life's deception, astride the vulture's flight.
If death can fly, just for the love of flying,
What might not life do, for the love of dying? (29)

Lowry's sense of death was an oxymoron—a welcome horror—and the spirit cuts across these poems as it did the book.

"The Cantinas" is a section of drinking poems, but only rarely do they score in the Shakespearean sense of inspired ribaldry. Lowry invokes only the "thirsty for disaster" aspect of addiction, never the domestic humor of it which illumined the Joycean Garden chapter of *Volcano*. "The Drunkards" is the best of the short ones:

The noise of death is in this desolate bar,
Where tranquillity sits bowed over its prayer
And music shells the dream of the lover,
But when no nickel brings this harsh despair
Into this loneliest of homes
And of all dooms the loneliest yet,
When no electric music breaks the beat
Of hearts to be doubly broken but now set
By the surgeon of peace in the splint of woe,
Pierces more deeply than trumpets do
The motion of the mind into that web
Where disorders are as simple as the tomb
And the spider of life sits, sleep. (40)

Earle Birney finds "Sestina in a Cantina," the longest poem in the edition, the most remarkable of the group, but it does not lend itself to brief extract.

The next section, "Venus," is concerned with various aspects of love, "lost love that leaves lightnings in its wake," or found love like "a new ship . . . waiting." Margerie Lowry showed me a group of penciled verse bits, written to her on those days when she took the bus for provisions and presented to her on her return as tributes to the vitality of their love. His was the persona of the animal lover and hers that of the "hartebeest." Such poems as those and the ones in "Venus" record moods of happiness where his and Margerie's intense interdependence on the remote beach provide the underlying *donnée*. "Yet," as Birney reminds, "the shadows cast by the light of his inner

hell, of addiction, of the fear and the symptoms of madness, loom, and
. . . even the very real and intense love he bore his wife could not
dispel the demons."

"The Comedian" reveals the self-mocking persona of which Conrad
Aiken and the late John Davenport always write. These poems present
the Lowry who was less disconsolate than anxious to deflate his own
self-pitying balloon. The rage not only to self-disparage but to self-
destroy is implicit everywhere and nowhere better than in the section's
finale, "Epitaph," quoted in Chapter 1.

"Songs from the Beach" are the most "Canadian" of the seven
groups. Lowry uses the beach, the shack, the forest path, the re-
fineries, the abounding wildlife as correlatives in an all-encompassing
conceit for the pilgrim's bittersweet voyage through life. "The Forest
Path to the Spring" is so flawless a work that it pales the poems in this
section.

The final section, "The Language of Man's Woe," contains poems
on the craft of poetry. It begins with a small prayer to Saints Rilke and
Yeats to help him to write, but there are other pieces which reveal
that he has schooled himself not with them but with the sonnets of
Shakespeare, and the lyrics of D. H. Lawrence, Shelley, and even
Ernest Dowson. There is evidence of multiple kinships—especially to
Aiken but also to the prose of Melville and Conrad.

Lowry managed in his lifetime to publish only a handful of poems
in Canada and only one outside Canada—a quatrain that was buried
in the Contributor's Column of the *Atlantic*. He soon gave up any
attempts to place his poems although he mentions *The Lighthouse
Invites the Storm* late in his life in one of those desperate attempts to
convince his New York editor that the advances he dearly needed
were justified by his attempts to complete work in progress. These lines
express Lowry's fears for the permanence of his poetry:

> When I am in the purgatory of the unread,
> Of the backward, of those with wandering attention . . .
> . . . .
> I shall not stir a metaphor in a poet's head
> Grown greyer than my book on his top shelf:
> I spoke too much of wounds that never mend,
> Of ships sailing that never come back.
>
> (excerpt, "This Dead Letter,"
> *Dalhousie Review,* Vol. 41,
> No. 3, Winter 1961, 384)

Chapter One

1. "For *Under the Volcano*," *Selected Poems of Malcolm Lowry* (San Francisco, 1962), 24.

2. Lowry, undated letter (probably 1933). U.B.C. Lowry Collection.

3. Besides the City Lights *Selected Poems,* noted above, other posthumous works, listed in order of publication, are as follows (all citations are to these editions, with shortened title and page numbers in brackets):

A. *Hear Us O Lord from Heaven Thy Dwelling Place* (Philadelphia and New York, 1961). Volume contains "The Bravest Boat" (13–28), "Through the Panama" (29–98), "Strange Comfort Afforded by the Profession," (99–114), "Elephant and Colosseum" (115–74), "Present Estate of Pompei" (175–200), "Gin and Goldenrod" (201–14), "The Forest Path to the Spring" (215–83).

B. *Selected Letters of Malcolm Lowry* (Philadelphia and New York, 1965).

C. *Dark As the Grave Wherein My Friend Is Laid* (New York, 1968).

D. *October Ferry to Gabriola* (New York and Cleveland, 1970).

4. "Biographical Note on Malcolm Lowry," *Presenting Lippincott Authors* (pamphlet), February, 1961.

5. At the time of Lowry's death—1957—there was no edition of either *Under the Volcano* (1947) or *Ultramarine* (1933) in print. However, Penguin (1958) and Vintage (1962) got out paperback editions of *Volcano* before Lippincott's simultaneous cloth and paperback reissue in 1965. All citations in this book, however, are to the original Reynal & Hitchcock edition of 1947, with shortened title, *Volcano,* and page numbers in brackets.

6. "The Jew in Search of a Son," *Eleven Essays in the European Novel* (New York, 1964), 27.

7. *Times Literary Supplement,* Jan. 26, 1967, 57.

8. "The Use of Literary Sources for Theme and Style in *Under the volcano*" (unpub. master's thesis, University of Toronto, 1965), *passim.*

9. "Myth in *Under the Volcano*," *Prairie Schooner,* XXXVII (Winter, 1963–64), 341–43.

10. *Selected Letters of Malcolm Lowry* (Philadelphia and New York, 1965), 28.

11. *The New Yorker* (Feb. 22, 1947), 149. However, sixteen years later, the magazine apparently recanted its brushoff of *Volcano,* referring to it in a brief review of *Ultramarine* as "the truly great novel *Under the Volcano*" (Dec. 13, 1961), 125.

12. "Through the Panama," *Hear Us O Lord from Heaven Thy Dwelling Place* (Philadelphia and New York, 1961), 86.

13. *Selected Letters*, 319.

14. "Lowry's Subjective Equipment," *The New Republic* (Jan. 15, 1966), 24.

15. All references and citations are to the 1934 Random House edition and will be noted by title and page number in brackets.

16. *Selected Letters*, 250.

17. Richard Ellmann, *James Joyce* (New York, 1965, paperback reissue), 745, 747.

18. *Selected Letters*, 3.

19. "Malcolm Lowry: A Note," *Canadian Literature* No. 8 (Spring, 1961), 30.

20. All references and citations are to the 1952 first edition published jointly by Duell, Sloan and Pearce, New York, and Little, Brown and Co., Boston, and will be noted by title and page number in brackets.

21. All references and citations to Aiken's fiction are to *The Collected Novels of Conrad Aiken* (New York, 1964), and will be noted by individual title and page numbers in brackets.

22. *Conrad Aiken* (New York, 1962), 61.

23. *The Modern Novel in Britain and the United States* (New York, 1964), 11.

24. "Europe's Day of the Dead," *Spectator*, Jan. 20, 1967, 74.

25. Ellmann, *James Joyce*, 647.

26. Ellmann, 534.

27. *Re Joyce* (New York, 1965), 135.

28. Lowry, "Hotel Room in Chartres," *Story*, V (September, 1933), 53–58.

29. "Malcolm Lowry, 1930," *Prairie Schooner*, XXXVII (Winter, 1963–64), 317–18.

30. I did not list *Lunar Caustic* among Lowry's posthumous works because a French version was published a year before his death (*Le Caustic Lunaire*, in *Esprit* (Paris) 24: 211–24, February, 1956, 340–55; March, 1956, 525–43; April, 1956). But Lowry said he allowed publication only out of a fear of losing the manuscript. An edition by Earle Birney and Margerie Lowry was published by *The Paris Review*, No. 29, Winter-Spring, 1963, 15–72, and by Jonathan Cape (London, 1968) and Grossman (New York, 1968). My references and citations are to the *Paris Review*-Cape-Grossman version and are noted by title and pages in brackets.

31. Lowry, *Ultramarine* (Philadelphia and New York, 1962). The first version of Lowry's first novel was published in England in 1933 by

Jonathan Cape and had been long out of print. No important changes were made for this first American edition, published posthumously. All citations and references are to the Lippincott edition and are noted by title and pages in brackets.

32. *The Argument of ULYSSES* (Columbus, Ohio, 1964), 299.

33. Margerie Bonner Lowry, "Introductory Note," *Ultramarine,* 7–8.

34. Stephen Spender, Introduction, *Under the Volcano,* ix–xii.

35. Sultan, *Argument of ULYSSES,* 307.

36. Hoffman, *Conrad Aiken,* 157–158n.

37. *Ibid.,* 65.

38. Sultan, 314.

39. "Of Tragic Joy," *Prairie Schooner,* XXXVII (Winter, 1963–64), 361.

40. *Selected Letters,* 177.

Chapter Two

1. *Selected Poems,* 28.

2. Letter to the University of British Columbia Library (U.B.C. Lowry Collection).

3. An unpublished letter from father to son, dated April 22, 1942 (U.B.C. Lowry Collection), reveals the father's attitude. The elder Lowry says that Cambridge, London, and France "left deep scars on my heart" and that Mexico and subsequent events "deepened these wounds." He tells Malcolm to read the story of the Prodigal Son in the Bible and not to try to justify himself but to ask forgiveness. He demands a frank statement "as to your having seen the error of your ways" and assurance that he has abandoned his old ways and will "live and act as your father and mother would wish." Malcolm wrote the required letter (two drafts exist in the U.B.C. Collection). His father seemed satisfied, for he replied that Malcolm had regained his former wholehearted confidence.

4. "Call It Misadventure," *The Atlantic* (June 1970) 106–12. All citations from this article will be noted in brackets by title and pages.

5. The most authentic version of Lowry's manuscript misadventures with *Ultramarine* has been written by Ian Parsons of Chatto and Windus, Ltd., publishers, London. (*Times Literary Supplement,* Feb. 9, 1967, 317) Parsons tells of the theft of the manuscript from his [Parsons'] automobile and the subsequent admission by a distraught Lowry that he had no carbon. Only by making the rounds of the various places where he had written parts of the novel was Lowry able to find, rescued from the wastepaper basket in the apartment of

a friend, a bundle of heavily corrected half-sheets of typescript. From these Lowry was able to redo the work.

6. In conversation, Savannah, Ga., March 27–28, 1967.

7. "Malcolm Lowry: A First Impression," *Encounter*, XXIX (September, 1967), 58–68. Subsequent citations will be noted by shortened title and pages in brackets.

8. *Dark As the Grave*, 20.

9. In conversation, Purdue University (W. Lafayette, Ind.), Feb. 28, 1966.

10. Charlotte Haldane, Introductory Note, *I Bring Not Peace* (London, 1932), iii. All citations will be noted in brackets by title and pages.

11. Aiken, in conversation.

12. Professor Dale H. Edmonds is especially forceful on this point. He traces the Consul's sense of sexual inadequacy to the Hell Bunker episode at Leasowe (related by Jacques Laruelle in Chap. I). The young Geoff is seen by Jacques as he emerges from the bunker after at least an attempt to make love with one of the village girls. "It seems that after this incident," Edmonds writes, "the Consul inevitably associated feelings of embarrassment and guilt with sex." ("*Under the Volcano: A Reading of the 'Immediate Level,'*" *Tulane Studies in English* XVI (1968), 97.

13. Christine Brooke-Rose, "Mescalusions," *London Magazine* (April, 1967), 103.

14. Aiken, *Ushant*, 349.

15. *Ibid.*, 348.

16. In a letter filed in the U.B.C. Lowry Collection, dated December 23, 1964, Miss Fredericka Martin, Casa Trece, Acenida Cuahtemoc 715, Cuernavaca, Mexico, writes significantly of what she learned of the Cuernavaca of the 1930s as a haven for drunken remittance men: "There is an aging woman from the States, who has been haunting Cuernavaca since 1937, who claims . . . to have seen Malcolm Lowry sitting on a cantina doorstep in the early morning holding his head, waiting to get another drink. . . . I cannot read *Under the Volcano* as it is too vivid for one who has been a bystander at too many such tragedies in the town of Cuernavaca."

17. Conrad Aiken, editorial letter, *Time* (June 16, 1961), 7.

18. Lowry, "Through the Panama," 44.

19. David Markson, "Malcolm Lowry: A Reminiscence," *The Nation* Feb. 7, 1966), 167.

20. Letter to me (Sept. 19, 1968).

21. Hermann Hesse, *Steppenwolf* (New York, 1963), tr. and with an introduction by Joseph Mileck, 17. Subsequent references to, and citations from, this novel are noted in brackets by title and page.

22. "In the Darkest Interior of Man," *New York Times Book Review* (Jan. 12, 1964), 1, 30.
23. Burgess, "Day of the Dead," 74.

Chapter Three

1. Edmonds, "A Reading of the 'Immediate Level,'" 64.
2. "A Noble Failure by a Corrupted Mystic," *New York Times Book Review* (Oct. 25, 1970), 5.
3. This extraordinary letter, which I discussed earlier (in the Foreword), occupies thirty-one pages in *Selected Letters* (pp. 57–88). I shall refer to it from now on as the Cape Letter.
4. Lowry, Cape Letter, 66.
5. *Volcano*, Introduction, xiv.
6. "In Terms of the Toenail," *New American Review No. 10* (1970), 53.
7. *Ibid.*
8. Edmonds, 69.
9. Burgess, 74.
10. Edmonds, 103.
11. Conrad Aiken, editorial letter, *Times Literary Supplement*, Feb. 16, 1967, 127.
12. "Of Tragic Joy," *op. cit.*, 361.
13. Fyodor Dostoevsky, *Notes from Underground*, tr. and with intr. by Ralph E. Matlaw (New York, Dutton, 1960), 20.
14. Stanley Jedynak, "*Under the Volcano*: An Existentialist Tragedy," *Thoth* (Spring 1959), 28.
15. *Ibid.*
16. *Ibid.*, 29.
17. David Benham, "Lowry's Purgatory," *Canadian Literature No. 44*, Spring 1970, 28.
18. "The Short Fiction of Malcolm Lowry," *Tulane Studies in English*, XV (1967), 67.
19. "Malcolm Lowry and the Outer Circle of Hell," intr. to *Lunar Caustic* (London and New York, 1968), 6.

Chapter Four

1. *Selected Letters*, Appendix 2, 422.
2. "The Literary Sixties, When the World Was Too Much With Us," *New York Times Book Review*, Dec. 21, 1969, 1.
3. *The Private Labyrinth of Malcolm Lowry: UNDER THE VOLCANO and the Cabbala* (New York, 1969).
4. Letter, *TLS*, 127.

5. "Another Season in Hell," *London Observer Weekend Review*, April 29, 1962, 26.

6. Arthur Barker, "Structural Pattern in *Paradise Lost*," *Philological Quarterly*, XXVIII (1949), 19–20.

7. Joseph Frank, "Spatial Form in the Modern Novel," *Critics and Essays on Modern Fiction 1920–1951*, W. Aldridge (New York, 1952), 44.

8. Lowry, Cape Letter, 85.

9. Letter, *TLS*, 127.

10. In a recent article, Victor Doyen is instructive on the significance of the number Seven: "Finally we have the number seven, a symbol in itself. In the first chapter Laruelle's Day of the Dead ends shortly after seven o'clock. The action of the central story takes place between seven a.m. and seven p.m. In an allusion to the Indian belief it is revealed that a cock crowing seven times announced death . . . : at the end of the novel, when the clock strikes seven times, the cock appears also. . . . The number seven has the connotation of perfection. For both Yvonne and Geoffrey it is the End of Time. In the context of the other Biblical allusions the seventh stroke of the bell reminds us of the opening of the seventh seal." ("Elements Toward a Spatial Reading of Malcolm Lowry's *Under the Volcano*," *English Studies* 50, 1968, 73).

11. The short story, repeatedly termed by Lowry the first version of *Under the Volcano*, was not published in Lowry's lifetime. However, in a special issue devoted to Lowry, *Prairie Schooner* printed the story (XXXVII, 4, Winter 1963/64), 284–300. Subsequent references, especially in this chapter, will be noted *Short Story*, and by pages in *Prairie Schooner*.

12. Cape Letter, 81.

13. For an account of the autobiographical overtones of this scene, see my Chap. 2 ("The Lowry-Aiken Symbiosis").

14. ". . . the mails brought an advance copy of the August [1936] *Esquire*. It contained the final draft of Ernest's story about the writer dying of gangrene in Africa." Carlos Baker, *Ernest Hemingway: A Life Story* (New York, 1969), 289.

15. Cape Letter, 70–71.

16. "Dazzling Disintegration," *The Saturday Review* (Feb. 22, 1947), 10.

17. "Malcolm Lowry," *Times Literary Supplement*, Jan. 26, 1967, 58.

18. Mexican Version, 8, 9, 34, 37, 38, 40, 41, 42.

19. Cape Letter, 69.

20. For a view of the novel as a major comic work, see Douglas Day's brilliant "Of Tragic Joy," *Prairie Schooner* (Winter 1963/64), 354–62.

21. Dale H. Edmonds, *Malcolm Lowry: A Story of His Life and Work* (unpublished Ph.D. thesis, University of Texas at Austin, 1965), 190.

22. Cape Letter, 80–81.

Chapter Five

1. "Malcolm Lowry: A Reminiscence," 167.

2. "Malcolm Lowry, New York Publishing, & the 'New Illiteracy,'" *Encounter* XXXV, 1, July 1970, 82.

3. *Ibid.*, 84.

4. See Lowry's story, "Strange Comfort Afforded by the Profession."

5. Cape Letter, 80.

6. "Another Room in Hell," *The Atlantic*, CCXXII (August, 1968), 85.

7. "Mega-Prone to Catastrophe," *New York Times Book Review* (Aug. 4, 1968), 5.

8. Matthew Corrigan is instructive on this and related points in "Lowry, New York Publishing," etc., *op. cit.*, 83.

Chapter Six

1. *Selected Letters*, 384.

2. "Under Seymour Mountain," *Canadian Literature No. 8* (Spring, 1961), 4.

3. *Selected Letters*, 222.

4. *Ibid.*

5. *Selected Letters*, 201.

6. *Selected Letters*, 22.

7. "'Why Has God Given This to Us?' But What God Gave, the City Took. The Story of Malcolm Lowry in Vancouver," *Vancouver Life* (January, 1968), 30.

8. Markson, "Malcolm Lowry," *op. cit.*, 164.

9. The first mention of Malcolm Lowry's death in an American newspaper may have been in Harvey Breit's column, "In and Out of Books," *New York Times Book Review*, July 13, 1957, 8, sixteen days after Lowry's death.

10. Conrad Knickerbocker reported the overdose as twenty sodium amytals, a miscalculation by a raging Malcolm Lowry. "Swinging the Paradise Street Blues: Malcolm Lowry in England," *Best Magazine Articles: 1967* (New York, 1967), 144.

11. "Publisher's Note," *Hear Us O Lord*, etc., unpaged.

12. "Lowry in Vancouver," *op. cit.*, 30.

13. *Selected Letters*, 383, 385.

14. "The Short Fiction of Malcolm Lowry," *Tulane Studies in English* XV (1967), 74.

15. Henry James, "The New Novel," in *Notes on Novelists, with Some Other Notes* (New York, 1914), 319.

16. Henry David Thoreau, *Walden & On the Duty of Civil Disobedience* (Holt, Rinehart and Winston, 19th Printing, June, 1966). All citations from and references to *Walden* in this chapter are to the Rinehart edition and are noted by title and page in brackets.

17. There is a mention of Thoreau, not an especially respectful one, in his last novel, *October Ferry to Gabriola:* "All in all they might have thought he was being yet more sardonic than the friend who's gibed at them about Thoreau" (155).

18. Charles R. Anderson, *The Magic Circle of Walden* (New York, 1968), 17–18.

19. *Selected Letters*, 266.

Chapter Seven

1. "Editor's Note," *October Ferry to Gabriola*, 335.

2. "Noble Failure by a Corrupted Mystic," *New York Times Book Review* (Oct. 25, 1970), 5.

3. For Lowry's replies to his editor Albert Erskine on the latter's criticism that the fictionalizing of the writer who writes about a writer's writing has little chance of gaining readers, see *Selected Letters*, 307, 320, 322, 331.

4. "Corrupted Mystic," *op. cit.*, 54.

5. "Editor's Note," *op. cit.*, 336.

Chapter Eight

1. Undated letter to Conrad Aiken (probably 1933), U.B.C. Collection.

2. Douglas Day, "The Scholar's Bookshelf," conversation with John Graham. Radio program presented Oct. 16, 1964, over the campus station of the University of Virginia.

3. *Selected Letters*, 373.

4. *Ibid.*

5. Aiken, in conversation with me, Savannah, Ga., March, 1967.

6. Quoted by Conrad Knickerbocker, "Malcolm Lowry in England," *op. cit.*, 136.

7. Douglas Day, Preface, *Dark As the Grave*, ix.

8. Lowry, *Ordeal of Sigbjørn Wilderness*, unpub. novel, unpaged. U.B.C. Collection.

9. "Another Room in Hell," *The Atlantic*, CCXXII (August, 1968), 85.

10. Day, Preface, xii.

11. Christine Brooke-Rose, " Mescalusions," *London Magazine* (April, 1967), 100.

12. George Robertson, "To the Volcano"; "The Forest Path." Television Documentary in Two Parts, Canadian Broadcasting Corporation, Trans-Canada Explorations Series, Nov. 29 and Dec. 6, 1961.

13. *Ernest Hemingway: A Reconsideration* (University Park, Pa., 1966), 18–19.

14. Margerie Lowry, letter to me, Sept. 5, 1968.

15. "The Revolt of the Demons," *The New Yorker* (May 23, 1964), 171.

16. Lowry, "The Bulls of the Resurrection," *Prism International*, Vol. V, No. 1 (Summer, 1965), pp. 4–11.

17. Anonymous, "A Prose Wasteland," *Times Literary Supplement* (May 11, 1962), 338.

18. Carl G. Jung, *Man and His Symbols: A Popular Presentation of the Essential Ideas of Jungian Psychology* (Garden City, 1964), 28.

19. *Ibid.*, 75.

20. *Ibid.*

21. Jung, *Man and His Symbols*, 78.

22. *Ibid.*, 67.

23. Edith Hamilton. *Mythology* (New York: Mentor Book, 1942), 133–34.

24. Carl G. Jung, "The Principal Archetypes," *The Modern Tradition: Backgrounds of Modern Literature*, eds. Richard Ellmann and Charles Feidelson, Jr. (New York, 1965), 654.

25. Carl G. Jung, "Psychology and Literature" from Jung's *Modern Man in Search of a Soul* (London). This essay reprinted in Brewster Ghiselin, ed. *The Creative Process* (New York: Mentor Book, 1961), 220.

Chapter Nine

1. *Selected Letters*, 59.

2. "Paperbacks in Review: Malcolm Lowry," *New York Times Book Review* (Nov. 8, 1964), 64.

3. Aiken, editorial letter, *op. cit.*, 127.

4. Aiken, in conversation with me, Savannah, Ga., March, 1967.

5. Robert B. Heilman, "Four Novels," *Sewanee Review*, LV (July-September, 1947), 492.

6. Robert B. Heilman, "The Possessed Artist and the Ailing Soul," *Canadian Literature No. 8* (Spring 1961), 16. This article is an expansion of Heilman's early review in *Sewanee*, above.

7. Aiken, editorial letter, *op cit.*, 127.

8. Aiken, in conversation with me, Savannah, Ga., March, 1967.

9. "Psychology and Literature," *op. cit.*, 218–19.

10. Space does not permit a full accounting of Lowry's bitter and, until the successful publication of *Under the Volcano,* fearful references to Charles Jackson's best seller. In Lowry's *Dark As the Grave,* Sigbjørn Wilderness, whose own novel has been rejected, sees a film ad for *Drunkard's Rigadoon* and the specter of that work, an undisguised parody of *Lost Weekend,* sets off Wilderness on a book-long excess of recriminations. References to *Lost Weekend* abound in *Selected Letters* (pages 45, 51, 61, 62, 63, 77, 84, 147, 188, 200, 292). Charles Jackson struck back in an unfavorable review of *Selected Letters:* "We Were Led to Hope for More," *New York Times Book Review* (Dec. 12, 1965), 4, 20.

11. Clyde Kluckhohn, *Mirror for Man* (New York, 1949), *passim.*

12. *Catastrophe and Imagination: An Interpretation of the Recent English and American Novel* (New York, 1957), 87.

13. Burgess, "Europe's Day of the Dead," *op. cit.*, 74.

14. "The *Volcano: 'Immediate Level,'*" *op. cit.*, 103.

15. Scobie and Bendrix are the heroes, respectively, of Greene's *The Heart of the Matter* and *The End of the Affair.*

16. Lowry, "Preface to a Novel," *Canadian Literature No. 9* (Summer 1961), 28–29.

17. Matthew Corrigan, "A Noble Failure," *op. cit.*, 5, 54.

18. Richard Ellmann, *James Joyce,* 566.

Selected Bibliography

PRIMARY SOURCES

The only important collection of Lowry papers is in the Special
Collections Division of the University of British Columbia Library,
Vancouver, B.C. For the purposes of this critical study the most useful
materials in the collection were the more than 1,100 pages of Lowry's
working notes. Included are the successive drafts of *Under the Volcano*,
from the short story under that title, written in Mexico in 1936, to the
final manuscript that was accepted a decade later by Jonathan Cape in
London and Reynal & Hitchcock in the United States and published
in February, 1947. The U.B.C. collection also provides testimony to
the large amount of fiction on which Lowry worked during the ten
years between publication of *Under the Volcano* and his death in 1957.
The manuscripts of three fragmentary novels were made available to
students, *La Mordida*, *The Ordeal of Sigbjørn Wilderness*, and *Dark
As the Grave Wherein My Friend Is Laid*. The latter was edited into
publication in 1968 by Margerie Bonner Lowry and Professor Douglas
Day, University of Virginia. A fourth novel, *October Ferry to Gabriola*,
Lowry's only book-length fiction on the Dollarton years, was published
in late summer 1970, edited by Mrs. Lowry. The single copy of the
manuscript and notes was held out of the collection throughout the
1960s by Mrs. Lowry, and I was unable to read it in that form.

The following bibliography lists alphabetically only the book publications and of these only the American and English titles. For a
complete listing of Lowry's individual poems and short stories, see
the Lowry bibliography, through 1964, prepared by Dr. Earle Birney
with the assistance of Mrs. Lowry. Fuller information on the Birney
bibliography is given later in this section under Secondary Sources—
Bibliographical Materials.

PUBLISHED NOVELS

Dark As the Grave Wherein My Friend Is Laid. New York: New American Library, 1968.

Lunar Caustic. London: Jonathan Cape, 1968, and New York: Gross-
man, 1968.
October Ferry to Gabriola. New York: World, 1970.
Ultramarine. London: Jonathan Cape, 1933.
Ultramarine. Philadelphia: Lippincott, 1962.
Under the Volcano. New York: Reynal & Hitchcock, 1947.
Under the Volcano. London: Jonathan Cape, 1947.
Under the Volcano. New York: Vintage-Random House, 1958, 1962.
First paperback edition.
Under the Volcano. Philadelphia: Lippincott, 1965 (cloth), and New
York: Signet (paperback). Both contain an introduction by
Stephen Spender.

PUBLISHED SHORT-STORY COLLECTION

Hear Us O Lord from Heaven Thy Dwelling Place. Philadelphia:
Lippincott, 1961.

PUBLISHED LETTERS

Selected Letters of Malcolm Lowry. Eds. Harvey Breit and Margerie
Lowry. Philadelphia: Lippincott, 1965.

PUBLISHED POETRY EDITION

Selected Poems of Malcolm Lowry. Ed. and with intr. by Earle Birney.
San Francisco: City Lights, 1962.

SECONDARY SOURCES

1. Bibliographical Materials
Birney, Earle. Four issues of *Canadian Literature*, a quarterly of
criticism and review, published by the University of British Co-
lumbia under the editorship of George Woodcock, contain the
first—and, at this writing, the only—bibliography of works by and
about Malcolm Lowry. This exhaustive compilation appears in
Issues 8 (Spring 1961, 80–88); 9 (Summer 1961, 80–84); 11
(Winter 1962, 90–95); 19 (Winter 1964, 83–89). The bibliog-
raphy is especially useful for its location of periodicals in which
Lowry's posthumous poetry has appeared. Of his bibliography,
Dr. Birney writes: "Although it is fairly complete in respect to
Malcolm Lowry's own writings . . . , it is very incomplete in

respect to published comment on his work and life." Dr. Birney was assisted by Mrs. Lowry in his endeavor. The accelerated interest in Lowry over the last decade, as indicated and spurred by a spate of posthumous publications, justifies a full supplement to Dr. Birney's bibliography.

Woolmer, J. Howard. *A Malcolm Lowry Catalogue.* Mr. Woolmer acknowledges a debt to the Birney bibliography as "the base upon which this collection was built." He adds his hope that the 65-page catalogue will serve as a check-list until a complete bibliography is published. This booklet, No. 2 of Woolmer's Focus Series (New York: Woolmer, 1969), contains essays by Perle Epstein and by this writer as well as a note on Lowry's poetry by Dr. Birney.

2. Biographies

The authorized biography was to have been written by Conrad Knickerbocker. Mr. Knickerbocker committed suicide on April 2, 1966, aged thirty-seven, while working on the biography. A lively and, to Mrs. Lowry, controversial report on Knickerbocker's "discovery" of the young Lowry—a series of intimate recollections of Lowry 1927–33, by people like John Davenport and Viscount Peter Churchill—appeared posthumously under Knickerbocker's byline in *The Paris Review* (Winter 1966) and was selected for *Best Magazine Articles: 1967,* ed. Gerald Walker (New York: Crown, 1967). Its sheer vivacity can only make one regret that he did not live to complete the biography. The assignment of official biographer was taken over by the able Douglas Day, who, besides having written a number of major essays on Lowry, had assisted Mrs. Lowry in preparing *Dark As the Grave* for publication.

3. Memoirs

The following unannotated list is selective. Although small in number, these remembrances of Lowry comprise a distinguished list. Each has been invaluable to me in writing this critical study. Their verve is testimony to what David Markson calls "the innocence, the mirth, the sheer abundance" of the man.

Aiken, Conrad. Editorial letter. *London Times Literary Supplement* (Feb. 16, 1967), 127.

———. "Malcolm Lowry: A Note." *Canadian Literature,* No. 8 (Spring 1961), 29–30.

Birney, Earle. "Glimpses into the Life of Malcolm Lowry," *Tamarack Review* (Spring 1961), 35–41.

Breit, Harvey. "In and Out of Books—Obituary." *New York Times Book Review,* July 14, 1957, 8.

Kirk, Downie. "More Than Music—Glimpses of Malcolm Lowry," *Canadian Literature No. 8* (Spring 1961), 31–38.

Knickerbocker, Conrad. "Swinging the Paradise Street Blues: Malcolm Lowry in England." *Best Magazine Articles: 1967.* Ed. Gerald Walker (New York; Crown), 1967, 64–65.

Lorenz, Clarissa. "Call It Misadventure." *The Atlantic* (June 1970), 106–12.

Markson, David. "Malcolm Lowry: A Reminiscence." *Nation,* Feb. 7, 1966, 164–67.

McConnell, William. "Recollections of Malcolm Lowry." *Canadian Literature No. 6* (Autumn 1960), 24–31.

Noxon, Gerald. "Malcolm Lowry: 1930." *Prairie Schooner* (Winter 1963/64), 315–20.

Stern, James. "Malcolm Lowry: A First Impression." *Encounter,* XXIX (September 1967), 58–68.

4. Critical Studies

The following annotated list is selective and limited, except in the case of a few major articles published in England, to works published in the United States and Canada. "The Lowry industry," as one critic put it, is burgeoning each year, and my list can only give a general idea of the huge amount of scholarship being accorded Lowry, especially since 1965. The annual *PMLA* International Bibliography and, until recently when it was discontinued, the *Modern Fiction Studies* biannual *Roll Call,* have listed scholarly-critical articles on Lowry. Here I have emphasized general studies rather than appraisals of individual works. Some review essays are included, especially those in which a major critic has "rediscovered" Lowry after missing him during the long period of silence after the original publication of *Under the Volcano.* Other sources are listed in Notes and References. All commentators whose works are cited in my text are listed in the general index.

A. Book-Length Studies

(1) Epstein, Perle S. *The Private Labyrinth of Malcolm Lowry: 'Under the Volcano' and the Cabbala.* New York: Holt, Rinehart & Winston, 1969, 241 pp. Mrs. Epstein's book was the first extended study of Lowry and of his masterpiece. It locates him where he lived; illuminates painstakingly the vital role of magic and mystery in Lowry's creativity. Once Professor Epstein moves from a perhaps necessarily turgid account of the history of the Cabbala to its relevance in *Under the Volcano,* her book is fascinating. My bias is Jungian-Archetypal; hers is Cabbalistic. I make use of the evidence that Carl G. Jung, after receiving a copy of the

novel, expressed the desire to consult with Lowry; she uses
as her point of departure Lowry's documented association
with Cabbalist Frater Achad (Charles Stansfeld Jones).
Under the Volcano, like *Ulysses,* is a book which yields its
secrets with lavish reluctance, and there is time enough for
both of us to be proved wrong. There are reasons, however,
to see Perle Epstein's line-by-line gloss as Cabbalist overkill.
Lowry had barely heard of the Cabbala when he composed
the essential drafts in Mexico—drafts containing, although
often undeveloped, many of the major motifs which Epstein
claims to be oriented in the Cabbala. See Chapter 4 above.

(2) Woodcock, George, editor. *Malcolm Lowry: The Man and
His Work.* Vancouver: University of British Columbia Press,
1971. This fine casebook provides for the first time in a
single volume an overview of critical response to *all* of
Lowry's prose works. George Woodcock has reprinted most
of the essays on Lowry that have appeared for the last
decade in his journal, *Canadian Literature,* and what an
impressive array they are. Certainly *CL* did more than any
other periodical in the world to keep interest in Lowry alive
at a time when not a single edition of *Under the Volcano*
or *Ultramarine* was in print. The highlights of previously
published material are Robert B. Heilman's expansion of
his original tribute to *Volcano* in the pages of *The Sewanee
Review*—surely a landmark; Lowry's own justly famous preface to the French edition of *Volcano,* translated from the
French by Editor Woodcock; poignant memoirs by William
McConnell and the late Downie Kirk. Another gem of a
memoir, published here for the first time, is that of Maurice
J. Carey, a Canadian Army sergeant general in 1939–40.
Carey reveals with a refreshing lack of hero worship aspects
of Lowry's drinking in those years which could lead to sad-
comic treachery (Lowry once hocked Carey's typewriter to
go on a bender and presented his children as a present a
kitten he'd filched next door). The essays are uniformly
excellent, and I have credited and cited many of them in
my text as well as later in this section.

B. Articles, Review Essays

(1) Allen, Walter. "The Masterpiece of the Forties," *On Contemporary Literature.* Ed. Richard Kostelanetz. New York:
An Avon Book, 1964, 419–21. Contains Allen's assessment

of *Under the Volcano* as the finest novel by an Englishman in the 1940s.

(2) Anonymous. "Malcolm Lowry," *The London Times Literary Supplement,* Jan. 26, 1967, 57–59. Despite a number of half-truths and unsubstantiated conjectures—so labeled by Conrad Aiken in a congenial corrective—this article presents much hitherto unpublished autobiographical material from the Mexican years to account for some of the motifs of *Under the Volcano.* Includes the likely source for the character of Jacques Laruelle.

(3) Anonymous. "A Prose Wasteland," *London Times Literary Supplement,* May 11, 1962, 338. One of the first major reassessments of *Under the Volcano* in Lowry's native country which ignored the book for fifteen years.

(4) Barnes, Jim. "The Myth of Sisyphus in *Under the Volcano,*" *Prairie Schooner,* Winter 1968–69, 341–48. Professor Barnes believes there can be little doubt that Lowry "consciously wove the myth of Sisyphus into . . . his narrative of the tortured Geoffrey Firmin." The article builds up steam after a slow start in which the Sisyphean parallels seem forced. However, like Sisyphus, Geoffrey certainly has been to hell and back: a man carrying personal and universal guilt throughout the infernal sojourn. This essay's contribution is its placement of *Under the Volcano* squarely in an absurdist—though *tragically* absurdist—tradition.

(5) Benham, David. "Lowry's Purgatory: Versions of 'Lunar Caustic,'" *Canadian Literature,* 44 (Spring 1970), 28–37. A much-needed demonstration of how Lowry sought to meld two versions of his Bellevue Hospital experience and how the merger itself fitted into Lowry's larger scheme.

(6) Birney, Earle. "Against the Spell of Death," *Prairie Schooner.* Winter 1963–64, 328–33. A concise and viable placement in time, place, and development of the Lowry poems selected by Birney for inclusion in the City Lights—the only, so far—edition of the verse.

(7) Burgess, Anthony. "Europe's Day of the Dead," *Spectator,* Jan. 20, 1967, 74. One would have expected this panegyric from the author of *Clock-Work Orange.* The Consul suggests to Burgess the Promethean rebel, a towering extension of Aiken's "Prufrock figures" which spawned him.

(8) Corrigan, Matthew. "Malcolm Lowry, New York Publishing, & the 'New Illiteracy,'" *Encounter* XXXV, 1 (July 1970), 82–93. A savage attack on the art-denying combination in

the New York publishing establishment of commercial zeal and literary ineptitude, with Lowry's misshapen posthumous novel, *Dark As the Grave,* as Corrigan's proof positive. Although he is too shrill in putting *all* the blame on Lowry's publisher for the fiasco of stitching together voluminous notes into a bad novel, Professor Corrigan displays admirable courage in taking on everyone who would exploit a dead writer's leavings in the hope of a commercial "kill." A truly compassionate plea for art over box-office.

(9) ———. "Masks and the Man: The Writer As Actor," *Shenandoah,* XIX (Summer 1968), 89–93. "Together the editors have done a remarkable job and almost every Lowry admirer will be grateful to them." Corrigan's praise of Douglas Day and Margerie Lowry in this review essay of *Dark As the Grave* contrasts with his subsequent position, expressed in the article capsulated above. Still, his review is the only one I have seen that comes to grips with an anomalous book in which Lowry reveals himself, not as a single persona, but as a wearer of masks.

(10) Costa, Richard Hauer. "Lowry/Aiken Symbiosis," *Nation,* June 26, 1967, 823–26. An attempt to give Conrad Aiken his full due in the development of the comic Hambo figure of *Ushant* to that modern tragic hero, the Consul.

(11) ———. "Lowry's Overture As Elegy," *A Malcolm Lowry Catalogue,* compiled and edited by J. Howard Woolmer, 1969, 26–44. An elegiac reading of the first chapter of *Under the Volcano.*

(12) ———. "*Ulysses,* Lowry's *Volcano,* and the *Voyage* Between: Study of an Unacknowledged Literary Kinship," *University of Toronto Quarterly* (July 1967), 335–52. An attempt to show how Lowry received a transfusion of Joyce through the veins of Aiken.

(13) Day, Douglas. "Of Tragic Joy," *Prairie Schooner,* Winter 1963–64, 354–62. The best essay yet written on the Falstaffian side of the Consul.

(14) ———. Preface, *Dark As the Grave Wherein My Friend Is Laid.* New York: New American Library, 1968, ix–xxiii. Professor Day cannot write uninterestingly about Lowry, but the fallout from his editorial labor with the scores of false starts by Lowry on *Grave* has taken its toll. This often brilliant preface was necessary, but Day's denigration of Lowry as novelist was not.

(15) Doyen, Victor. "Elements Toward a Spatial Reading of

Malcolm Lowry's *Under the Volcano*," *English Studies* 50 (1968), 65–74. This essay by a young Belgian scholar demonstrates that, as with *Ulysses*, Lowry's novel is best read as one reads poetry—continually fitting fragments together and keeping allusions in mind until, by reflexive reference, a coherent poetic web of meaning is arrived at.

(16) Durrant, Geoffrey. "Death in Life: Neo-Platonic Elements in 'Through the Panama,'" *Canadian Literature* (Spring 1970), 13–27. Professor Durrant links Lowry's most self-revealing story to neo-Platonic myth. His synthesis enables him to show how Coleridge's *Ancient Mariner*, whose lines Lowry appended to the margins of his text, serves as a kind of mythic gloss for Sigbjørn Wilderness's voyage.

(17) Edelstein, J. M. "On Re-Reading *Under the Volcano*," *Prairie Schooner*, Winter 1963–64, 336–39. A moving tribute to *Volcano* from one of its original admirers who stresses the originality of the book which makes annual rereadings of the novel ever new experiences.

(18) Edmonds, Dale. "*Under the Volcano*: A Reading of the 'Immediate Level,'" *Tulane Studies in English*, XVI (1968), 63–105. Professor Edmonds, whose 1965 doctoral dissertation at the University of Texas launched Lowry scholarship at that level, believes that it is on "the level of people, places, events and circumstances within a fictional world that much resembles our own that [*Under the Volcano*] communicates most effectively." He proves his contention with one of the two or three indispensable essays on Lowry's book. A treasure of Volcanic and Consular lore.

(19) Gass, William H. "In Terms of the Toenail: Fiction and the Figures of Life," *New American Review No. 10* (1970). Novelist-philosopher Gass has been "talking up" Lowry and *Volcano* among his students at Purdue and elsewhere for a decade or more. This essay, using *Volcano* for its main thrust, relates metaphor to life in a way that only a creative writer of the first order could do.

(20) Heilman, Robert B. "The Possessed Artist and the Ailing Soul," *Canadian Literature No. 8*, Spring 1961, 7–16. This essay is an expansion of Professor Heilman's early review of *Under the Volcano* (*Sewanee Review*, LV, July–September 1947), the first tribute to the book from a major scholar. Heilman, although not entirely happy with this new writer who "never corks his cornucopia of evocative images and symbols," nevertheless assigned vital significance to "the power of Lowry's possessed art" from the beginning. By an

accident of the alphabet, the essays by Edmonds, Gass, and Heilman—perhaps the three most indispensable ones—are here noted in succession.

(21) Hicks, Granville. "One Great Statement," *Saturday Review*, Dec. 4, 1965, 39–40. Lavish praise, not only for the novel (which Hicks like many another missed on its original appearance) but for Lowry's letter to Jonathan Cape.

(22) Hirschman, Jack. "Kabbala/Lowry, etc." *Prairie Schooner*, Winter 1963/64, 347–53. Poet Hirschman was the first to dare a Cabbalistic reading of *Under the Volcano*. He saw Lowry's reference to elaborate symbolics, such as those of the Cabbala, as not merely literary devices but for stratifying levels of meaning.

(23) Janeway, Elizabeth. "A Legacy, a Man and a Legend," *The New York Times Book Review*, May 21, 1961, 1 and 16. When a 14-year silence was broken by the appearance of Lowry's posthumous *Hear Us O Lord*, Miss Janeway was among the first to greet the book as an invaluable legacy of the creative spirit triumphant despite the demons.

(24) Jedynak, Stanley. "*Under the Volcano*: An Existentialist Tragedy." *Thoth* (Spring 1959), 25–29. An existentialist reading in which Professor Jedynak gives a philosophical accounting for the curious diffusion—uninvolvement, really —which characterizes the Consul's progress to destruction. This essay is all the more remarkable for it originated as a graduate paper at Syracuse University where, in the late Professor Leonard Brown, Malcolm Lowry had a devoted admirer from the start.

(25) Kilgallin, Anthony R. "Faust and *Under the Volcano*," *Canadian Literature No. 26* (Autumn 1965), 43–54. The best of a number of Faustian readings of *Volcano*.

(26) ———. " 'Why Has God Given This to Us?' But What God Gave, the City Took: The Story of Malcolm Lowry in Vancouver," *Vancouver Life*, January 1968, 29–31, 48–52. A passionate appeal for belated recognition for Lowry in the Canadian city, virtually in whose midst the writer penned his best work. Professor Kilgallin has obviously spoken at length to every surviving Canadian who knew Lowry, and his forthcoming book is anticipated warmly.

(27) Knickerbocker, Conrad. "The Voyages of Malcolm Lowry," *Prairie Schooner*. Winter 1963/64, 301–14. An authoritative capsule of Lowry's life which Knickerbocker was expanding into the official biography at the time of his suicide.

(28) Markson, David. "Myth in *Under the Volcano*," *Prairie Schooner*. Winter 1963/64, 339–46. Novelist Markson was a close friend of Lowry's in the later years. His imperishable memoir is cited earlier in these pages. This essay, a portion of Markson's 1951 thesis at Columbia, is an Odyssean-Joycean reading of *Under the Volcano*.

(29) McCormick, John. *Catastrophe and Imagination: A Reinterpretation of the Recent English and American Novel.* London and New York: Longmans Green & Co., 1957. Despite some factual errors, McCormick's five-page (85–89) discussion of *Under the Volcano* was among the first to declare that the novel was about "the nature of love in a fragmented society."

(30) New, W. H. "Lowry's Reading: An Introductory Essay," *Canadian Literature No. 44* (Spring 1970), 5–12. Professor New's fine essay leads off another stimulating Lowry issue of *CL*, this one devoted to Lowry's extra-literary interests. New not only reveals Lowry's reading but shows generally how the influences of his reading—especially his reading in the occult—crept into his fiction.

(31) Shorter, Kingsley. "Lowry's Private Trip," *New Leader*, Sept. 15, 1969, 14–16. Mr. Shorter is unconvinced that either occultism or the Cabbala is seminal to *Under the Volcano* ("a feat literary rather than alchemical. . . ."). He sees Lowry's comic gift and chronic sense of doom as needing no metaphysical authentication. "Magnificent as the book is, . . . *Under the Volcano* remains a very private trip."

(32) Spender, Stephen. Introduction, *Under the Volcano*. Philadelphia: Lippincott, 1965, vii–xxvi. Mr. Spender later acknowledged that he had not read Lowry's letter to Jonathan Cape when he wrote this essay. Although full of biographical half-truths, the essay is notable for its view of the novel as cinematic and, in its subjectivity, at an opposite pole from Joyce and *Ulysses*.

(33) Tiessen, Paul G. "Malcolm Lowry and the Cinema," *Canadian Literature No. 44* (Spring 1970), 38–49. "In cinema technique, Lowry finds not only a method but also a metaphor to express the tormented, surrealistic world of his characters." (Lowry was more than a film buff, and Professor Tiessen's essay, long needed, accords full attention to Lowry's cinematic grasp of fiction.)

(34) Tindall, William York. "Many-Leveled Fiction: Virginia Woolf to Ross Lockridge." *College English*, X, 2 (November

1948), 68–69. Not all scholars missed *Under the Volcano* first time round. Professor Tindall was one who didn't.

(35) Toynbee, Philip. "Another Season in Hell," *The Observer*, April 29, 1962, 26. Philip Toynbee was one of those who did miss *Volcano* first time round. He atones richly: "I am now persuaded Lowry was a great writer, and that *Under the Volcano* is one of the great English novels of this century."

(36) Tuohy, Frank. "Day of a Dead Man," *Spectator* (Aug. 27, 1961). An unusually frank reassessment of Lowry's position. After stating shortcomings of *Volcano,* Tuohy comes down hard in favor of its recognition as a major work of the century.

(37) Wain, John. "Another Room in Hell," *The Atlantic,* CCXXII (August 1968), 84–86. A perceptive warning of the wrong turn into which the Novel is being led by a sensibility like Lowry's which is unable to project beyond itself.

(38) Woodburn, John. "Dazzling Disintegration," *Saturday Review of Literature,* Feb. 22, 1947, 9–10. Original devotees of *Under the Volcano* committed to memory such portions of this dazzling review as the following: "I have never before used the word in a review, and I am aware of the responsibility upon me in using it, but I am of the opinion, carefully considered, that *Under the Volcano* is a work of genius."

(39) Woodcock, George. "Under Seymour Mountain," *Canadian Literature No. 8,* Spring 1961, 3–6. Along with Earle Birney, George Woodcock has been a Canadian writer who recognized from the start the immensity of Lowry's achievement and who has said so in a dozen articles. This essay helped me place Lowry in the tradition of Proust, writers who "conceive all their work as one great inter-related pattern on whose parts they work continuously and simultaneously." I have not been able to do full justice to the Woodcock-edited book on Lowry, published as this book went to the printer.

(40) Widmer, Eleanor. "The Drunken Wheel: Malcolm Lowry and *Under the Volcano,*" *The Forties: Fiction, Poetry, Drama,* ed. Warren French (Deland, Fla.: Everett/Edwards, 1968), 217–226. Professor Widmer joins Robert Heilman as recognizing the defects of Lowry's virtues. She sees the novel as containing too many disparate elements. "The intense moment of encompassing poetic vision both creates and restricts this novel, allowing small possibilities for irony or the capriciousness of chance."

(41) Wright, Terence. *"Under the Volcano:* The Static Art of Malcolm Lowry," *Ariel,* I, 4 (October 1970), 67–76. Professor Wright joins Victor Doyen and others who find the novel evoking the esthetic response of poetry, music, and the visual arts.

Bibliographical note: I was unable to obtain copies of two recent brief critical studies on Lowry in time for inclusion. They are Daniel B. Dodson's Malcolm Lowry *(Columbia Essays on Modern Literature, 1971) and Anthony R. Kilgallin's booklet published by Copp Clark of Toronto.*

Index

Index